FAMOUS LAND BATTLES

From Agincourt to the Six-Day War

ВОИНЫ КРАСНОЙ АРМИИ!
КРЕПЧЕ УДАРЫ ПО ВРАГУ! ИЗГОНИМ НЕМЕЦКО-
ФАШИСТСКИХ МЕРЗАВЦЕВ С НАШЕЙ РОДНОЙ ЗЕМЛИ!

Above :
Russian war propaganda, Second World War vintage,
appeals for feats of arms against the hated invader

Overleaf :
Scotland for Ever by Lady Elizabeth Butler : the charge of
the Scots Greys at Waterloo

Contents pages :
Even in the missile age the victors' flag still indicates 'We
are here' : the Israeli flag flies over abandoned Jordanian
positions in Jerusalem's Old City in the Six-Day War of 1967

Endpapers :
Hell by Georges Leroux – a bitter allegory drawn from the
unspeakable battlefields of the Western Front in the First
World War

FAMOUS LAND BATTLES

From Agincourt to the Six-Day War

RICHARD HUMBLE

Maps by David Worth and Jennifer Mexter

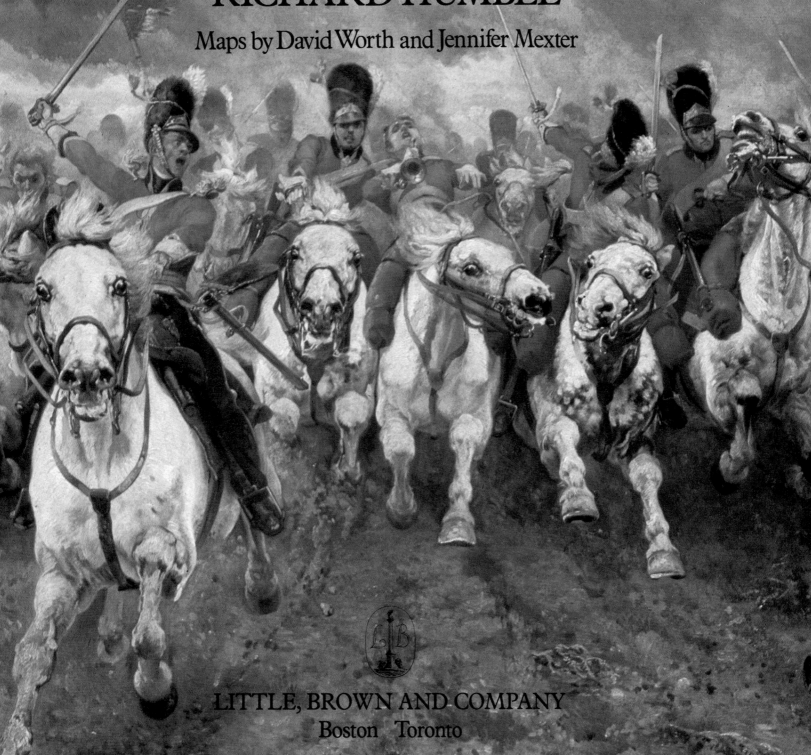

LITTLE, BROWN AND COMPANY

Boston Toronto

For my family

ISBN 0-316-38145-4

Library of congress catalog card no. 79-1527

FIRST AMERICAN EDITION

PRINTED IN ITALY

CONTENTS

BATTLES LONG AGO

'Now tell us all about the war, And what they fought each other for.'

I N Robert Southey's poem *After Blenheim,* Old Kaspar's reply to this question from his grandchildren, though admirably brief, is less than adequate :

> *'It was the English,' Kaspar cried,*
> *'Who put the French to rout ;*
> *But what they fought each other for*
> *I could not well make out.*
> *But everybody said,' quoth he,*
> *'That 'twas a famous victory.'*

Southey wrote that poem about 150 years ago, and quite a few 'famous victories' have been won since then; yet Old Kaspar is still with us. Despite the best (or worst) that modern education can achieve, we do tend to remember famous battles with only the vaguest notions of why they were fought, where they were fought, who fought them, and what happened afterwards.

Keeping these four questions in mind, this book examines eighteen battles dating from the medieval longbow to the age of the nuclear missile. All of them are unquestionably 'famous' battles, and the aim is to help the Kaspars (old and not-so-old) of the late twentieth century to understand them better. Certainly the original Old Kaspar would have found it useful: his 'famous victory', Blenheim, comes in Chapter 4.

The textbook road to battle

Once you are at war, strategy is the broad plan of how you intend to win and tactics are the details of how you go about it. Both will be useless unless they are flexible enough to cope with the enemy's own strategy and tactics, which are bound to get in the way. And when this happens some kind of battle is inevitable, because your armed forces and those of the enemy end up on collision courses.

Battles have been fought for no better reason than pride, or political pressure back home, or because neither general could think of anything better to do than to 'have a battle'. There have even been battles in which the troops of each side started to fight before their generals were ready – Gettysburg (Chapter 10 in this book) is a perfect example. However military theorists may deplore the fact, as many battles have been won for all the wrong reasons as for the right ones.

The first armies

Even in the very first civilizations known to history, organization and weapons had already produced soldiers and armies. Rulers were already being judged on their ability to defend their people from armed aggression and themselves to conquer neighbouring lands. The quest for military glory was an accepted facet of human existence; and, whether we like it or not, has undeniably remained so for the last five thousand years.

From around 3000 BC, the early civilizations of Egypt, in the Nile valley, and Sumer and Akkad in Mesopotamia (between

the rivers Tigris and Euphrates in present day Iraq), all fought their wars with armies of foot soldiers armed with bronze-headed spears and carrying rectangular shields. There were no horsed soldiers, though by 2000 BC high-ranking spearmen were riding to battle in clumsy chariots. The only armour in this period seems to have been a light helmet made of bronze, or, in the case of the social elite, splendidly fashioned from gold. The tomb of one of these worthies, Mes-kalam-shar of Ur, excavated in the late 1920s, yielded a magnificent helmet, a gold-shafted spear, an axe-head and gold-mounted daggers – luxury war gear for a rich officer caste.

Battles fought between these spearmen-armies had to be fairly simple affairs, decided by one hedge of spearmen out-thrusting and out-shoving the other. To harry an approaching formation with stinging attacks and to take up the chase once the enemy line had been broken, light infantry – not burdened with shields and armed only with axes, daggers or light spears – had been adopted by the end of the millenium. Such were the troops who carved out the first genuine empire in the history of the world for the Akkadian ruler Sargon the Great (3000–2305 BC), who reigned from the Mediterranean to the Persian Gulf.

The Egyptian kings of the upper and lower Nile who founded the 'Old Kingdom' of Egypt in the same period (about 2850–2300 BC) also relied on heavy and light spearmen, and were the first to enlist the specialized aid of warriors from abroad. The Egyptians had formidable neighbours on their southern border: the Nubians, a negro race adept in the use of the bow and arrow, whose fire-power Egypt harnessed by employing Nubian

archers on a regular basis. This made the Nubians the first in a long line of specially-recruited 'foreign legionnaires' reaching down the centuries to the Highland and Gurkha regiments of the British Army, the Cossacks of Russia and the North African colonial *goums* in French service.

The introduction of archers to the battlefield was a vital innovation. The bow gave armies the ability to destroy enemy troops at a distance for minimal risk. Before the bow, stones were the only way of

Above: Massed infantry look on during a dramatic chariot action in the Battle of Kadesh in Syria, fought about 1290 BC between the armies of Ramses II of Egypt and the Hittite King Muwatallis

Below: Vivid portrait in stone of a monarch in the saddle reveals one of the key weapons which made the Assyrians overlords of the ancient world: the bow

engaging troops at a distance, the stones being either flung by hand or whirled and released with great force from a sling. As stones are the cheapest and most abundant ammunition in the world, and as a sling is far easier to make than a bow, slingers retained their military importance for many centuries before vanishing from the scene in the Middle Ages. But in the hands of an expert the bow could kill at double or treble the distances over which a shower of slung stones merely proved an irritant.

As a long-range firearm with a high rate of fire, the bow remained unchallenged until the emergence of the breech-loading rifle in the second half of the nineteenth century. In all those 4,000 years only a handful of military peoples used archery to its full advantage. The first to do so were the Assyrians, who conquered the whole of the known world east of the Mediterranean between about 1100 and 612 BC, when their capital, Nineveh, fell. The Assyrian

rampage across the Middle East came about because they were the first people to put the making of war on a scientific basis.

Their secret, broadly speaking, was to take every known weapon and use it in its most effective role. This particularly applied to archers. The Assyrians used foot archers, chariot archers and horsed archers – the latter being by far the best way to use the bow, because a mounted archer could gallop into range, fire off a few shafts and then gallop away again with no risk to himself. (Saracen horsed archers used this tactic with deadly effect on the Crusaders of western Europe in the twelfth century AD, while the Mongol horsed archers conquered their way from the China Sea to eastern Germany largely by using the same tactic.) Not content with getting the maximum firepower out of the bow, the Assyrians also developed body and leg armour for both horsed and unmounted soldiers; they used horsed spearmen and heavy lancers to ride down and break enemy troops already whittled to distraction by arrow fire. They added to the specialized needs and performances of the light and heavy infantry, and in addition brought in engineers or sappers to breach the walls of enemy cities.

In short, the Assyrians developed every arm used in land warfare before gunpowder firearms and, ultimately, the ground-attack aircraft. Yet their career of conquest, prolonged though it was, could end only one way: Assyrian conquests proved too widespread to be maintained against repeated revolts.

Their successors as military top-dogs were the Persians, whose genius for superior organization won them an empire stretching from the Black Sea to India and then prevented their new subject warrior-peoples, the Assyrians foremost among them, from carrying arms on a scale large enough to encourage revolt. For sheer splendour and manpower the Persian Empire seemed unbeatable – but when its 'Great Kings' started to take on the obstreperous city states of Greece they came up against a totally new military system which proved their ruin.

The Greeks produced a new breed of heavy infantry, the like of which had never been seen: protected with helmet, cuirass and shield, and armed with long spears and double-edged swords for close-in work, the hoplites marched and fought in formation to a marvellous discipline. They could hold out in a near-unbreakable shield wall, or charge home, as at Marathon in 490 BC,

Below : From the Greek heroic age: Achilles, super-hero of the Trojan Wars, in action with the Queen of the Amazons. He is wearing the high-crested 'Attic' helmet with its wide cheek-pieces, a heavy, enclosing 'bell' corselet and moulded greaves to protect the lower leg. Later Greek armour would give the heavy infantry far less massive protection, but greater mobility in return

with devastating effect. Peltasts – light infantry – and slingers completed their battle array and made for flexibility of tactics; frequently the hoplite host rode to battle on horseback, dismounting to fight, thus gaining that other military virtue, mobility of action.

The kings of Macedon, Philip (359–336 BC) and Alexander the Great (336–323 BC) proved themselves master-technicians with armies of hoplites and phalangites – massed pikemen – and armoured cavalry. They used the hoplites and pikemen-mass, called a *phalanx*, to pin down the enemy centre while the cavalry routed the enemy flanks. This infantry/cavalry teamwork, plus a strong blow at the enemy's weakest point, was the secret of Alexander's conquest of the entire Persian Empire together with Egypt. It enabled the Graeco-Macedonian army to smash the huge Persian hosts, as H.G. Wells put it, 'as a stone smashes a bottle'. Alexander's empire fell apart after his early death at Babylon in 323 BC, but the reign of the phalanx/cavalry combination on the battlefield endured until the next advance in weaponry and tactics.

This came from Italy in the form of the Roman legion, originally the biggest building-block in a citizen army with the habit of fighting its battles three lines deep, the toughest spearmen being held back in the third line. Originally, too, the Romans relied as heavily on the thrusting spear as anyone else, but abandoned it in favour of light throwing javelins backed up by stabbing swordplay at close quarters. It is far easier to kill a man with a stab than with a sweeping cut, and the Romans were able to conquer all comers largely because they drilled this fact into their line infantry.

After a series of murderous defeats at the hands of the great Carthaginian general Hannibal, who rampaged all over Italy between 218 and 204 BC, the Romans also learned to break down the legion into handy sub-units (maniples and centuries) to meet all the crises of battle without losing cohesion. Hannibal found it easy to lure the old-style legions into a trap and cut down the hemmed-in legionaries like cattle. Disciplined infantry was not enough: sound cavalry was also needed to protect the flanks. The Romans learned fast. At Zama in 202 BC – the Waterloo of the wars with Carthage, fought on Carthaginian soil in North Africa – Hannibal was decisively beaten in precisely the same style as his own former triumphs over the Romans. Victory over Carthage gave Rome the mastery of the western Mediterranean; clashes with

Greek colonists in southern Italy and Sicily led to all-out war with the Greeks. It was the end of the line for the phalanx, which was chewed apart by the smaller, handier Roman maniples at Cynoscephalæ (197 BC) and Pydna (168 BC).

Rome's subsequent advance to world empire was marked by one hideous defeat which Roman strategists preferred to forget rather than learn from: Carrhae, in 53 BC. In a vainglorious attempt to subdue the Parthians, heirs to Alexander's generals and to ancient Persia, Marcus Crassus led seven legions to destruction in the Syrian desert. Parthian heavy cavalry destroyed the Romans' skimpy cavalry screen, laying open the mass of the legions to decimation by the fire of horsed archers.

Horsed archers never did become an integral part of the Roman military machine, but the Roman army of the later Western Empire (from about AD 192–410) was very different from the army that had beaten the Carthaginians and Greeks back in the second century BC. The hard-marching infantry legions became obsolete, replaced in prime importance by divisions of heavy armoured cavalry which raced from one leak in the imperial frontiers to another. Nor were regular forces

Above : Portrait of a hoplite on a Greek red-figure vase of about 480 BC depicts the superbly-drilled infantryman who met and broke the armies of Persia at Marathon and Plataea. He still sports greaves on his legs but his body-armour is far lighter than the old 'bell' corselet. When in action the helmet was pulled forward and down to protect the face

Above : This vivid scene from the Acropolis shows what happens when cavalry comes up against good infantry. Damage to the carving has removed the right arm of the hoplite together with the long spear, which is making the Persian charger recoil while the hoplite cannily shelters behind his shield

Right : The hoplite's opponent: a Persian 'Immortal', so called because when one fell another would immediately step into his place. He is an archer-spearman, carrying his curved bow, with a quiver slung from the shoulder. The gorgeously equipped Persian infantry found that they had a very short life expectancy against armoured troops determined to come to hand-to-hand fighting

sufficient: barbarian tribes were taken into alliance as armed *federati*. Sometimes they did fight for Rome, more often than not they proved a Trojan Horse for other invaders. Rome's last great general, Stilicho, was not even Roman but a Vandal. He was one of the greatest masters of mobile warfare known to military history, keeping the Western Empire intact through a string of victories against incredible odds between AD 396 and 410. However, there was only one Stilicho. When the Emperor Honorius, fearing treason, had Stilicho murdered in 408, Rome fell to the Goths within two years.

The Eastern Empire, with its capital at Constantinople, lived on after the fall of Rome. In the reign of Justinian (527–65) it even produced a Greek reincarnation of Stilicho, Count Belisarius, who recovered North Africa and Italy briefly for the Empire – again by the masterly use of heavy cavalry. But from the seventh century AD the Empire was a shrinking island of bureaucracy, palace revolutions and religious faction-fighting, ringed by a sea of turbulent foes.

The Goths, Vandals and Franks, having wrecked the Western Empire, at last settled down and aped the civilization they had destroyed. A jumble of barbarian kingdoms grew up in the ruins of the Roman West. In time they accepted Christianity, and it became the new medium of learning and the peaceful arts. Not so the Arabs who, fired by Mohammed and his teaching, came raging out of the desert after 632. Arab armies of horsed warriors – swordsmen, lancers and archers – swept the board in Palestine, Persia, North Africa and Spain. The Arabs even crossed the Pyrenees into southern Gaul, only to be flung back at Tours by the Frankish general Charles Martel in 732. Thoroughly shaken, Europe was now confronted and contained to the south and east by an alien and ideologically hostile civilization.

What the Arabs were to the Mediterranean world, the Vikings of Scandinavia were to north-west Europe: a terrifying scourge which demanded determined fighting and the right tactics to reduce to human proportions. The Viking style of fighting owed its success to an interesting blend of features. Viking warbands and armies knew all about mobility – they would make mass round-ups of horses to ride across country from one victim to the next. Their warriors preferred to fight decisive battles on foot, behind a disciplined shield-wall. In time the Vikings, like every military race before them – be it Assyrian, Persian, Greek or Roman – found that foot soldiers had their limits. An armoured warrior on horseback could always achieve more; and it was from an area of Viking settlement in northern France – Normandy – that the armoured knight came riding out to dominate the military scene in Europe.

The original Norman knights of the eleventh century had all the versatility of their Viking forebears. Lethal in the saddle with longsword, throwing javelin and lance, they could also dismount to fight on foot; also like the Vikings, they made excellent mercenary warbands and served in foreign pay as far east as Constantinople and the Holy Roman Empire itself. But they were certainly not invincible. William of Normandy's victory at Hastings in 1066, so often hailed as proof of the supremacy of the mounted knight, was nothing of the kind. The Normans did not win at Hastings: the English threw away a certain victory by prematurely breaking formation. Before they did so the Normans were on the verge of panic, all their mounted attacks having been repulsed. The knights only came into their own after William had used archers to cut the English shield wall down to a size which the knights could manage.

When Europe's Crusading knights came up against Saracen horse archers in the Middle East a hundred years later, the result was a general stalemate, only broken when one side or the other made a mistake. A new infantry weapon, the crossbow, helped force the Saracens to keep their distance; Saracen mobility prevented the European knights from riding down their elusive enemy. There was no stalemate, however, about the stunning Mongol invasion of eastern Europe in the thirteenth century. The Mongol regiments of disciplined horse archers, having bowled over all comers across the entire length of Eurasia, had begun the devastation of Hungary, Poland and eastern Germany when the Great Khan died in 1241 and the Mongols went home to elect a successor. Fortunately for Europe the next Khans, Mangu and Kubilai, concentrated on the conquest of southern China; and memories of the rout of the Poles and Germans at Liegnitz in 1241 remained as an awful reminder of what might have been.

The Mongol Empire lasted for an even briefer period than Alexander's empire – it had vanished by 1370. The armies of Europe learned as little from the short-lived Mongol supremacy as the Roman army had learned from the defeat at Carrhae. The terrible efficiency of the horsed archer was never understood or emulated in the Christian West, where the mounted knight, heavy and light infantry crossbowman and foot archer continued to dominate the military scene until gunpowder firearms wrought a bigger revolution than even the horsed archer had ever accomplished.

Below : The mailed knights of Normandy ride out to crush the upstart English army at Hastings in 1066. Notice that their main weapon is not the lance but the throwing javelin, enabling them to make repeated hit-and-run attacks. At Hastings the Norman knights got the shock of their lives, failing totally to panic the shield-wall of armoured spearmen and axemen waiting for them on the ridge. At one stage it was the Normans who were on the verge of panic, before Duke William drew off his knights and ordered up the foot archers to decimate the English shield-wall with massed volleys of arrows

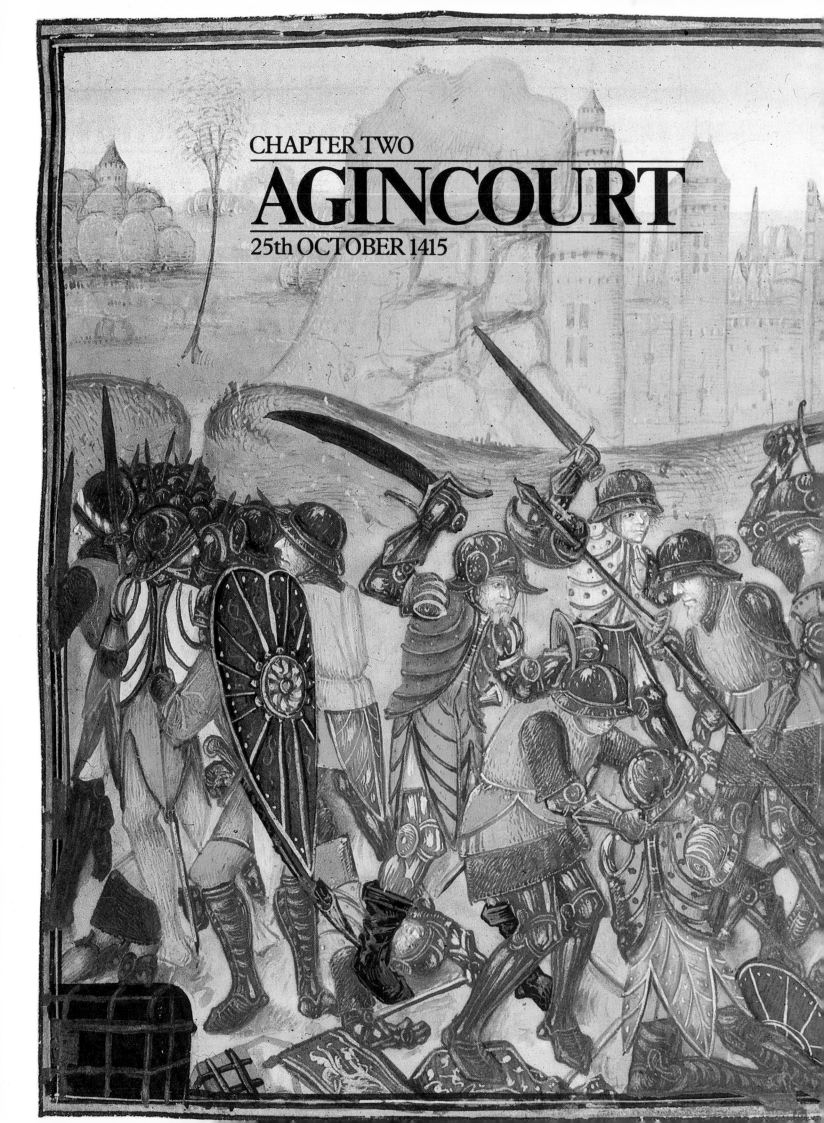

CHAPTER TWO
AGINCOURT
25th OCTOBER 1415

Right: 'The mirror of all Christian Kings': Henry V prays to St George, who is portrayed in the insignia of the Order of the Garter founded by Edward III. An undisputed master of the calculated risk in war and certainly a superb leader of soldiers, Henry's cold bigotry made him a singularly unattractive figure who needed all the glamour that Shakespeare was later to provide

Previous pages: A vivid reminder of the viciousness of Agincourt – the results of Henry V's order to kill all prisoners, issued to prevent any chance of a 'fifth-column' comeback against the outnumbered English. A group of men-at-arms is hacking down a French knight in the foreground; further to the rear another knight, wounded, helpless and already stripped of his leg armour, is having his throat cut. On the right of the picture, two Englishmen are haggling over some loot. Henry's men were shocked at the order to kill the prisoners – not on chivalrous grounds, but because this would deprive them of possible fortunes in ransom money

Hopelessly trapped by the armoured masses of France, Henry had to make them attack where it suited him best

The war

IN the 350-odd years since 1066, when William of Normandy had become King of England, English kings had never ceased to press their claims to Normandy and other lands in France; and for a young English king to revive these claims was nothing new. Twenty-five years old when he became king in 1413, Henry V had spent his formative years in English civil wars, fighting on behalf of his father Henry IV, who had seized the crown from Richard II. A renewal of the old feud with France was an ideal opportunity to sink all domestic quarrels, unleashing the resentment and ambition of the English nobility against a foreign and thoroughly familiar enemy.

Henry V's great-grandfather, Edward III, had fought a series of wickedly expensive but successful wars in France, securing a bridgehead of territory at Calais and a coastal strip around Bordeaux in the south.

In the fire-power of their foot archers, adept in the use of the powerful longbow, the English had discovered a potent weapon against the ponderous armies of French knights, and they looked back with pride and confidence to the victories of Crécy (1346) and Poitiers (1356).

Henry V could therefore contemplate a war against France with enthusiasm and confidence. His first move would be aimed at Normandy, the old Duchy foremost in his claims, involving a cross-Channel invasion followed by the capture of a firm base. Henry gave himself plenty of time to raise and equip his expeditionary force of archers, infantry men-at-arms, knights and siege gunners, armed with the new cannon, before sailing from Southampton on 11 August 1415. His total force seems to have been around 9,000 men, but all figures for this (and for most medieval campaigns) are conflicting and suspect.

The campaign: from Harfleur to the Somme

Henry assumed correctly that the French would expect him to cross the Dover Narrows and begin operations from the existing English base at Calais; the English landing on the north shore of the Seine estuary was therefore unopposed and the French were caught decidedly on the wrong foot at the outset of the campaign. Henry's first objective was the capture of the walled city of Harfleur, but he had not bargained for the spirited resistance put up by Harfleur's garrison. The siege began on 18 August and dragged on until 22 September, by which time Henry's troops were riddled with dysentery; 2,000 of them were dead or unfit for further service; he had to earmark another 1,000 to garrison Harfleur; which left him barely 6,000 men with which to continue the campaign. Nearly all his noble advisers argued against doing anything more ambitious than making sure of Harfleur. The English army had lost too many men and a cold, wet autumn was already well advanced.

Henry, however, was determined to take the field and trail his coat through Normandy from Harfleur to Calais. Gambling on the hesitation and inactivity of the French army which had already cost them Harfleur, he calculated that ten days should be ample to see the English safely into Calais, thereby winning an important moral victory by marching through France at their leisure. (A sound propagandist,

Henry had from the outset of the campaign posed not as a foreign invader, but as a rightful king coming to claim his own.) The march to Calais began on 6 October.

At first it seemed that the English would get away with it. By the thirteenth they were already eighty miles out of Harfleur and over half-way to Calais, with only one major river crossing, the Somme, in front of them. But with only six miles to go to the vital ford at Blanchetaque, Henry received frightening news: 6,000 Frenchmen were waiting for him at the Somme.

If there was no way through to Calais, there could be no turning back to Harfleur either; for the English would almost certainly be pursued all the way and finally taken in flank and crushed by the main French army moving north-west. Henry, however, was still determined to cross the Somme and continue his march to Calais. He set off up the Somme valley, hoping to find a place where he could slip his army across, but the French kept pace with him on the opposite bank. The English were foiled at Abbeville, Pont Rémy, and Hangest-sur-Somme, Crouy, Picquigny, Amiens, Boves and Fouilly – a miserable week of marching through sluicing rain in ever-increasing hunger with the French always one step ahead on the far bank of that cursed river.

At Fouilly, on the eighteenth, Henry decided to cut across country instead of

Above: A mêlée between French and English men-at-arms. Medieval armour had its limitations; a man could be stunned or temporarily paralysed by a smash on the helmet with a hammer, giving the attacker ample time for a deadly knife-thrust through a joint in the armour. Two-handed cutting or slashing against an armoured opponent was often far less effective than a shrewd stab in the joints with a thrusting weapon

Below : One very good reason for English confidence in 1415: a detail of an illumination from Froissart's *Chronicles* showing the battle of Crécy, the famous rout of the French back in 1346

following the northerly meander of the Somme between Boves and Bethencourt – a decision that yielded the English their miracle. Peasants interrogated on the line of march told the English of fords at Bethencourt and Voyennes. Their information was sound, and the English army struggled across to the north bank mere hours before the French advance guard arrived on the scene. The Somme was behind the English now – but as they resumed their march towards Calais on the twenty-first they began to sight the tracks of a numberless host which was clearly marching ahead of them and slightly to the east. Throughout the twenty-second and twenty-third the armies steadily converged.

Neither the French king nor his son the Dauphin was with the French host, which was commanded by Charles d'Albret, Constable of France. D'Albret had pulled off a copybook piece of interception and he had no intention of spoiling it by rushing into a premature engagement. Throughout the twenty-fourth the English scouts watched the dense French columns streaming onwards, curling west round the wood of Tramecourt to lie massively across the English road to Calais by nightfall.

In *Henry V*, Shakespeare uses the wait through the night to great dramatic effect, depicting the cocky and splendidly equipped French making bets on how many Englishmen they will kill, while the weary and down-at-heel 'poor condemned English' wait glumly for the slaughter. But if the chronicler Enguerrand de Monstrelet is to be believed it was the other way around, with depressing silence from the French camp:

'*Scarcely any of their horses neighed all night, which many took to be an omen of evil to come. The English played music on their trumpets and other instruments throughout the night, and the whole neighbourhood re-echoed with the sound of it.*'

The armies deploy

Daylight on 25 October showed the French barely half a mile away and apparently invincible in numbers. Their strength is today considered to have been around 25,000 to the English 5,700 and they merely lay there, waiting. The position as the English saw it, however, offered a certain amount of hope. Ploughland speckled with recently-sown corn led towards the French through a narrowing hour-glass of open ground between two woods, which seemed certain to prevent the French from out-flanking the English army and swallowing it whole. This levelled the odds considerably, for the English army could fill the neck of the hour-glass comfortably – but the French would not be able to open out and use their numbers to full advantage. They would have to attack on the same frontage as the English, and if their first line ran into trouble their second and third lines would then find themselves blocked by their own men.

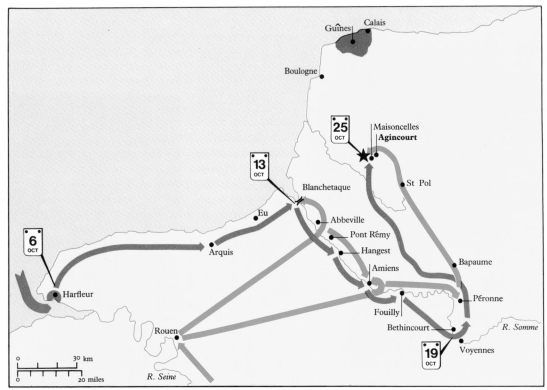

Left : The crisis of the campaign – Henry's attempted march from Harfleur to Calais and its interception on the lower Somme. Force-marching ever further and further away from safety, the English (*red*) were facing starvation and exhaustion by the time they finally managed to get across. But d'Albret and the immensely powerful French field army (*blue*) blocked their resumed march to Calais with ease.

There was another advantage for the English: as an army of foot soldiers they did not have to worry about firm ground for their horses, while the French did, or should have. It had been raining heavily for the last fortnight and the armies were facing each other across soggy ploughland – the worst possible terrain over which to walk a horse, let alone spur it to a charge. It needed only half the front-line French knights to be knocked over to cause chaos for the following masses advancing through the hoof-churned slurry; while any thrown knight, flat on his back in the mud, would be helpless as a capsized beetle.

At Agincourt, therefore, Henry's main concern was to get the French committed to a head-on attack before they had realized their weaknesses. He deployed his own army between the two woods, the men-at-arms interspersed with archers in their wedge-shaped *herce* formation which permitted the maximum number of arrows to be aimed at any given spot. Each archer planted a sharpened stake in the ground before him, presenting a bristling palisade to the enemy. When Henry saw that the French were not going to charge him, the archers were ordered to uproot their stakes and stand ready to move forward. The king himself gave the command: 'Banners advance! In the name of Jesus, Mary and St George!' and the line rolled forward. To repeated cries of 'St George!' and silence from the astonished French, the English line advanced to within three hundred yards of the French first line. The stakes were planted again, and the archers drew their first shafts.

Slaughter in the mud

As a trained archer could loose at least six arrows in a minute, and assuming that 4,000 archers let fly more or less simultaneously, this meant that the knights and dismounted men-at-arms of the French first line suffered a rain of as many as 24,000 arrows in the first minute. The French troops reacted with the blind and uncoordinated rage of a fighting bull bitten on the nose by a terrier, and charged forward to piecemeal destruction.

The first Frenchmen to assault the English line at least had the benefit of advancing over comparatively solid ground, but as soon as the knights started to move they created a deepening quagmire. Forced to ride across the line of advance of their own men-at-arms by the constricting woods, the knights were easy targets for the

simple reason that a man on horseback is so much easier to hit than a man on foot. It was sufficient merely to wound the French chargers, a hideously easy task with long-bow volleys at 100 yards or under, and the formations of knights dissolved into chaos.

The biggest danger for the English were the dismounted French men-at-arms in the centre, who actually reached the English line and traded blows with their tormentors. To do so they were forced to struggle forwards so closely packed together that they could not even use their sword-arms or swing their maces. The English, on the other hand, had all the room they needed for knifework through helmet-slits and armour joints, and for stunning blows with the war-hammers they carried slung from their belts. Thousands of French corpses were found after the slaughter without a wound on them; either stunned or tripped in the crush, they had been unable to get to

Above : Hand-to-hand fighting between French and English knights. This sort of close combat, giving the French no chance to open out and use their superior numbers to full advantage, was precisely what Henry wanted

Below : The English trump card: longbowmen. Accurate fire was less important than their ability to keep pouring rapid volleys of arrows into the same narrow area, like pounding a mallet into a column of advancing ants

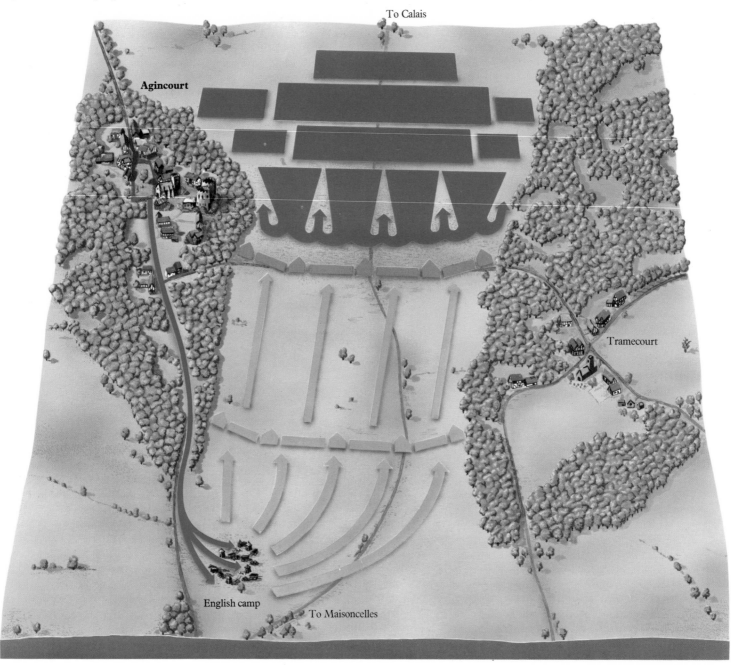

To Calais

Agincourt

Tramecourt

English camp

To Maisoncelles

Above : Henry's prime concern at Agincourt was to provoke the French (*blue*) into attacking down the constricting hourglass of open ground between the woods of Agincourt and Tramecourt. When they made no move against the English (*red*) in their original position, Henry deliberately advanced to a range short enough for his archers and made the French an offer they could not refuse

their feet and were suffocated by the weight of other victims on top of them.

It seems that the English archery ceased after the first forty-five minutes or thereabouts. After that the archers threw away their bows, hefted their knives, billhooks, hammers and other hand weapons, and clambered over the steadily thickening carpet of prostrate French bodies to pull down more and more. English soldiers were seen stark naked and barefooted, plastered in gory slime, out of their minds with battle-fury; others found time to single out individuals who looked rich enough to be worth a good ransom. So many prisoners were taken that Henry was faced with a new worry. The French third line had still to move; alone, it outnumbered the entire English army. The growing tally of French prisoners also

represented a potential threat because there was no way of keeping them safely disarmed. Should the French third line manage to reverse the initial English victory, it would be easy for the French captives to snatch up weapons and avenge the massacre their army had suffered by inflicting one of their own.

Revenge of a sort was exacted, but only of a feeble and underhand nature, and the excesses it triggered off were terrible. At some time in the afternoon a small band of French knights and men-at-arms who had fled the battle led a force of 600 peasants against the undefended English baggage-train and plundered it. In itself, this posed absolutely no danger to the English forces but it prompted Henry to an order which made him infamous. The French third line was still intact and hundreds of prisoners were ready to take up arms again at a second's notice. Suddenly, this flare-up of activity occurred behind the English line – it was a recipe for disaster, and Henry reacted by ordering that all the prisoners were to be killed. This was received by his men with outraged disbelief – not on humanitarian grounds, but because of the lost fortunes in potential ransom-money that it implied. Henry, however, was a commander who saw to it that any order he thought fit to give was promptly obeyed, and a new massacre began. It was only called off when it became obvious that in fact the French third line was melting away without daring to enter the fray.

It was all over by late afternoon. Henry and his commanders were already touring the battlefield when Montjoye, the French herald, arrived to make formal acknowledgment of France's defeat. Casualty figures for both sides are difficult to assess. The French lost seven to ten thousand men, although fifteen to sixteen hundred aristocratic prisoners were lucky enough to escape Henry's order to kill the captives. The English dead numbered no more than five hundred, among them the commander of the right wing, Henry's uncle the Duke of York. He was found dead but un-wounded in his armour under a heap of bodies. As he was an elderly, corpulent man, he probably died of a heart attack. The whole battle lasted four hours at the most, and had been largely confined to an area 700 yards by 600.

Although the only field army of France and the cream of France's military commanders had been wiped out, the war dragged on for another four years. After a triumphant return to England via Calais, Henry returned to Normandy and fought a more orthodox campaign – of modest marches punctuated by sieges – capturing Caen and Bayeux in 1417, Falaise in 1418 and Rouen the following year. In 1420, by the Treaty of Troyes, Henry was named as the French king's heir, and he married the Princess Catherine. In 1422, however, he was robbed of everything he had fought for by premature death at the age of thirty-four. Had he lived another three weeks he would have been king of France, for King Charles died almost immediately after him.

The accession of Henry V's baby son – the only English monarch to be crowned king of both England and France – left the English troops in France under the command of capable generals who continued to win victories for a while, but there was never any question of France meekly

acquiescing to English rule. Within thirty-six years of Agincourt the last English soldiers had been driven from France, apart from the Calais garrison, and that too was lost in 1558.

A major battle in 1415 was inevitable once the French had found out that Henry was crossing the Channel; they certainly intercepted him with energy and skill, more than atoning for the apathy which had led to the loss of Harfleur. But good strategy and bad tactics do not mix and the French tactics at Agincourt were appalling. During the previous 400 years, enough had been learned about the art of warfare and the proper use of armoured troops to leave the French with no excuse for just sitting and waiting until Henry goaded them to attack exactly where it suited him best. For his part, Henry undoubtedly proved himself an inspired leader of men and a master of the calculated risk. On that march to Calais he came within a hair's width of disaster, and of being written off by history as a headstrong young man who took one risk too many.

Above : English celebrations of the victory at Agincourt, which proved to be hollow indeed. Henry's bid to become king of both England and France failed with his early death and left the English with an exhausting and ever more expensive war against a revived and defiant France

CHAPTER THREE
NASEBY
14th JUNE 1645

Rupert's wild cavalry charge, fatally successful, left the king's last army wide open to Cromwell's counterblow

The war

THE armed struggle between King Charles I and the English Parliament in the 1640s is always called '*the* English Civil War', which is like calling the Napoleonic Wars '*the* war with France'. Between 1066 and the 1640s there had been at least eight full-blooded civil wars in England, the most persistent of which – the Wars of the Roses in the fifteenth century – had dragged on for decades.

The medieval civil wars have a lot of relevance to the great Civil War of 1642-6, because it was really the last of England's medieval wars. When rebellion broke out there were no regular troops in the country at all: they had to be raised by both sides in the old medieval way, out of the purses of the local lords and gentry. There was one vital difference: 230 years before, when Henry V had raised his army for the war of Agincourt, it was far easier to create an 'instant' army of high fighting potential because of the feudal mould of society, in which one's duties to one's lord included providing troops when required to do so. But both Charles I and Parliament had to improvise armies and discover their fighting potential as quickly as possible without this natural raw material; and the side which created the best army – Parliament – eventually came out on top.

Seventeenth-century armies

Looking at the weapons and tactics used by foot and horse soldiers in the seventeenth century, the impression is one of warfare in the melting-pot. Clumsy gunpowder firearms had ousted the far more efficient longbow, the cumbersome muskets of the day being good only for a couple of shots before the rival lines of battle clashed and the muskets became used as elaborate clubs. Pikemen were back – hedgehog formations of foot soldiers armed with long spears, whose basic function was to repel enemy horsemen with a bristling wall of spears after pushing their opposite numbers off the field. The real revolutions, however, were in the artillery and cavalry.

Guns on wheeled carriages now rumbled along with an army on the move; they served to punch holes in the enemy line before the pikemen collided, and to hammer at fortifications, making a breach for attacking troops. But the cavalry had altered out of all recognition from the armoured masses that had charged to gory destruction at Agincourt. Soldiering on horesback was in fact half-way through an evolution from the medieval armoured knight to heavy cavalry for breaking up enemy formations in battle, and light cavalry for reconnaissance and pursuit.

Seventeenth-century cavalry units were becoming smaller and learning to charge in extended lines rather than ponderous masses. More important perhaps, they were becoming better disciplined, capable of being halted and re-formed by the most expert cavalry leaders for repeated charges. Armour was shrinking to a simple pot helmet with extensions for protecting the face and neck, and back-and-breast body armour. A totally new breed of cavalryman was the dragoon, capable of riding swiftly to take up a position and dismounting to fight, using the firepower of carbines and long pistol. More orthodox cavalry weapons still included the lance, but the most modern cavalry doctrine relied on charging home with the sword alone. The shield carried on the left arm was now a thing of the past.

These new soldiers were expensive to recruit, equip and train. Both sides found themselves short of cash during the Civil War, but the best long-term solution, as Parliament had learned by the year of Naseby, was the intensive drilling of a permanent conscript army. Charles, relying on volunteers, scored his most impressive victories early on in the war, but lost out to the painfully-acquired expertise of his more professional enemies.

Apart from the permanent military sore of Ireland, central Europe had been tearing itself to bits in the Thirty Years War ever since 1618, and many Englishmen with a fancy for military glory had learned their trade in the German wars. The most famous of these was King Charles' young nephew, Prince Rupert of the Rhine, who had learned how to lead cavalry charges

Previous pages : Charles I in his field headquarters, dictating dispatches to Sir Edward Walker, his Secretary at War. It is easy to forget that Charles was his own commander-in-chief, and by no means an unsuccessful one. In 1644 he took the main Parliamentary army most capably, at Lostwithiel in the West Country. But the following year his worst fault – an eternal readiness to see things in their most optimistic and unrealistic light – brought his army and his cause to disaster at Naseby with a good deal more ferocity and dash than cool tactical judgement. Parliament had no Ruperts of its own when the war began, but by the year of the Naseby campaign they had a formidable cavalry leader in Oliver Cromwell, Member for Cambridge and self-taught soldier.

The campaign of 1645

In 1642 Charles had fled a hostile and dangerous London to raise an army at Nottingham. After an indecisive brush with Parliamentarian forces at Edgehill, the King had shrunk from the prospect of a bold march on London until it was too late to take the capital; he retreated and set up his court at Oxford. By far his best year was 1643, when the North and West of England were secured for Charles by the victories of Adwalton Moor and Roundway Down; Prince Rupert took Bristol, the second city of the kingdom.

By 1644 Parliament was in such straits that it hired the Scottish army to come south and assist in the recovery of Yorkshire, helping the northern Parliamentarian army to smash the king's northern army at Marston Moor (2 July). But Charles countered by rounding up the entire western Parliamentarian army at Lostwithiel in Cornwall (2 September). He refused to consider the loss of the North as anything worse than a temporary setback; and as the summer campaigning season of 1645 approached he still bid high for victory.

There was one bastion of Parliamentarian resistance in the West, however: Taunton, still holding out defiantly, and only feebly besieged by the Royalist army in the West under Lord Goring. Taunton was natural bait with which to lure Parliament's 'New Model Army' (or 'New Noddle', as the Royalists sneeringly called it) into territory where it could be cut off and destroyed.

From the point of view of Parliament, raising the siege of Taunton was the natural starting-point for a campaign to reconquer the West. The result should have been a battle somewhere in the Taunton region, but both sides soon got their priorities – and, as a result, their strategies – in a hopeless tangle.

Charles could not campaign in the West or anywhere else without leaving Oxford dangerously exposed to the New Model

Below : Streeter's famous engraving of the armies deployed at Naseby, seen from the Parliamentarian side. The massive strength of Cromwell's cavalry force on the Parliamentarian right wing is stressed. Notice, in front of the Parliamentarian infantry, the little force known as the 'Forlorne Hope of Musquettiers'. This detachment was intended to do maximum damage to the advancing enemy line and generally take the sting out of its attack

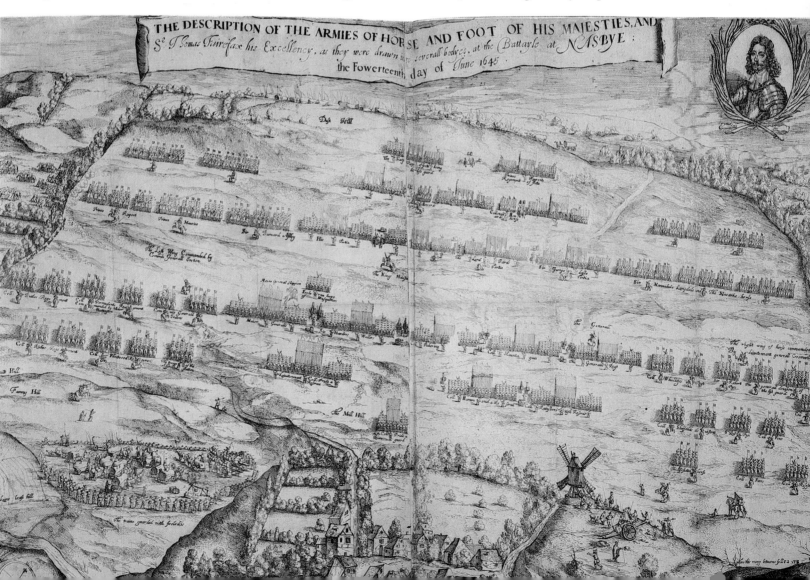

Above : A musketeer of the early seventeenth century, showing the burning match which, when snapped into the firing-pan by the released trigger, fired the piece. Long, heavy and with too slow a rate of fire for more than a couple of shots before the infantry lines clashed, these muskets were usually used as clubs in the thick of the action

Above right : The changing face of armour. Full suits of plate were now museum pieces : even the long, jointed 'tassets' to cover the front thigh were on their way out. Back-and-breast body armour, including shoulder and arm protection for the more conservative, would linger on to the close of the century

Below : Prince Rupert, the king's nephew – arrogant, headstrong, and a berserk leader in the attack

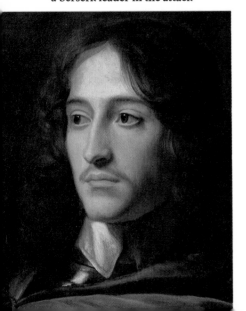

Army : if he could only manage to trap and destroy the New Model, as he had done with Essex's army at Lostwithiel, he would be able to go where he liked. For their part the Parliamentarians were lured by the prize of Oxford, and at the same time deterred by the strength of the Royalist forces there. As a result the New Model's commander, Sir Thomas Fairfax, was plagued by a series of contradictory orders from London, and the initiative in the 1645 campaign was left to Charles.

The King began by concentrating his forces, calling in Goring and his cavalry for a grand Royalist muster at Stow-on-the-Wold on 8 May. This concentration caused the Parliamentarian leaders to order Fairfax, who had arrived at Newbury during his march into the West, to go no further for fear of being overwhelmed. Instead of ordering a campaign against Fairfax Charles now decided to take his army north. Up in Scotland the Royalist Marquis of Montrose, in a splendid hit-and-run campaign with tiny forces of Highland clansmen, had won several victories for the King over the Scots and was clearly on a winning streak. This left the Parliamentarians in northern England on their own and offered a chance of recovering the North and avenging the Marston Moor defeat, if Charles came up from the South with his army.

But this wildly optimistic strategy hopelessly over-extended the Royalist forces. Charles sent Goring back to the West with 3,000 cavalry, one of the costliest mistakes he ever made. For the march to the north had only got as far as the Midlands when Charles and Rupert learned that the Parliamentarians were massing for a siege of Oxford. Messages were sent to Goring, ordering him to rejoin the King's army ; but Goring argued that the siege of Taunton must come first, and stayed where he was. An erratic, lethargic drunkard, Goring more than anyone else was the cause of disaster for the King's hopes when suddenly, on 5 June, the New Model Army and Cromwell's cavalry left Oxford to its own devices and headed north to intercept Charles and Rupert.

The sack of Leicester

On 22 May, having heard of the threat to Oxford, Charles and Rupert shelved the grandiose plan for recovering the North. Saving Oxford was of paramount importance. If they raised Cain in the Midlands, they might perhaps distract the New Model

Army from Oxford ; and as they were expecting Goring's cavalry to join them from the West they looked forward to a battle with confidence. As a start, Charles and Rupert decided to take Leicester, a rich Parliamentarian stronghold with plenty of booty to keep the Royalist troops happy.

Rupert's speciality was taking towns by storm. He appeared before Leicester on 29 May, blasted breaches in the walls during the following day, and attacked at midnight on the night of 30-31 May. Resistance was all over within a couple of hours. The plunder was splendid and the troops had a few days' contented rest while Charles and Rupert decided what to do next.

A real problem for both sides was the time it took for news to travel. It was not until 7 June that Rupert and Charles heard that the danger to Oxford was over for the moment, that Fairfax and the Parliamentarians were coming north, and that therefore the Royalist army, now heading for Oxford via Daventry, was set on a collision course with the New Model. Fairfax was now keen to force a battle. Apart from his blunt orders from Parliament to avenge Leicester, he had had a windfall : an intercepted letter from Goring explaining why Goring was staying in the West, while Charles and Rupert remained ignorant of this delinquency.

Between the ninth and the thirteenth the two armies continued to grope for each other within the triangle formed by Daventry, Northampton and Market Harborough. Rupert, deeply disturbed at the continued absence of Goring and with vivid memories of Marston Moor, did not want a battle ; he pressed for a swift disengagement via Leicester and a resumption of the march to the North. Charles saw the choice as one between retreat and battle. There had been a lot of silly stories in the Royalist camp about the Parliamentarian generals coming to blows, morale in the New Model Army being at rock bottom, and similar wishful thinking. Rupert, as a professional soldier, believed none of this, but Charles did and he decided to stand and fight. By nightfall on the thirteenth it was clear that the following day would see a battle somewhere between Market Harborough and Naseby, a little town one-third of the distance between Market Harborough and Daventry.

Deployment of the armies

By the early morning of 14 June 1645, the armies were in contact and searching earnestly for the most suitable ground on which to confront each other. It was Rupert whose choice decided the site of the battlefield. He selected Dust Hill, two miles north of Naseby, as the best place to assemble the Royalist host. Lord Astley's infantry were in the centre; the cavalry on their right flank was commanded by Rupert and his brother Maurice, that on the left flank by Sir Marmaduke Langdale.

The slopes of Dust Hill led down to a level field called the Broad Moor, some 600 yards across and screened down its western edge by a line of bushes and scrub known as Sulby Hedges. South of the Broad Moor and hidden from the Royalist infantry by a

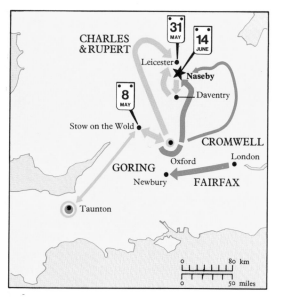

Left : The wandering tracks of the armies during the Naseby campaign. The refusal of Charles to concentrate on the destruction of Fairfax in the south, where the biggest concentrations of Royalist troops were deployed, was a fatal error, though Goring's insistence on staying in the West decided the issue in the Midlands

slight ridge were the Parliamentary forces: Henry Ireton's cavalry on the left facing the princes, Major-General Skippon's infantry in the centre, and Cromwell commanding the right-flank cavalry wing. Cromwell was commander of all the Parliamentarian cavalry and, to strengthen the left wing, sent Colonel John Okey's regiment of dragoons to dismount behind Sulby Hedges and give covering fire.

On the Royalist side, Goring's defection now stood out in all its gravity. Rupert's cavalry (about 4,500 in all) was outnumbered by 2,500; the total strength of the Royalist army was around 9,000 as against 14,000 Parliamentarians. Remembering painfully how Cromwell had seized the initiative at Marston Moor with a

Left : A selection of standards carried into action during the Civil War of 1642–6, with the names of the officers who commanded the various companies and regiments. All the deep division of the country during the conflict is reflected by the mix of religious and political mottoes and slogans under which the troops went into battle

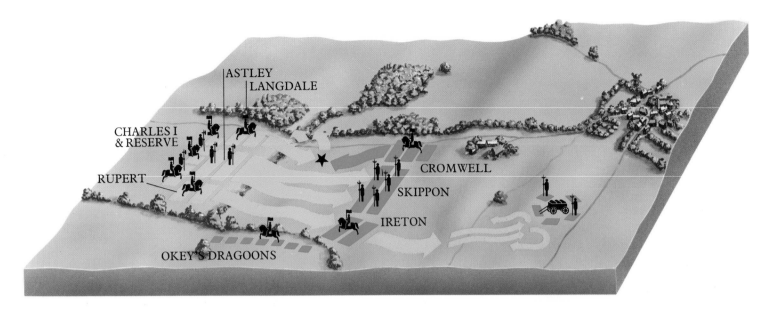

Above : The two main phases of the action at Naseby, which was decided by Rupert's failure to rein in his cavalry (*orange*) and Cromwell's iron control over his own (*blue*)

sudden charge, Rupert was determined to make the running himself this time. Shortly after 10 a.m., colours fluttering and sunlight glinting off weapons and armour, the Royalist line rolled forward to the attack.

Rupert's charge: when success can be fatal

Thundering at the head of their squadrons, Rupert and Maurice bore down on Ireton's cavalry with tremendous *élan*. They had to run the gauntlet of fire from Okey's dragoons behind Sulby Hedges, but the princes crashed into Ireton's troopers and scattered them. In the first minutes of the battle, Rupert had ripped the left-flank cavalry cover clean off the Parliamentary infantry, but it all went for nothing. He failed to hold in and re-form his men who charged madly onwards, far into the rear of the Parliamentarian lines. Finally they

came up to the New Model's wagon-train, which was stoutly defended by a ring of musketeers. Only then did Rupert recover his men and turn them round – only to find that the battle was already lost.

Astley's charge: collision of the infantry

While Rupert's cavalry charged forward on their right, Astley's infantry marched gallantly across the Broad Moor in impressive array, keeping their formations well. They drove back the advance formation or 'forlorne hope' of Parliamentarian musketeers who were stationed in front of Skippon's front line to take the sting out of the Royalist charge. Cheered by the sight of Ireton's cavalry already on the run, Astley's infantry lowered their pikes and came manfully to 'push of pike' with the New Model's infantry. Outnumbered though they were, the Royalist infantry drove their opposite numbers back, and the entire Parliamentarian centre began to buckle.

Cromwell's charge: the decisive right hook

Cromwell's charge on the right flank of the battle was a mirror-image of Rupert's attack on the left: complete victory over the opposing cavalry. But there was one vital difference. Once it was clear that Langdale's cavalry was decisively broken, Cromwell halted his squadrons, re-formed them and wheeled to the left. Then they charged for the second time deep into the unprotected Royalist left flank. Over on the far side of the battlefield, Okey's dragoons rushed to their horses and came charging in on the Royalist right flank while the shaken infantry of the New Model Army, saved in the nick of time by the successes of their cavalry, rallied and counter-attacked in the centre. Appalled at the speed of the reversal and the menace of the three-sided trap thus closing in on them, the hemmed-in Royalists began to drop their weapons and surrender by the hundred.

By the time Rupert brought his cavalry back to the field there was nothing he could do to save the day. The New Model infantry and Cromwell's cavalry were still virtually intact; Charles, at the head of his life guards, had striven unavailingly to patch up some kind of front with the surviving Royalist cavalry, but there was nothing for it but to retreat, abandoning even Leicester in the overriding need to get clear of the triumphant New Model forces.

Aftermath and losses

The New Model Army lost only about 150 men in the battle, a small price to pay for the capture of half the Royalist army. Royalist losses were much heavier, though well under 1,000. But as well as destroying the King's only field army, the New Model had captured his baggage and artillery train. The loot included Charles' correspondence, the latter containing damning proof of the King's willingness to bring Catholic Irish troops over to fight his English subjects. When these letters were published they appalled and alienated many who had loyally supported the King's cause since the beginning of his conflict with Parliament.

The aftermath of Naseby was in total contrast to the fumble and confusion with which the 1645 campaign had opened. The New Model Army's first objective after recovering Leicester was to attack Goring's force in Somerset, which was defeated at Langport on 10 July. In August Charles failed to penetrate Lancashire in order to join hands with Montrose and was eventually forced back to Oxford. The New Model Army then turned on Bristol, now under Rupert's command, and captured the city on 11 September; South Wales followed; Devon and Cornwall were next early in 1646; finally Oxford itself surrendered in June 1646, bringing the war to a decisive end.

Naseby's status as a famous battle is therefore indisputable. It reflected a key stage in the evolution of modern cavalry tactics; it was the first victory of the first professional standing army in English history. But above all Naseby opened the floodgates of defeat for the Royalist cause, and the tremendous sequence of political events which followed the battle surpassed those of many other more celebrated actions.

Above : A comparatively little known portrait of the victor of Naseby: Oliver Cromwell, for once depicted not as a scowling, armour-plated stormtrooper but as a country gentleman looking rather ill at ease in velvet

CHAPTER FOUR
BLENHEIM
13th AUGUST 1704

Previous pages : Marlborough directing operations on the field of Blenheim, from the famous commemorative tapestries at Blenheim Palace. This battle was not won by issuing orders, sitting back and letting subordinates do the fighting : Marlborough was constantly on the move along the whole British front, keeping everything under his own eye

Marlborough's 'famous victory': a perfect example of how to impose your will on the enemy and make him dance to your tune

The war

IF 1940, the year of Dunkirk, was Britain's most appalling experience of fighting on the continent of Europe as part of an alliance against a joint foe, then 1704, the year of Blenheim, was unquestionably the most triumphant. As grandiose in scale as it was intricate in detail, the Blenheim campaign represents the greatest single act of service that Britain has performed for her allies in any war.

The mastermind of the campaign, Britain's Duke of Marlborough, had a far harder job than Montgomery trying to beat Rommel at Alamein, or even Wellington trying to throw Napoleon's armies out of Spain. Marlborough was an Eisenhower of a general. He was as much a tactful chairman as a military commander, always obliged to play the diplomat, consult the allied governments, respect the sensitivities and weaknesses of individual allies, fend off the whims of politicians back home, and use political subterfuge to survive against enemies who sought to pull him down.

'Generalissimo' is the slick term for these co-ordinator generals. Nearly all of them (and again Eisenhower is the best modern example) have exercised their power far from any battlefield, with copious staffs to handle details of planning, supply, strategy and tactics. Marlborough, however, was unique : a diplomat and politician, quarter-master and engineer, strategist and tactician, all in one. The Blenheim campaign proved that he had two other priceless qualities : the courage to come up with a daring plan and stick to it, and the sense to keep all the details to himself and prevent his masters from sinking the plan at birth.

By 1702 most of western and central Europe was ranged in alliance against the France of Louis XIV. Louis' ambitions, stratagems, and constant wars of expansion had caused intense trouble for the previous thirty-five years; Louis had adopted the motto *Nec Pluribus Impar*, 'Not Unequal to Many', and had a track record of diplomatic and military victories to prove it justified. But now the 'Sun King' was attempting to make his grandson, the Duke of Anjou, king of Spain. Anjou's claim was as good as anyone else's but the real problem lay in what would happen to the Spanish Empire, the biggest in the world. Apart from the territories in the Americas and the Pacific there were Spain's extensive lands in Europe : modern-day Belgium and Lux-emburg, the Duchy of Milan, Sardinia, Sicily and the Kingdom of Naples. And it was the spectre of the Spanish Empire passing under French domination in a naked take-over bid that brought the 'Grand Alliance' into existence.

The architect of the Grand Alliance was William of Orange, who had been fighting Louis all his life as Stadholder of the Dutch Republic, and who in 1688–9 had become king of England as well. He brought in the Holy Roman Emperor, the Habsburg Leopold I, ruler of Austria, thus enabling the allies to fight the French in the Low Countries, the Rhine and Italy. The treaty of alliance was negotiated by William's captain-general and ambassador-extra-ordinary – Marlborough – and signed at The Hague in September 1701. There was no little panic when William died in February 1702 and his sister-in-law Anne became queen of England, but the new queen upheld the alliance. She also upheld the appointments of her best friend's husband – Marlborough.

However, the Dutch were not so sure. William had been their Stadholder for

Right : Kneller's portrait of Marlborough crowned with the victor's laurels. An unquestioned military genius, Marlborough blended an acute tactical sense of his opponents' weaknesses with patience and a refusal to be pressurized into changing his plans. Always saddled with the tremendous job of preventing monarchs and politicians from excessive meddling, he never forgot that no victory can be won without destroying the enemy's armies in the field

the offensive only allowed the French to strengthen their armies on the upper Rhine; he had been right, and now it looked like being too late to do anything about it. The Holy Roman Emperor's envoy in London appealed to Queen Anne for immediate help, which could only come from the Low Countries.

Marlborough had toyed with a plan for taking the British army up the Rhine as far as Coblenz, swinging south-west into the Moselle valley and forcing the French into a campaign on their own frontier in Lorraine. Though this would have little effect on the war in southern Germany, it would have the advantage of being infinitely more acceptable to the Dutch than a march to the Danube. Marlborough promised the Austrian Imperial envoy to march the British Army to the Danube provided that the Holy Roman Empire guaranteed the collaboration of an army under Prince Eugene of Savoy, the Empire's leading general. He then persuaded the Queen to give him an Order in Council to 'send a speedy succour' (nature unspecified) 'to His Imperial Majesty'. Finally (April 1704) he laid the Queen's Order before the Dutch and told them that he would campaign on the Moselle that year. To this the Dutch had no choice but to agree.

Left: Prince Eugene of Savoy, the leading general of the Holy Roman Empire and the colleague in whom Marlborough placed complete trust. The partnership between the two generals, begun in the Blenheim campaign, was to endure through many trials in the painful years which lay ahead

thirty years and his death left them with a deep sense of insecurity. They also profoundly distrusted Anne's loyal but misguided efforts to get her husband, Prince George of Denmark, accepted as allied commander-in-chief over Marlborough. The Dutch did not want a foreign commander to run their army for them, but were prepared to accept Marlborough as nominal commander provided that he agreed to consult representatives of the Dutch government, the States-General, at every turn.

Throughout 1703, while Marlborough fretted non-stop over the inadequacies of the Dutch, the war's centre of gravity was swinging from the Low Countries to southern Germany. The Elector of Bavaria went over to the French, leaving the loyal Margrave of Baden isolated on the upper Rhine, and southern Germany and the Danube valley open to Louis' armies. A decisive French advance in 1704 seemed likely to capture Vienna and knock Austria with the Holy Roman Empire clean out of the war. Marlborough had repeatedly warned the Dutch that their refusal to take

The long march: planning and execution

To get to the Danube, Marlborough had to work out how to march an army of 40,000 men over 250 miles through unfamiliar and difficult, if friendly, terrain replete with unbridged rivers and mountain ranges. Along the route he would be joined by allied German contingents to a total of about 20,000. The route ran right round

Left: Marlborough's line of march (*red*) from the Low Countries to the Danube valley. Nothing on this scale had ever been attempted by a British army, and it would never have stood a chance of success without meticulous preparation

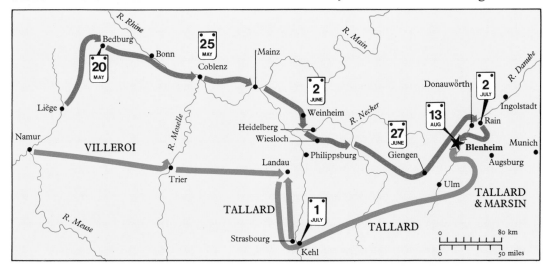

Above: All the panoply and splendour of the army of Bourbon France, the most efficient product of Louis XIV's long reign and his favourite instrument of foreign policy. Before Blenheim, no French army had been beaten in over forty years

Below left: British infantry attacking along the bank of the Danube towards Blenheim village

Below centre: British cavalry cutting down the opposition in the swamps bordering the Nebel in the centre of the battlefield

Below right: Prince Eugene in action against the French and Bavarian left flank. His timely charge in support of Marlborough averted a French breakthrough in the Oberglau sector during the battle's most crucial phase

France's eastern frontier and looked dangerously exposed to flank attack, but the risk Marlborough was taking was a nicely calculated one. As far as Coblenz, the French would reckon that he was bound for the Moselle. As far as Heidelberg, they could not rule out an allied invasion of Alsace. But once the allies had vanished south-east into Baden it would be obvious where they were going, and by then they would have completed two-thirds of the long march.

Making the march possible was the biggest job. Nothing like it had ever been attempted and the supply problems were immense. The army would need a travelling treasury to buy food, forage and replacement transport and draught animals. Advance depots must be set up to supply the troops at the end of each stage of the march. Inevitably the cavalry would outstrip the infantry and artillery, but there could be no more than two or three days' rest to keep the army reasonably

well concentrated. That Marlborough and his Quartermaster-General, William Cadogan, solved all the essentials in just over three weeks – even down to arranging that the infantry would get an issue of new shoes half-way along the march – was an amazing achievement, but there it was: Marlborough told the States-General in The Hague what he was going to do at the end of April 1704; and on 20 May the march began from Bedburg, fifty miles north-east of Liège.

The pattern of the march was easy stages for the foot and guns, with Marlborough riding ahead with the cavalry and sending back appropriate orders to the main body once he had surveyed the line of march. Nepotism helped him greatly because the main body was commanded by his brother, General Charles Churchill, who became the recipient of a stream of letters containing the natural history of the march. 'March with the whole directly to Heidelberg, since the route we have taken through Ladenburg will be too difficult for you.' 'We came most of the way up hill, so that you must take care beforehand to ease your artillery horses all you can.' 'I hope this warm weather you take care to march so early as to be in your camp before the heat of the day.' Few armies can have marched with such care, precision and minimal fatigue to the troops since the heyday of the Roman legions. Coblenz was passed on 26 May; eleven days and 100 miles later the army was at Wiesloch, south of Heidelberg, the last point from which an invasion of Alsace could be mounted. On 7 June the last leg of the march began: east and south-east, away from the Rhine, striking out decisively for the Danube.

The French marshals in eastern France, Villeroi and Tallard, were taken completely by surprise. Having joined forces at Landau to repel what looked like being a certain invasion of Alsace – Marlborough had reinforced the illusion by having a bridge built over the Rhine at Philippsburg – the marshals were nonplussed when Marlborough marched for the Danube. By the time they had referred the whole conundrum to Louis XIV, who ordered Villeroi to stay where he was and Tallard to march into Bavaria, it was 23 June and Marlborough, Prince Eugene and the Margrave of Baden had already met to concert their strategy. Tallard's men had not even crossed the Rhine when on 27 June, Marlborough's army closed up at the end of its long march at Giengen, only eighteen miles north-east of Ulm.

Attack upon the Village of BLENHEIM in which taken Twenty Eight Battallions & Twelve Squadrons | *a Brigade of French Foot in ÿ Center of ÿ Field of Battle near BLENHEIM cut* | *Prince EUGENE of SAVOY attacking ÿ Left Wing of ÿ French Army at ÿ Battle of BLENHEIM commanded by ÿ Elector*

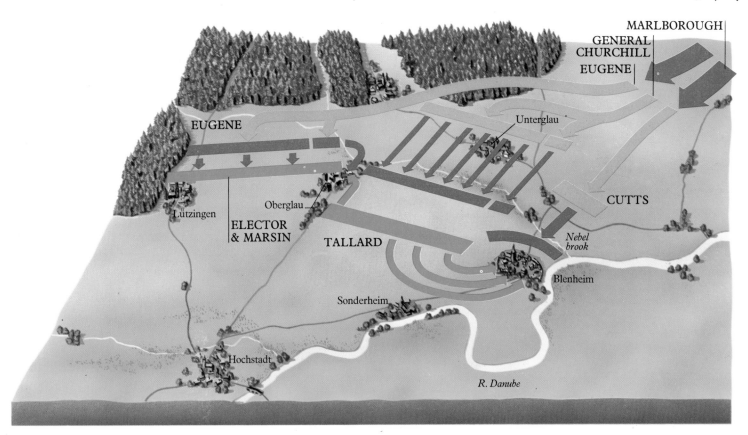

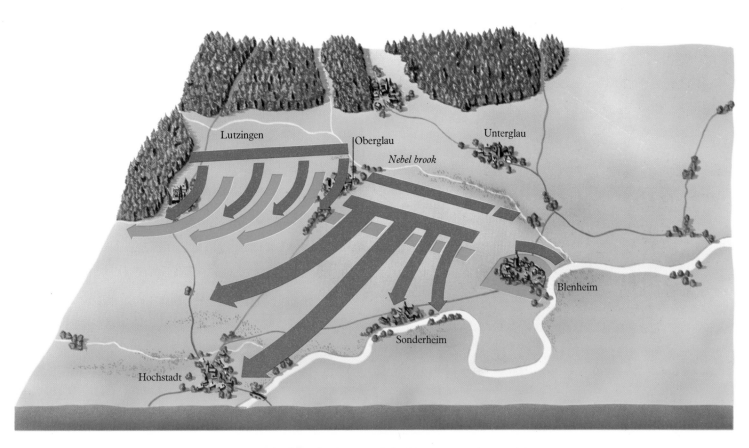

Above: The pattern of the battle, with Marlborough (*red*) first having to wait for Eugene to get into position, then weakening the French centre (*blue*), and finally breaking clean through with the decisive assault

Above : Lord Cutts' infantry presses towards the blazing buildings of Blenheim village – the crucial 'wave of the matador's cape' on the left flank which distracted Tallard from the coming blow in the centre

The campaign in Bavaria, 27 June-12 August

The allies had agreed that Eugene would block any French attempts to reinforce the armies of Bavaria and Marshal Marsin, the latter to be tackled by Marlborough and Baden. But the Margrave had not supplied the siege guns promised to Marlborough before the long march, and proved a touchy and unhelpful ally. He and Marlborough stormed the Schellenburg heights and captured Donauwörth on 2 July, thus capturing an important base on the Danube, but they failed to follow it up. Tallard was already across the Rhine and all Eugene could do was to leave enough troops to bluff Villeroi into staying in the Black Forest, and then march east to join Marlborough.

Keen to recover the initiative from Marlborough as quickly as possible, Tallard joined up with Marsin and the Elector of Bavaria on 5 August. Marlborough, Eugene and the Margrave met for a council on the sixth. It was agreed that the Margrave should take 20,000 men and besiege Ingolstadt, an independent command which pleased him and relieved Marlborough and Eugene of the Margrave's inhibiting caution. Eugene's army was to stay put around Hochstadt on the Danube and look temptingly isolated, with Marlborough keeping carefully in touch some twenty miles to the east.

On 10 August, two days after the Margrave had set off for Ingolstadt, Eugene informed Marlborough that he was in contact with the Franco-Bavarians. He held on at Hochstadt until he was sure that the combined Franco-Bavarian army was coming for him, then pulled out on the eleventh and withdrew to the east, joining forces with Marlborough on the twelfth. The two commanders made a joint reconnaissance, found the French and Bavarians making camp, and decided to attack on 13 August.

The armies deploy

Tallard's position had been chosen with great care. Its right flank was anchored on the Danube at the small village of Blenheim, and its left flank, three-and-a-half miles away, at Lützingen on the fringe of dense woodland. Midway between Lützingen and Blenheim, the village of Oberglau served as a central bastion, while the centre and right, left temptingly open, consisted of marshy ground on either side of a sluggish stream, the Nebel. To attack this position the allies would have to drop any ideas of turning the flanks. It would have to be a central attack, running the gauntlet of French fire from Blenheim and Oberglau.

Tallard and Marsin had 56,000 men against the allies' 52,000. They outnumbered the allies in guns (90 against 66) and infantry (70 battalions against 66), but the allies had the edge in cavalry (178 squadrons against 143 French and Bavarian). Marlborough, however, planned to attack the two villages with enough force to oblige Tallard to weaken the French centre. Meanwhile bridges were built across the Nebel and Marlborough's line shifted forward to the French side of the stream. But he could do nothing until Eugene had deployed into line opposite the Elector of Bavaria and Marsin, between Lützingen and Oberglau, and this took until 12.30 in the afternoon.

The attacks on Blenheim

Marlborough opened the battle with a fierce attack on Blenheim village which was most satisfactorily held – satisfactorily, because the French reacted by packing more and more troops into Blenheim to make sure of their right flank. Lord Cutts (nicknamed 'Salamander' Cutts because he revelled in the hottest fire) did a perfect job of keeping Tallard's attention fixed on Blenheim by attacking repeatedly until there were so many French in the village that they could hardly move. Marlborough meanwhile directed the bridging and crossing of the Nebel; eventually he told Cutts to stop attacking and concentrate on keeping the French hemmed in, and prepared to repeat the process at Oberglau.

Oberglau: crisis of the battle

The attack on Oberglau, launched at about 3 p.m., was intended to leave Tallard's centre wide open for a decisive attack, but it was a disaster. Heartily counter-attacked by the Irish 'foreign legion' of the French army, the ten battalions led against Oberglau by the Prince of Holstein-Beck broke and fled. Now it was Marlborough's centre that was exposed. The French attacked repeatedly, hoping to widen the gap beyond repair, and Marlborough only held out thanks to a cavalry charge from Eugene's detachment.

The French cavalry broken

By 4 p.m., however, Marlborough could see that his strategy was working. The cream of Tallard's infantry was locked up in Blenheim; the Oberglau sector, thanks to Eugene's troopers, was now secure. Between Blenheim and Oberglau Marlborough deployed 14,000 infantry and 5,000 cavalry in alternate lines. Tallard's attenuated centre was facing disaster and the battle had been turned inside out. Instead of Marlborough being forced to attack on ground of Tallard's choosing, Tallard was now forced to throw in his cavalry on ground of Marlborough's own choosing.

As the French cavalry swept in to the attack the English cavalry fell back, exposing the long lines of infantry musket-barrels at the ready. Murderous volley-firing broke the French cavalry attacks and pushed the French troopers back again.

Coup de grâce in the centre

By 5 p.m. Eugene's detachment was still locked in furious combat with Marsin and the Elector of Bavaria out on the allied right, but Tallard's last reserves were spent. Marlborough rode down the line for the last time and ordered in his massed cavalry. Then 8,000 fresh troopers swept forward, supported by cheering infantry and artillery, and shattered the weary screen of cavalry that was all that Tallard could put in their way.

With the centre gone, there was nothing for it but retreat for Marshal Marsin and the Elector of Bavaria, whose men had fought off three attacks from Eugene and were still deeply engaged. Faint hopes of a French rally were dashed by the energy of the allied pursuit and the early capture of Tallard. While some die-hard regiments fought on until 9 p.m., the end of the battle came around 6 p.m. when the twenty-seven trapped battalions surrendered the blazing ruins of Blenheim village.

Losses and achievement

The news of the allies' victory at Blenheim stunned Europe: it was the first time ever that one of Louis XIV's armies had been routed in battle. For a total loss of 13,000, Marlborough and Eugene had inflicted a French loss of 20,000 killed and wounded and 14,000 prisoners. Another 7,000 French deserted during their retreat back to the Rhine.

Blenheim did not end the 1704 campaign. Not content with reversing the course of the war, saving Vienna and the Austrian Empire, and winning the greatest English victory on European soil since Agincourt, Marlborough marched west to the Rhine and crossed it. He invaded Alsace and pushed north to the Moselle, taking Landau, Trèves, and Trarbach – all splendid bases for the following year's campaign. Even then his work was not done: he had to race off to Berlin, 400 miles away, and persuade the King of Prussia not to withdraw his troops. Next he journeyed to Hanover, to arrange the details of Hanover's contingents for 1705; then on to The Hague to consult with the delighted Dutch; and finally home to a hero's welcome in England.

Few battles have ever had such tremendous consequences as Blenheim, but the victory did not end the war. Allied disunity – first in euphoria and then in excessive caution – kept the war dragging on for another ten years.

Below : The end at Blenheim. Marshal Tallard, his army scattered and in full retreat, surrenders to Marlborough

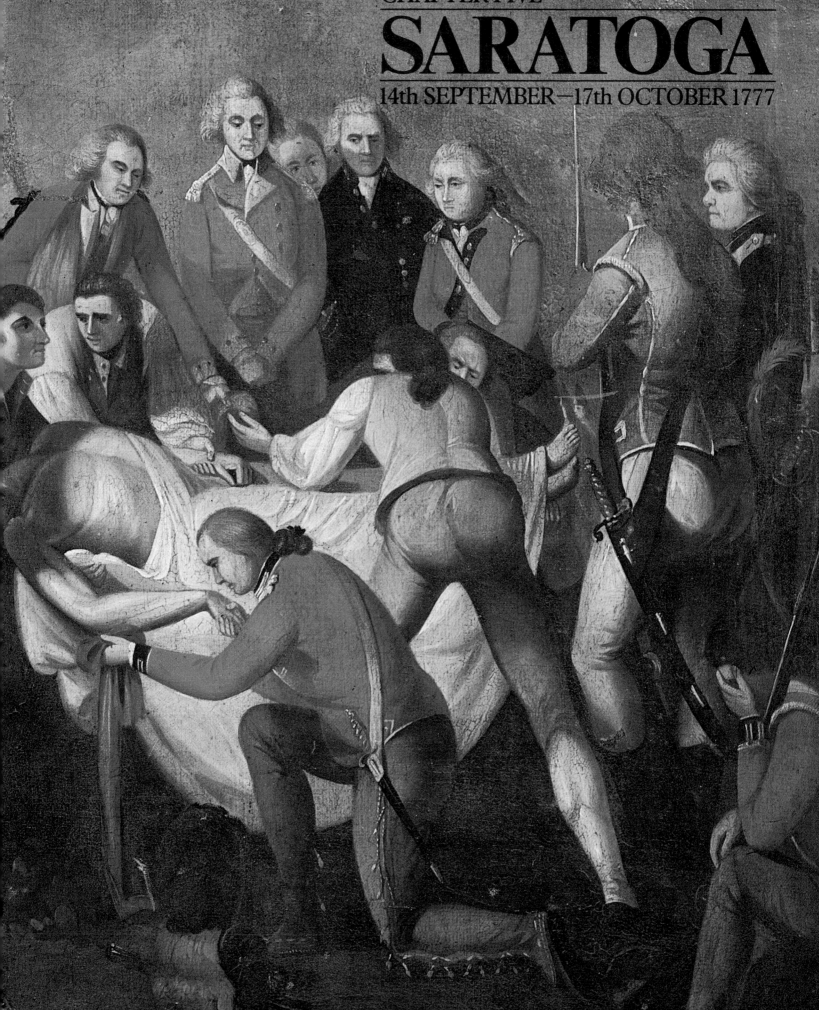

Previous pages : The burial of General Fraser under American fire during the second battle at Freeman's Farm, which sealed the fate of the trapped British force. It was typical of the whole campaign that the only subject considered suitable for a commemorative battle painting was this melancholy event

Guerrilla war in the American colonies engulfs a powerful British strike force; the pattern for Vietnam is set

The war

Below : 'Gentleman Johnny' Burgoyne, the British commander at Saratoga. There were only two things wrong with his master-plan for reconquering the rebel colonies : he was miserably let down by his superiors and colleagues, and he persisted in carrying out his part of the plan far past the point of no return

SEVENTY-THREE years after scaling the heights of glory at Blenheim, the British hit the lowest depths of humiliation at Saratoga during the American War of Independence, the Vietnam of the eighteenth century. Until then, success in warfare had seemed to belong to the professional standing army, with its drilled and disciplined manoeuvres and firepower. But Saratoga was a startling phenomenon: a people's army of backwoodsmen defeating regular troops, the 'amateurs' proving more than a match for the 'professionals'.

It was particularly stupid of King George III's government to antagonize the American colonists, because the mere facts of geography had always made the colonists particularly good at looking after themselves. In the Seven Years War with France (1756–63) the colonists had played a considerable part in helping to break the French hold on Canada. When the war was over they felt pretty pleased with themselves, happy enough to think of themselves as British yet aware that much of the victory was due to their own efforts. Almost at once, however, George's government 3,000 miles away began saddling the colonists with new and heartily resented taxes, overriding all protests and mulishly escalating the wrangle into a full-scale confrontation.

As the colonists saw it, there was no choice but to get organized as a political entity, raising their own funds, passing their own rules and regulations and forming their own militia units. In short, the United States of America started life as one of the biggest, earliest trade unions in history, bent on breaking an unpopular government financial policy by militant action.

Militant confrontation became a shooting war in 1775, the year of Lexington and Concord, when the New England colonists stopped British troops from marching about at will and penned them up in Boston. The 'Battle of Bunker Hill' followed, a bloody and inconclusive slaughter carried out to chase the colonial militia off the heights commanding Boston. This gave the colonist 'patriots' their first real war heroes; it should have persuaded George's government to think again and start negotiating. Instead the British government set about hiring German troops to send to America in order to put down the revolt – and this was an insult which did much to produce the Declaration of Independence of 4 July 1776.

This should have made life considerably easier for the British because it brought matters into focus. Now there was an enemy capital to take, Philadelphia in Pennsylvania, and an enemy army to beat, the rebel colonists' 'Continental Army' under General Washington of Virginia. If

the British and their mercenaries could take and hold Philadelphia and defeat Washington's forces at every engagement, the rebel government would never get the chance to put down any roots.

By December 1776 the British seemed well on the way to victory. The colonists had tried an invasion of Canada, which had proved a calamitous failure; General William Howe had seized New York, then thrown Washington out of not only New York State but neighbouring New Jersey as well; substantial troop reinforcements had already crossed the Atlantic and more were scheduled for 1777. Plans had been put forward for an advance from Canada to meet up with a northward drive from New York up the Hudson River, thus cutting off all the New England colonies and paving the way for a future advance to recover Boston. The initial success of the colonists now seemed petty and empty in the face of the recent string of British victories.

Washington, however, proved everyone wrong – both the dispirited colonists and the over-confident British – by bouncing back across the Delaware River on Christmas Night 1776 and inflicting two stinging defeats at Trenton and Princeton. This miniature of a campaign (on both sides involving fewer men than the English Civil War's Naseby campaign) had consequences extending far beyond its immediate nuisance-value. For the rebel colonists it was a wonderful tonic, restoring and boosting morale after a daunting run of failure; it showed them that they were still in the ring and able to beat the British. For General Howe in New York, it served as emphatic proof that Washington's army must be the major objective for 1777.

But as Bernard Shaw put it in *The Devil's Disciple*, 'The British soldier can stand up to anything except the British War Office'. The war against the rebels was being directed from over 3,000 miles away, in Whitehall. This automatically created a serious time-lag between orders going out to America and the course of events there. Not once, during the entire conflict, did a British general receive orders from London that made sense when set in the context of the current strategic situation.

This naturally led to an exaggerated sense of independence on the part of the British generals, each of whom felt free to go to the government with his own ideas on how the war should be won. But the weakest link in the chain was the 'man at the top', Lord George Germain, Secretary of State for the American Colonies – generally

despised, cashiered from the Army for cowardice nineteen years previously, but a smooth diplomat who had learned the pliant art of court politics and enjoyed King George's confidence.

It was Germain who gave his approval to two different plans for the 1777 campaign, each contradicting the other, without telling either of the generals who had submitted the plans what the other was supposed to be doing.

At the end of 1776 General John Burgoyne had come to London and convinced the king and council that he was the man to lead an army south from Canada, join forces with Howe at Albany on the Hudson, and slice off the New England colonies. A month after Burgoyne's plan had been approved, Germain approved Howe's plan to march in the opposite direction against Washington, invade Pennsylvania and take Philadelphia. Not once did he point out to the two generals that one operation precluded the other's best chances of success. Not once did he remind them that dispersal of effort violates one of the first principles of war: *never* leave yourself weak everywhere and strong nowhere. Nor did he warn the generals that

Above : George Washington as a young officer of Virginia militia, long before Britain's breach with her American colonies. Washington's appointment to command the rebel 'Continental Army' was an inspired one : he was the man who proved to his countrymen that they could fight the British and win

Above : Burgoyne drumming up Indian recruits for the invasion of the rebel colonies. There was nothing new about enlisting Indians for military service : it had been a permanent feature of all the American colonial wars against the French. But Burgoyne's attempts to use the Indians as a 'terror weapon' with which to cow the rebels backfired, driving thousands to join the rebel colours

colonial forces might block Burgoyne's advance while Washington's army remained in being as a fighting force.

In short, Germain should have told Howe that Washington and Philadelphia could wait until the junction with Burgoyne had been made and the isolation of New England accomplished; or told Burgoyne that New England could wait until Howe had finished off George Washington. Instead he passively approved the two contradictory schemes, leaving both Howe and Burgoyne with written confirmation that each pet scheme had won the government's approval as top priority.

Burgoyne: the energetic amateur

Burgoyne's appointment was an accurate reflection of the over-confidence of the British by 1777: he had absolutely no experience of commanding an army in America. As things turned out this had little effect on the energy and speed with which he got his army moving. What did

matter was his fatally low opinion of the colonists. He shared the widespread view that the colonists were a namby-pamby lot who would never stand up to professional troops – wishful thinking permissible back in 1775 but certainly not in 1777 after Bunker Hill, Trenton and Princeton. Totally misjudging their mentality, Burgoyne thought that the colonists would cower at home in the face of his threat to let loose the Indian tribesmen in British pay. On the contrary, they reacted with disgust to the notion that a British general, calling himself an officer and a gentleman, could stoop to using savages against women and children. The Americans flocked to the colours to enlist on the colonial side.

The force Burgoyne led south was a motley but formidable host: 3,700 British troops and 3,000 German, about 200 loyalists and French Canadians, 500 Indian braves and 38 guns – a very high artillery complement for so small a force. Facing him was General Philip Schuyler's militia, scattered all over Vermont and New York. Schuyler's only concentration was the garrison of Fort Ticonderoga at the south end of Lake Champlain, some 3,500 strong.

In Burgoyne's eyes there was every reason for confidence, for Schuyler could not possibly meet, simultaneously, Burgoyne's thrust from the north and Howe's anticipated thrust from the south. There was also to be a third thrust – up the Mohawk Valley from Lake Ontario to Albany, commanded by Lieutenant-Colonel Barry St Leger, with an army consisting mostly of 1,000 Iroquois Indians. As these three pincers closed in on Albany they would either scatter or destroy the American militia, eventually joining up together to form an unbeatable host.

Burgoyne takes Ticonderoga

On 21 June 1777, Burgoyne's force embarked at the head of Lake Champlain in an imposing fleet: 200 transports, 20 gunboats and 3 frigates. By 3 July the troops and guns were ashore and ready to attack Ticonderoga, where Burgoyne expected to meet the toughest resistance of the campaign. Instead he had a walk-over. The garrison had neglected to defend the crest of Sugar Loaf Hill, which dominated the fort, and Burgoyne's gunner-general, William Phillips, promptly had two guns put there. General St Clair, the garrison commander, wasted no time in acknowledging his error and decided not to throw his troops away in futile resistance. He evacuated the fort that night and on the night of the sixth broke out with a loss of 400 men in a rearguard clash at Hubbardton.

The fall of Ticonderoga without a shot was a tremendous shock to the colonial forces, who had confidently expected it to hold out for weeks. Nor did Burgoyne dally there. He pushed on and on 10 July reached Skenesboro, a mere sixty miles from Albany. For the loss of only 200 men he had come over a hundred miles in twenty days, and captured the strongest fort in America with 128 guns.

After Ticonderoga: Burgoyne's mistakes

Burgoyne can be excused for thinking, with Ticonderoga in his hands, that the worst of the campaign was over. In fact it was just beginning, and two bad errors of judgment meant that it was his fault. The first was the decision to continue to advance by land, when he could have retired to Ticonderoga,

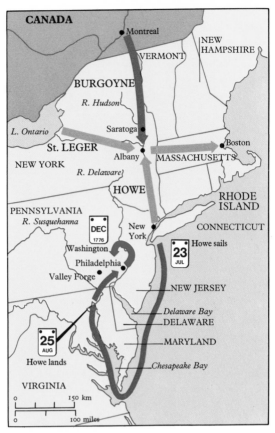

re-embarked his men and sailed south down Lake George, halving the overland distance to Albany. Instead he plunged his men into the tortuous terrain, dense woods and water-courses of Wood Creek, leading to Fort Edward on the upper Hudson. This mistake was made worse by his determination to take along the strongest possible artillery train, 52 guns in all, for which he had repeatedly to stop and wait.

Here, for the first time in modern history, was revealed a mistaken faith in fire-power as a medium which *must* win against irregular forces – a creed which, 200 years later, brought European and American troops to grief in Vietnam.

Thus from Skenesboro to the upper Hudson Burgoyne was commanding a different army from the one with which he had begun the campaign. It was now 1,100 men weaker: 200 casualties suffered at Hubbardton, 900 left to hold Ticonderoga, and even more encumbered with guns and ammunition wagons. The new line of march turned out to be a nightmare obstacle course, for Schuyler's militia had used axe and crowbar to fell countless trees across the narrow tracks and choke the water-courses with rock obstacles. Until these were cleared Burgoyne's wagon-trains could not move a yard, and when they did grind forward it was only to meet new obstacles a little further on. It took twenty days to struggle the twenty miles from Skenesboro to Fort Edward, reached on 29 July. The bold drive from the north had slowed down to a crawl of a mile a day.

Left: The British grand design for the 1777 campaign against the rebels, as it should have been (*light red*) and as it actually turned out (*dark red*). At the moment when Howe's troops should have been marching up the Hudson valley to join hands with Burgoyne at Albany, they were in fact getting seasick on a voyage in the opposite direction – the expedition against Philadelphia

Above : In a wild charge against a Hessian emplacement at Saratoga, Benedict Arnold's horse goes down (*centre*). Arnold's bravery and energy did much to persuade the colonist rank and file that they could not only stop British troops, but beat them

Opposite : The road to Saratoga. The march began brilliantly with the rapid capture of Fort Ticonderoga, which Congress had expected to hold out for months. But then the pace of Burgoyne's advance (*red*) fell off to a crawl. He could have halved the distance to Albany by re-embarking his forces and shipping them down Lake George, but chose the direct overland route instead. The time thus lost was used to full advantage by the rebel forces (*blue*) under General Horatio Gates

Burgoyne isolated

In the first week of August 1777, while Burgoyne waited for his artillery and supply wagons to join him at Fort Edward, the finishing touches were being put to the ruin of the British strategy.

Howe's army, far from moving swiftly into Pennsylvania, taking Philadelphia and then switching substantial forces back to the lower Hudson to help Burgoyne, was literally at sea. Howe had wasted nearly four months of good campaigning weather in assembling an invasion fleet with which to sail up Delaware Bay and pounce on Philadelphia from the sea. He sailed with 19,000 troops on 23 July, leaving 8,000 in New York under the command of Sir Henry Clinton; made a last-minute decision to head for the Chesapeake instead of the Delaware; and never even got his troops ashore until 25 August. By then Howe had already written to Germain that Burgoyne could expect no help from him, and by the time Germain received this frightening information it was far too late to do anything about it.

Burgoyne's other intended source of reinforcement, Barry St Leger's advance up the Mohawk, also failed to materialize. St Leger's little force was held up by the spirited colonial defence of Fort Stanwix, and his Indian allies melted away at the

false news that an army of 3,000 men was advancing against them. This left St Leger with no alternative but retreat; and Burgoyne, who had moved forward another painful seven miles to Fort Miller, was on his own.

Defeat at Bennington . . .

The writing on the wall began to appear on 16 August. On that day a column of 700 Hessians and loyalists, sent by Burgoyne into the Green Mountain country to forage for horses, food and wagons, was cut to pieces by 2,000 colonial troops at Bennington. A relief force of 650 was driven back to Fort Miller after being badly mauled. Bennington cost Burgoyne over 200 dead and 700 captured, more than ten per cent of his army, but he was still determined to press on to Albany, thus fulfilling his role in the original grand design for 1777.

What he did not know was that 7,000 colonists were now waiting for him, dug in on Bemis Heights, and that more American militiamen were taking the field by the thousand. General Gates had replaced the pessimistic Schuyler, and now Gates had the energetic aid of Benedict Arnold, fresh from his triumph over Barry St Leger in the Mohawk Valley. Gates was confident that by fighting a defensive battle in wooded terrain, where Burgoyne's regulars would

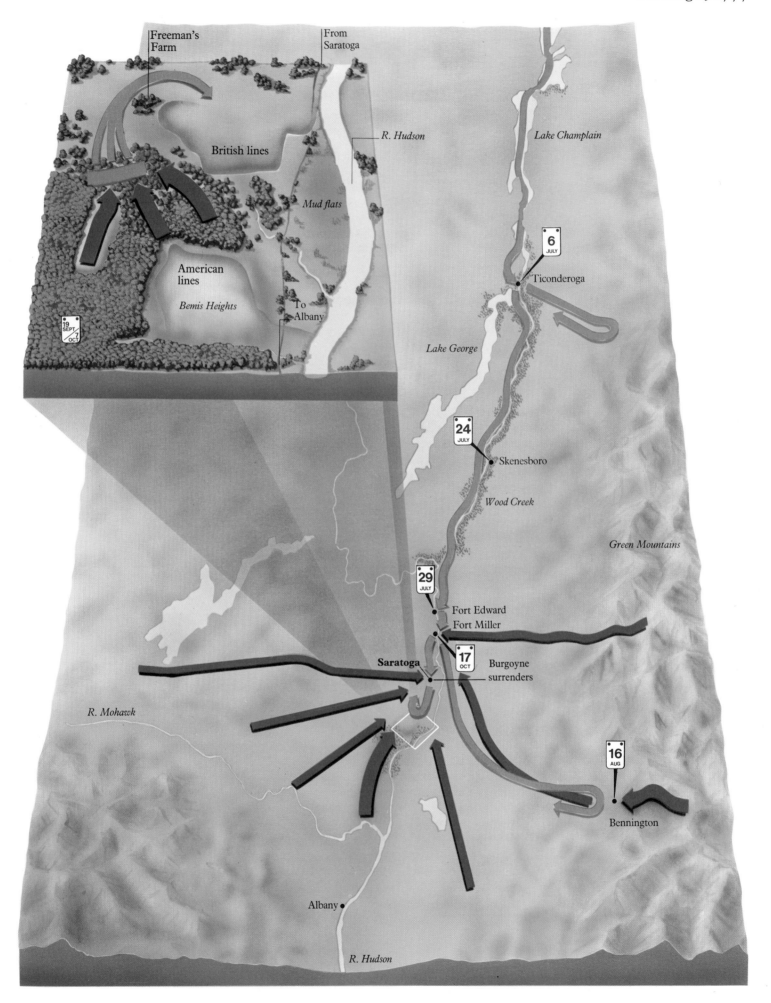

Freeman's
Farm

From
Saratoga

British lines

R. Hudson

Mud flats

American
lines

Bemis Heights

To
Albany

19
SEPT
7
OCT

Lake Champlain

6
JULY
Ticonderoga

24
JULY
Skenesboro

Lake George

Wood Creek

Green Mountains

29
JULY

Fort Edward
Fort Miller

17
OCT
Burgoyne
surrenders

Saratoga

R. Mohawk

16
AUG

Bennington

Albany

R. Hudson

be unable to deploy to bring their full fire-power to bear, he could continue to halt and grind down the invading army.

... and at Freeman's Farm

Burgoyne advanced for the last time on 13 September, marching through Saratoga towards the American position. On the nineteenth he launched three columns through the woods, hoping to out-flank Gates' line; but Benedict Arnold detected the flanking move and broke it up. In a fierce fight around Freeman's Farm, Burgoyne's columns were pushed back by superior numbers, having lost another 600 irreplaceable men.

For nearly three weeks Burgoyne lay immobile, hoping that Gates would be imprudent enough to attack – but Gates stayed where he was, his reinforcements swelling daily while Burgoyne's men went on to half rations and their morale slumped. He shrank from the prospect of fighting a retreat all the way back to Canada through forests thick with invisible marksmen, and pinned all his hopes on another attack to break through to Henry Clinton on the lower Hudson.

By 7 October, the date of Burgoyne's second attack, Clinton had opened up the Hudson and pushed a small force of 2,000 men upstream. Clinton's main priority was the defence of New York, and the growing desperation of Burgoyne's position was never made absolutely clear until it was too late. For on the seventh, in another bruising fight at Freeman's Farm, Burgoyne was beaten again with the loss of another 700 men. He was left surrounded by the enemy, with few more than 5,000 increasingly hungry and dispirited men to face over 17,000 exultant rebels.

Burgoyne held on until 12 October, hoping against hope for miraculous news that Clinton's foremost troops had advanced far enough to make a breakthrough and link-up possible; but on the thirteenth he bowed to the inevitable and bargained for the best possible terms. His men would lay down their arms and be allowed to embark for England, on condition that they pledged never to serve in America again. Gates accepted these terms because he too was looking south, for he feared a last-minute relief march by Clinton; he also wanted to have Burgoyne's men safely disarmed as soon as possible. On 17 October, therefore, he formally received Burgoyne's surrender – but the Convention of Saratoga was later repudiated

by the American Congress, and Burgoyne and his men went into captivity.

Aftermath

The most important result of the Saratoga fiasco was that it brought first France, then Spain and Holland into the war on the colonists' side. Having scored first the defeat and then the capture of an entire British army, the colonists had earned the right to be taken seriously by Britain's bitterest enemies. A French expeditionary force crossed the Atlantic to fight beside Washington; the French fleet challenged the British hold on the American seaboard and broke it for long enough to enable the Americans to win victory and indepen-

dence from their British colonial masters.

Saratoga cost the British the northern colonies, except for a foothold in New York which they held until the end of the war in 1783. They won several impressive successes in the south, but the arrival of the French made the odds too high and the cost too heavy. The real damage to the British cause had already been done – at Saratoga, where the colonists realised for sure that they could win. It was indeed a victory which won a war and cemented the brotherhood of a new nation.

Clearly, there is no one culprit on whom the blame for Saratoga can be placed. The real villain of the piece was the complacent British assumption that when it came to the crunch the American colonists would not stand and fight against professional troops. The original strategy for the campaign had been sound enough, but it was fatally changed by Howe, and Burgoyne's own attempt to carry out his part single-handed was unrealistic. Tactically, Burgoyne's army was like a fish out of water, forced to march and fight in an unfamiliar environment for which it had never been trained.

There will probably never be a clear-cut solution to the problem of how to fight determined irregular forces on their home ground with regular forces intended for totally different battlefields. Burgoyne and his men had the bad luck to be the first guinea-pigs in a long series of fruitless experiments; they were not to be the last.

Above : The end. Burgoyne surrenders to Gates on 17 October having accepted that there was no hope of relief by Clinton's force from New York

CHAPTER SIX
VALMY
20th SEPTEMBER 1792

Previous pages : A French engraving of the cannonade of Valmy as seen from behind the French lines, with French staff officers apparently being mown down like flies by exploding shells. The Prussian guns can be seen in the far background, and the columns of their abortive advance are just to the right

A general loses heart: the non-battle that kept the French Revolution alive

The war

Below : French hussars, with their ornate *sabretaches* still bearing the crowns and monograms of the *ancien régime*. Michel Ney, one of the most famous of all Napoleon's marshals, was still an NCO with a hussar regiment at the time of Valmy

THERE are natural similarities between Saratoga and Valmy, though tactically the two actions were as different as chalk from cheese. Both were collisions between raw patriot troops on one side and highly-disciplined foreign regulars; both saw the 'professionals' lose to the 'amateurs'; both became symbols of the emergence of a new republic. But there the similarities end.

The French revolutionary troops did not beat the Prussians at Valmy because the old French royalist army had been swept away by a new and dynamic force. On the contrary: they won because the Revolution had *not* scrapped the royalist army.

Few of the events in Versailles and Paris in 1789-91 affected the French Army directly. The aristocratic officer corps did not, as some accounts suggest, emigrate *en masse*, leaving hundreds of vacancies to be filled by promotions from the ranks and elections of popular candidates by the troops. The fact was that the French Army had been one of the country's first institutions to be touched by the vague movement towards reform and modernization that sought expression in France from the 1760s on. New royal military colleges had been set up, at one of which a scruffy Corsican teenager named Napoleone di Buonaparte received his training for the French artillery in 1779–84. Superfluous regiments had been amalgamated with others or abolished; above all the artillery had been completely overhauled, making it the best in Europe.

Some idea of how little the Revolution changed life in the French Army for the first two years is given by taking a few of the men who became generals under the Republic and marshals under Napoleon. Michel Ney, for instance, joined up as a trooper in the 'Régiment Colonel-Général' in 1787 and by January 1791 had risen only to quartermaster-corporal; it took another thirteen months before he was made troop sergeant. Nicolas Jean-de-Dieu Soult enlisted in the 'Régiment Royal-Infanterie' in 1785; he had risen to corporal by June 1787, but it took him until July 1791 to move on up to sergeant. Louis-Nicolas Davout joined the 'Régiment de Royal-Champagne-Cavalerie' straight from the Paris Military Academy in February 1788 as a second lieutenant; he was such a fanatical supporter of the principles of the Revolution that he was first arrested and finally dismissed the service in 1791. (He was immediately elected lieutenant-colonel by the local regiment of volunteers.)

When France went to war in April 1792, therefore, the trained soldiers of the regular French Army were beginning to look

elsewhere for more rapid advancement. The Revolution had produced the idea of a new 'citizen's army' of volunteers, 100,000 strong, with officers elected on performance and merit; but barely a third of the hoped-for flood of volunteers had come forward. However, those who had done so needed training, so the officers and rankers who resigned from regular units and transferred to the volunteer battalions were eagerly snapped up. Such transfers, of course, only weakened the regular units; and while the volunteers were learning the rudiments of their trade the French Army was emphatically not fully battle-worthy.

The war was the deliberate creation of comparatively moderate revolutionaries in Paris; they saw a declaration of war against Austria, France's traditional foe and now a haven for exiles and counter-revolutionaries, as the ideal way of getting King Louis to declare either for the Revolution or against it.

Ranters and demagogues harangued the volunteers as they trailed enthusiastically off to the frontiers – patriotism, the ideals of the Revolution and the will to conquer would carry them to victory. However, most of the green troops had barely learned such essential preliminaries as how to load and fix bayonets, let alone the disciplines of close-order drill and the need to form square when charged by cavalry. Their officers did their best, but the first frontier clashes with the Austrians were disastrous. Units broke and took to their heels, yelping that they were betrayed; some murdered their officers. After three months of virtually uninterrupted military failure, the revolutionaries in Paris had all the ammunition they needed to launch a second revolution. They captured the King and jailed him, proclaiming a National Convention and a crusade of terror against all internal enemies of the nation.

The enemy at the gates – eventually

Had Austria and Prussia so desired, they could have marched their armies into Paris by the high summer of 1792; but Austria, Prussia and Russia were all obsessed with claiming the widest possible territories from defenceless Poland, and the best royalist German forces were deployed in the east, not in the west and along the French frontier. Not until 19 August did the Duke of Brunswick lead a coalition army of Prussians and Austrians against France, and no sooner had he done so than

the weather broke. Week after week of sluicing rain turned the countryside into a vast bog and slowed down the pace of the allied columns to a muddy crawl.

The Army of the North

Brunswick's invasion route was the one once used by Marlborough up the Moselle valley: Coblenz-Trier-Longwy-Verdun-Châlons and so direct to Paris. Facing

Above: French officer and infantryman, sporting tricolour cockades and engaged in some extremely polite musketry drill

51

Above: General Dumouriez, commander of the Army of the North. The first hero of the French republican army, he had joined the service under Louis XV

Above right: The crisis facing France by September 1792, when the armies of the royalist coalition (*pink*) rolled across the frontier towards Paris, bent on saving King Louis XVI and restoring him to his original power

Brunswick was the 'Army of the North', deployed from northern Lorraine to Belgium and commanded by General Charles François Dumouriez, an ebullient 53-year-old who had first seen service under Louis XV in the Seven Years War (1756–63). Dumouriez also had under his orders General Charles-François-Etienne-Christophe Kellermann's 'Army of the Centre', on the Moselle sector. A resilient character, exuding confidence, Dumouriez was just the man for the job; he had taken up his command with plans for an offensive in Belgium, but confidently undertook to defend Paris from Brunswick.

The disastrous spring and summer months had not been completely wasted for the French. The surviving volunteer units had gained vital battle experience, albeit of the toughest kind; and commanders had learned to stiffen their volunteers with regular regiments close by. There wâs far less temptation to shout '*sauve qui peut!*' and bolt when the flanking regiments were calmly standing their ground. It was this, combined with the excellence of the regular artillery batteries at their disposal, that was to prove the best card of Dumouriez and Kellermann.

The Argonne passes

Brunswick cracked the frontier obstacle of Longwy on 23 August, when the town tamely surrendered after one day's bombardment. Struggling on through the rain to the Meuse, he took Verdun on 2 September. But the next hurdle for the invaders was the densely forested ridge of

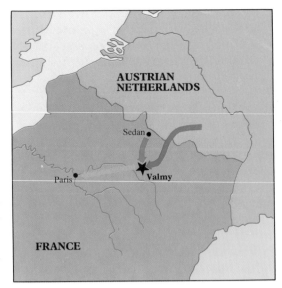

the Argonne, fifty miles long and twenty wide – a natural barrier pierced by only a few roads, whose exits should bave been easy to defend.

Promising Paris that he would defend the Argonne passes 'like the Spartans at Thermopylae', Dumouriez marched down from Sedan on 1 September with 33,000 men while Kellermann came from Metz with 18,000. By 8 September, when Brunswick's army pushed into the Argonne in three columns, Dumouriez and Kellermann seemed to have all the key exits on the other side safely closed. But Dumouriez proved unequal to the task of watching all three mouse-holes at once. On 12 September Clerfayt's Austrian corps, 11,000 strong, forced its way through the pass at Croix-aux-Bois and debouched into open country. Now faced with encirclement, Dumouriez and Kellermann fell

Right: The Duke of Brunswick points out the French positions at Valmy to King Frederick William of Prussia, while his artillery teams (apparently on a collision course) dash aimlessly to and fro in the background. Disconcerted by the resolution shown by the French, Brunswick inertly ordered a retreat after his cannonade and feeble infantry advance had failed to make the French stampede

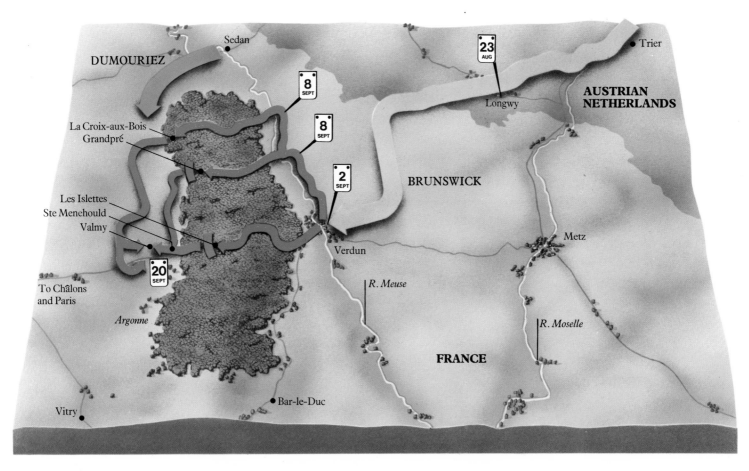

Sedan

DUMOURIEZ

23 AUG

Trier

8 SEPT

La Croix-aux-Bois
Grandpré

8 SEPT

Longwy

AUSTRIAN NETHERLANDS

2 SEPT

BRUNSWICK

Les Islettes
Ste Menehould
Valmy

Verdun

Metz

20 SEPT

To Châlons
and Paris

R. Meuse

Argonne

R. Moselle

FRANCE

Vitry

Bar-le-Duc

Above : The extraordinary manoeuvres which landed the Army of the North (*blue*) with its back to the wall at Valmy, with Brunswick's army (*pink*) between the French forces and Paris

back and concentrated at Sainte-Menehould, but the price they had to pay was leaving the road to Paris wide open.

Brunswick's reaction was the correct one: destroy the enemy army first. With his long communications he had, in fact, little choice in the matter; it would have been suicide to march on Paris with Dumouriez loose in the rear. On the seventeenth, as soon as the other two allied columns were clear of the Argonne, Brunswick wheeled ponderously south behind Dumouriez and Kellermann, cutting off their only line of retreat down the Vitry road. The entire mass of the invading army was now actually between Paris and the French forces; and on 20 September Brunswick rolled forward to deliver the *coup de grâce*.

The 'cannonade of Valmy'

On the face of it, the French were doomed. In five months' disastrous campaigning they had never once stood up to a determined attack; nor had they ever been in such a dangerous position. But all was not well with Brunswick's army. Its original strength of 75,000 had been considerably reduced by chronic dysentery during the advance. As for Brunswick's supply lines, they were strung out all the way back up the Moselle. Longwy and Verdun had been

windfalls: the allied siege train had been far to the rear when the French garrisons surrendered. And by 20 September things were even worse, with the Prussian field bakeries back at Verdun and the flour supplies as far away as Trier. It was a soaked, sickly and under-strength force that prepared to assault Dumouriez and Kellermann on the twentieth.

The French commanders, however, were a seasoned lot, every man of them a veteran officer of the pre-revolutionary army. The most experienced of them was the Comte d'Abovile, 63 years old, who had first seen action against the British at Fontenoy in 1745 and was now commanding the French artillery. Correctly deployed on the high ground around Valmy and Yvan, the French looked across a shallow, muddy valley to the height of La Lune, where the Prussians deployed on the foggy morning of the twentieth. The intense weakness of the French position was strategic, not tactical; it could not be rushed by a *coup de main*, nor blasted wide open by short-range artillery fire. Brunswick decided to open the battle by softening-up the French with a long-range bombardment.

When a watery sun had half-heartedly dispelled the morning fog Brunswick's guns crashed out, and the French gunners

immediately replied. The mere fact that French guns were shooting back won the first trick for Dumouriez because his infantry stayed where it was, cheering the gunners on instead of bolting. Little damage was done by the Prussian guns, partly because of the range, partly because the muddy ground prevented shot from bouncing murderously through the ranks. And all the while d'Abovile's batteries continued to trade shot for shot.

Around noon Brunswick decided that the time had come for a general advance. This must have been nothing more than a last attempt to panic the French, for their lines were still holding and their guns had not been silenced. On the other hand, the terrain did not permit a swift, head-on infantry attack; the advancing Prussians would have to plod through the mud under increasingly destructive artillery fire.

What happened was perhaps the biggest anti-climax in military history. As the long Prussian lines came down the slopes of La Lune the French still stayed where they were, their fire unabated. The lines began their crawl across the plain – and then, still comfortably out of musket-shot, they stopped. French morale soared when it was seen that the Prussians were not working their own guns forward, and turned to sheer joy when the Prussian advance proceeded to turn itself into a withdrawal. Both sides managed to hold their positions until nightfall, but the Prussians withdrew during the night.

Aftermath

Once extricated from his near-certain death-trap at Valmy, Dumouriez was able to re-position his army astride the road to Paris. Ten days later, with the weather as vile as ever and casualties from sickness now appalling, the allied army was reduced to 17,000 effective fighting men. Brunswick decided on retreat.

The non-defeat of Valmy was justly hailed by the French as a great victory. So it was, but a victory on the moral, not the physical plane. The soldiers of a new France had stood and fought with the weapons of the old, and their enemies had retired abashed. Inevitably Valmy became a mighty symbol, for while the French guns were firing the Republic was being proclaimed in Paris. It seemed like an omen, and when the Republicans abolished the old calendar with its weeks, months and

saints' days and instituted their own, 20 September, the day of Valmy, became Day One of Year One of the Republic.

Dumouriez did not remain on the scene for long. Idolized in Paris as the Republic's first hero, he led the great French invasion of Belgium in 1793 but – like Benedict Arnold in the American War of Independence – abandoned his country and its cause, and went over to the allies. An exile for the rest of his life, he died in England in 1822. His epitaph at Henley-on-Thames, where he is buried, says that he is 'waiting for his country to do him justice'.

Kellermann, however, stayed with the tricolour and became one of the great heroes, first of the Republic and later of the Empire. Napoleon made him a marshal and created him Duke of Valmy. The father of an equally famous cavalry general, Kellermann, like Dumouriez, outlived the incredible years that came after Valmy, dying in Paris in 1820.

Above : Another addition to the myth of Valmy, showing battered but indomitable French infantry protecting a wounded officer and apparently preparing to fight to the death. In fact, the dreaded Prussians called off their advance before they got anywhere near the French lines, thus sparing Dumouriez's men from the supreme sacrifice. But this does not seem to have proved too much of an obstacle to this splendid piece of Revolutionary artistic licence

CHAPTER SEVEN
AUSTERLITZ
2nd DECEMBER 1805

Napoleon's masterpiece: central break-through, flanking wheel, crushing victory

The war

FOUGHT thirteen years after Valmy, Austerlitz and its preceding campaign formed Napoleon's classic victory, and his first as Emperor of the French. It was also the first of many triumphs for his unique creation: the *Grande Armée* which, with its glittering crop of marshals under the command of Napoleon, marched into every capital in Europe save London.

The *Grande Armée* took shape in training camps along the coast of the English Channel, for Napoleon's main project for the year 1805 was the invasion and conquest of England. But as the months went by the English not only declined to give the French a clear run across the Channel: they brought in Austria and Russia to keep Napoleon busy on the mainland of Europe. In 1805 as in 1792, the year of Valmy, France was menaced by a coalition of her enemies.

Valmy had been the product of defensive strategy plain and simple: the republican army had fought the enemy invaders on republican soil. But the Austerlitz campaign was an example, on an enormous scale, of what is today known as the 'pre-emptive strike'. Instead of waiting to see what the Austrians and Russians would do, Napoleon shot the *Grande Armée* deep into enemy territory and delivered a knock-out blow hundreds of miles from France. As an audacious piece of strategy, nothing like this campaign had been seen since Marlborough's march to the Danube 100 years before. It made terrific demands on the stamina of the French troops, who had to march some 800 miles from the Channel to Czechoslovakia in fourteen weeks with a full-dress battle waiting for them at the end of the road. Nothing on this scale had ever been seen in war.

Equally unprecedented was the manner in which Napoleon had recast the French army into the *Grande Armée*. He had formed it into seven corps, each one a miniature army with its own complement of infantry, cavalry and artillery and under the command of a marshal or of a general marked down for promotion to marshal. The idea was that all the corps should follow different lines of march, keeping just close enough to each other to be able to come

together at the required time and place for a decisive battle. In his deployment of the corps of the *Grande Armée* for the invasion of England, Napoleon had hedged his bets. He had placed three of them at Hanover, Utrecht and Bruges, ready for an eastward move should the need arise.

Napoleon had beaten the Austrians twice, each time in northern Italy (in 1796–7 and again in 1800). Knowing how the Austrians thought and fought, he guessed, correctly, that they would again be expecting the main action of a new campaign to develop in Italy. Napoleon had not fought Russian troops before but two of his marshals (Soult and Mortier) had, and he was confident that the Russians would not be difficult to defeat. In any

event, shackled as they would be to the Austrians, he did not imagine that the Russians would give him any serious trouble on their own. Napoleon therefore planned a lightning invasion of Bavaria and the Danube valley to seize the initiative from the Austrian and Russian armies, throw them off balance and destroy them piecemeal.

First stage: the march to Ulm

The English have always told their children that Nelson's victory over the French fleet at Trafalgar (21 October 1805) saved England from invasion – a myth more than somewhat undermined by the fact that by the time Trafalgar was fought the invasion camps had been empty and the invasion forces had been marching steadily in the opposite direction for the previous eight weeks. The move from the Channel began on 27 August and after thirty days of hard marching the *Grande Armée* had reached its first concentration line.

This is best represented by an open hand, thumb down – the thumb resting on Basel and the tip of the forefinger on Würzburg. Now Napoleon was stealthily reaching out, like a poacher preparing to 'tickle' a fat trout, to catch the westernmost Austrian army: 70,000 men under General Mack, centered on Ulm in the upper Danube valley. Ostentatious moves by the French cavalry kept him watching the exits from the Black Forest, which was where he expected the French to come from. What he actually got was an enveloping net, closing first from the north and east and so cutting him off from any help, then from the south and finally the west.

Some Austrian generals urged Mack to call in all the detachments scattered around Ulm, concentrate his army and break out – either south towards the Tyrol or east down the Danube to join up with the advancing Russians – but he did nothing apart from making an extraordinarily bad set of guesses about what the French were really up to. In the end he had no choice but to surrender on 20 October. Barely 10,000 managed to escape out of his original 70,000 and in total disarray. For Napoleon an important bonus to the elimination of Mack was the welcome support offered by the Elector of Bavaria, who now came over

Above : David's extravaganza, 'The Dedication of the Eagles on the Champ de Mars', depicts the kindling of the legend of the *Grande Armée*. Napoleon, in his neo-Classical coronation robes, plays Caesar at left while the newly-created Marshals flourish their batons in salute as the gleaming new eagle standards are dipped in homage. The colour-bearers in the foreground already wear the prize which Napoleon's soldiers came to covet above anything else: the cross of the *Légion d'Honneur*

59

to the French side in gratitude for the 'liberation' of his country.

Second stage: the march to Vienna

Napoleon's next objective was the Russian army of General Kutuzov which had pushed up the Danube valley during October to support Mack and was concentrating at Braunau on the River Inn, 160 miles east of Ulm, when Mack surrendered. A major worry was that Kutuzov might decide to join up with the strong Austrian forces across the Alps, and to keep him safely sealed in the Danube valley Napoleon now detached three corps and sent them off to hold the line of the Alps. For his part, Kutuzov had no intention of being lured into a set-piece battle with the French: he was going to make a fighting withdrawal back down the Danube, all the way to Vienna and beyond if necessary, in order to bring the main allied armies to full concentration.

The second phase of the campaign began on 24 October, and it saw mixed successes for both sides. Napoleon failed to destroy Kutuzov south of the Danube, as he had intended; Kutuzov crossed to the north bank at Krems on 9 November, burning the wooden bridge behind him; he then turned clumsily on the French forces on the north bank and gave them a bad mauling at Dürnstein on the eleventh. This escape to the north bank more than compensated for the fact that Napoleon had bounced Kutuzov out of every defensive position the Russians had tried to hold, forcing them to retreat over 130 miles in three weeks.

Napoleon now ordered a drive on Vienna itself, with a crossing of the Danube immediately north of the city and an advance to Hollabrunn to cut off Kutuzov's

army. This depended on the capture of the Tabor Bridge at Spitz, which the Austrians had left guarded and mined for demolition. The French took it with a piece of military cheek, bluffing the dim Austrian commander that a truce had been signed giving the French the right of passage. The French cavalry commander, Murat, had outwitted the Austrians at the Tabor Bridge; but when he came up against Kutuzov's rear-guard at Schöngrabern on 15 November he mistook it for the whole Russian army. Seeing Murat's hesitation, Kutuzov entered into fake truce negotiations and thus gained a whole day for the

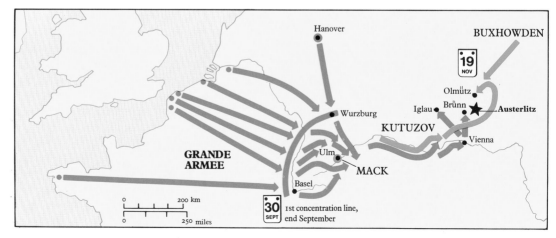

Russian main body to make good its escape from Napoleon's trap. Marching on into the Czech province of Moravia, Kutuzov joined up with the first relief Russian column under General Buxhöwden on 19 November.

Building and baiting the trap

Kutuzov's escape and the ensuing concentration of the Austro-Russian armies at Olmütz seemed to change the whole campaign. Tired and disordered after their scorching pursuit down the Danube valley, the scattered French corps were now faced by 80,000 men, apparently with time on their side and more reinforcements to come from Russia and the Alpine sector. It was hard to see how the allies could lose now. But in fact Napoleon was now looking for a decisive battle to end the campaign at a single blow, and he knew already where he wanted to fight it.

On 21 November, riding forward with his staff from his HQ at Brünn, Napoleon had traversed the country round the village of Austerlitz. He noted that the area was dominated by a central plateau, the Pratzen Heights, which would surely catch the attention of the allied army when it advanced against him from Olmütz. Rule One for dominating any battlefield has always been 'take the high ground', and as the allies loved campaigning by the book they would automatically occupy the Pratzen and think the French had made a howling error for not taking it themselves. It was natural bait, but Napoleon spent the whole of the twenty-first surveying the area to make sure. 'Never', wrote Baron Thiébault, an Austerlitz eye-witness, 'was any battlefield better examined or better prepared.'

Napoleon's plan was to hover on the edge of the Austerlitz area and look as invitingly weak as he could. The Austrians and Russians, now under the command of the young, romantic and naïve Tsar Alexander, wanted a battle; for the first time in the compaign, Napoleon would now play hard to get. As the allies approached the French would simulate retreat, encouraging the allies to follow up and occupy the Pratzen Heights as they did so. But as soon as the allies moved off the Heights Napoleon would hit them with everything he had, having at the last minute brought in the corps of Bernadotte and Davout from Iglau and Vienna respectively.

Timing was crucial. If Bernadotte and Davout should be delayed, Lannes, Napoleon and the corps of Soult and Lammes, together with Murat's cavalry, would almost certainly be wiped out. If the allies came too fast and too hard, the French would be pushed right off the battlefield Napoleon had chosen. But the allies finally lumbered out of Olmütz on the twenty-seventh, and Napoleon gave them another day before sending the orders for Bernadotte and Davout to come racing to the

Above : French dragoons surprise and capture a Russian supply convoy. Kutuzov, commanding the advance Russian army in the Danube valley, fought a well-executed retreat down the Danube after Ulm, extricating his army and joining up with the main allied forces before Austerlitz

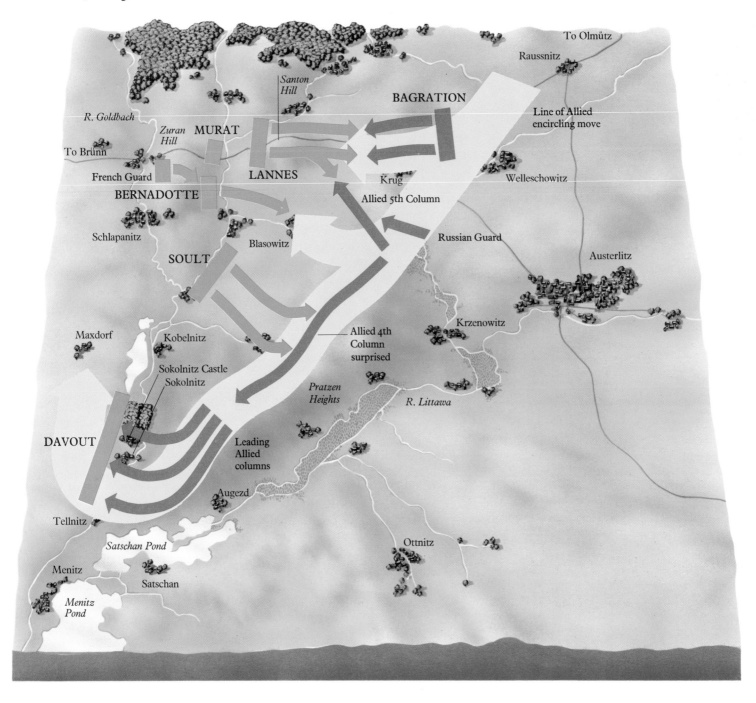

Raussnitz

To Olmütz

BAGRATION

Line of Allied
encircling move

R. Goldbach

*Zuran
Hill*

MURAT

*Santon
Hill*

To Brünn

French Guard

LANNES

Krug

Allied 5th Column

Welleschowitz

BERNADOTTE

Schlapanitz

Blasowitz

SOULT

Russian Guard

Austerlitz

Maxdorf

Kobelnitz

Allied 4th
Column
surprised

Krzenowitz

Sokolnitz Castle
Sokolnitz

*Pratzen
Heights*

R. Littawa

DAVOUT

Leading
Allied
columns

Augezd

Tellnitz

Satschan Pond

Menitz

Satschan

Ottnitz

*Menitz
Pond*

Above : The destruction of the
Austro-Russian host (*red*) at
Austerlitz. Napoleon had originally
hoped to wheel the whole French
army (*blue*) south to trap the allies,
but the French left flank was
checked by the tough resistance put
up by Bagration

scene. On the twenty-ninth and thirtieth
the French retreated across the Austerlitz
plain according to schedule and the allies
kept on coming. The following day they
were lured on to the Pratzen, their central
mass swinging south off the road to Brünn,
and Bernadotte and Davout arrived. By
nightfall all was ready for the springing of
the trap. In the morning the French would
continue to 'retreat'; the allies would attack
from the Pratzen and trigger off the French
counter-blow.

The allied plan could hardly have suited
Napoleon better if he had written the
orders himself. It consisted of a massive left
hook by the bulk of the Austro-Russian
forces, organized into three ponderous
columns, to roll down off the Pratzen

Heights across the muddy valley of the
Goldbach stream. A fourth column would
attack the French centre and a fifth, with
the Russian Imperial Guard, would drive
in the French left. But merely copying out
the intricate move orders in both Russian
and German took all night, and some allied
commanders found themselves in action
next morning without a clue as to what they
were supposed to be doing. Moreover, the
allied plan contained no margin for troops
going astray or running into unexpected
resistance at the wrong place. To be
attacked confidently by enemy troops who
obviously knew what *they* were about
proved to be a moral blow for the allies even
before battle was fairly joined.

First light on 2 December yielded the

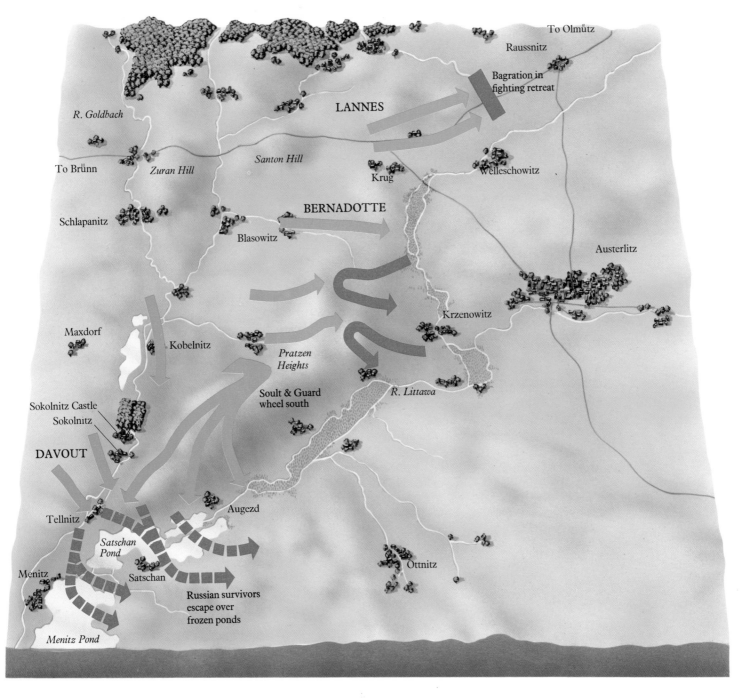

French another advantage, one both practical and psychological: a dense fog clinging to the low ground, masking the true deployment of the French as the allied columns began to crawl forward. They were forced to descend into obscurity and the shock of unexpected resistance; the French had the wonderful moral boost of climbing out of the mist into brilliant sunshine and catching their enemies both unawares and in disorder. For the allies, who began to move soon after 6.30 a.m. were soon in confusion, with some columns falling badly behind right from the start while others reached their objectives on time but in isolation.

The first shots of the battle were fired in the lower Goldbach at about 7 a.m., French light infantry engaging the head of the leading Russian column. This was Davout's Third Corps, still recovering from its scorching march up from Vienna and only intending to put up a token resistance before falling deliberately back to tempt the allied columns onwards. Down at regimental level, however, the men had other ideas and an increasingly spirited battle-within-a-battle flared up on the lower Goldbach. By 8 a.m. two out of the three outflanking allied columns were still stuck and the third column, having pushed the French out of the village of Tellnitz, had halted.

As the growing light revealed the crest of the Pratzen Heights looming above the mist, Napoleon had asked Soult how long

Above : The evening of Austerlitz. Wounded Russian prisoners face a miserable night in the snow

his Fourth Corps would need to ascend the hills. 'Twenty minutes, Sire', was the crisp reply; and shortly after 8.30 a.m. the great central push began. Soult was as good as his word, and the Pratzen was rapidly occupied; but on the far side the French found the Russian fourth column labouring belatedly into action. Caught totally by surprise, the Russians and Austrians tried furiously to recover the Pratzen and came close to succeeding; but the French infantry were better marksmen and Soult rushed forward the entire artillery reserve of his corps whose guns tore bloody lanes in the allied masses. The left-hand division of Soult's corps pushed onwards until it was threatening the hill on which the two allied emperors had started the day, causing near-total panic at the top on the allied side.

Up on the northern flank of the battle zone, the French (Murat's cavalry and Lannes' Fifth Corps) and the Russians (Bagration with the former allied advance guard) had gone forward to collide head-on, but sterling work by the French heavy cavalry broke up the Russian attack and by noon Bagration was falling steadily back down the road to Olmütz.

By about 11 a.m., therefore, Napoleon had already put the allied plan badly out of gear. The allied flanking columns were stuck fast; their centre was menaced by the French on the Pratzen to which Bernadotte's First Corps and the French Imperial Guard were also moving up; meanwhile the allied right was being driven back. This left only one uncommitted allied unit on the field: the Russian Imperial Guard, 10,000 men strong. Shortly after 11.30 a.m. the Russian Guard brought on the crisis of the battle by launching a ferocious blow against Soult's Fourth Corps on the Pratzen and captured the only allied trophy of the battle: the eagle standard of the French 24th Light Infantry Regiment. The Russian guardsmen were driven off only by the cavalry of the French Imperial

Guard – the French foot guards, weeping with frustration at being held back, never got into action at all – and after a desperate hour's fighting the menace receded. The French had punched an enormous hole right through the allied centre.

Napoleon's original plan had envisaged a general wheel to the south by the whole of his line to destroy the entire allied army, but Bagration's obstinate resistance in the north had made this clearly impracticable. Napoleon therefore had to be content with wheeling the French centre against the hapless allied flanking columns in the Goldbach valley. In their ensuing flight the shattered columns were forced to retreat across the splintering ice of two broad but mercifully shallow fishponds at Satschan and Menitz, across which the allies were floundering in total rout by the time the sun set at around 4 p.m.

Results and assessment

Out of their original strength of about 89,000, Austerlitz cost the Austrians and Russians about 27,000 killed, wounded and captured. This made a total of about one-third allied losses, of which by far the highest burden was borne by the Russians. The French counted only 9,767 Russian prisoners; Russian lists admitted to 23,502 casualties. High Russian mortality was due largely to their desperate habit of fighting to the last gasp with bare hands and teeth rather than surrendering. The French troops' reaction was to bayonet the Russian wounded in the heat of the action to be on the safe side.

French losses were low by comparison, nearly 9,000 out of a total force which stood at 75,000 on paper, but which may have been as low as 60,000 after the stresses and strains of the campaign. Of these losses only 1,305 were killed; 573 were captured and 6,940 were wounded.

Austerlitz did not end the war for Napoleon: the victors of the *Grande Armée* did not see France again for three years, and that was only passing through on their way to open a new campaign in Spain. But Austerlitz did knock Austria clean out of the war until 1809, making Napoleon the arbiter of central and southern Germany; it did force the Russians to seek an armistice, and it did enable Napoleon to attack the unsupported Prussians and flatten them at Jena in 1806. If Napoleon had been content to build a powerful France and restructure Germany under French patronage, leaving the East to Russia, Austerlitz would have been far more than a prominent and gaudy milestone on the road to Waterloo.

Above : The closing stages of the battle. Napoleon, in his famous grey top-coat, watches Soult's corps and the Imperial Guard drive south against the allies. The turbanned figure on Napoleon's right is Roustam, the Emperor's bodyguard – a legacy of Napoleon's campaign in Egypt and Syria in 1798, as were the Mamelukes of the Guard, one of the more exotic units of the Imperial Guard's cavalry, two of whom can be seen on the right of the picture

CHAPTER EIGHT
WATERLOO
18th JUNE 1815

When delegation is fatal: three days of errors that cost Napoleon his last campaign

The war

TEN years after Austerlitz, when Napoleon fought his last battle at Waterloo, his old *Grande Armée* no longer existed: it had finally marched to destruction as a fighting force in the Russian campaign of 1812. All that was left to Napoleon in 1813 and 1814 was a skeleton of survivors, fleshed out with raw young conscripts and cloaked with a tradition of military glory that no other European nation could boast.

The ghost of the *Grande Armée* was not strong enough to save France from invasion and conquest in 1814. Even so the men who had fought for Napoleon remained an explosive force when their emperor had been exiled to Elba and the Bourbon King Louis XVIII had been restored to the throne of his ancestors. The French felt as the Germans were to feel after World War I – betrayed, cheated, robbed and insulted by the post-war regime and the insolence of the victors. They certainly felt little guilt at having set Europe by the ears for the last twenty-two years. When Napoleon escaped from Elba and landed in southern France on 1 March 1815, France was heartily sick of eleven months of Bourbon rule and welcomed him with open arms.

That, at least, was the popular version of the Napoleonic legend, much of which was written up by Napoleon himself on St Helena. In reality his position after the return from Elba was a good deal more shaky. Loyalties were deeply divided: his old generals and marshals had accepted service under Louis XVIII to preserve the wealth and titles given them by Napoleon, and only a handful came back to the Emperor on his return. Substantial areas of France had always retained a deep loyalty to the Bourbons; the country as a whole had been bled white and worn out by twenty years of war.

When Napoleon became Emperor again in 1815, France was faced with almost a repetition of the allied invasion of 1814. The allies had pronounced Napoleon an enemy of mankind and vowed a joint campaign – Britain, Prussia, Austria and Russia working in concert – to root him out of France for good.

It was all very well for Napoleon to promise 'no more wars, no more conquests', and go through the motions of setting up a constitutional monarchy. He was threatened with war whether he liked it or not, against odds that would only increase as the weeks went by. He had to strike first, breaking up the allied coalition before it was fully formed, or go under. In a strictly limited sense, Napoleon in 1815 decided to do what he had done in 1805: seize the initiative and destroy his enemies.

The armies of 1815

In the spring of 1815 Napoleon was much better off for troops than he had been during the previous year. The prisoners of war were all home and available, and the thousands of walking wounded who had played no part in the 1814 campaign were healed, fit, and largely eager for another campaign. Napoleon was able to reconstitute the Imperial Guard from this formidable pool of available veterans from earlier campaigns, and raise a field army of 124,000 men by the middle of June. Conscription would have amassed more cannon-fodder, but by the time that this raw material had been gathered the Austrians and Russians would have entered the game. Napoleon therefore prepared to drive into Belgium with this mass of 124,000, split apart the armies of Wellington and Blücher and destroy the allies one after the other. As at Austerlitz, absolute precision and timing would be needed to bring it off, but out of the brilliant team of marshals who had won the day at Austerlitz, Napoleon had only Soult with him as chief-of-staff. Davout, now Minister of War, was back in Paris. All the others were dead, disgraced, or retired.

There was one exception: Michel Ney, 'bravest of the brave', the man whom Napoleon had called 'a lion' for his bravery on the field of battle. Remembered above all for his heroic leadership of the rear-guard during the retreat from Moscow, here surely was a man Napoleon could depend on. But Ney had led his fellow-marshals in insisting that Napoleon must abdicate in 1814; he had promised Louis XVIII to bring back Napoleon 'in an iron cage' after the escape from Elba.

Emotionally burned out at the prospect of civil war, Ney had eventually gone over to Napoleon again, full of lame excuses for his conduct. As events were soon to prove, he was a desperately sick man possessed of a lurking wish to expiate his mistakes by dying in battle. The kindest thing Napoleon could have done would have been to restore Ney to all his titles and pension him off – but the Emperor was so short of corps commanders that he gave Ney the command of *two* corps: the entire French left wing. Determined though it was by circumstances, this appointment was the first fatal error of the campaign.

Ney's appointment shows how astonishingly bad Napoleon could be at picking the right man for the right job. He was planning to remove the allies from Belgium with two powerful wings and a central reserve. For this he needed two first-rate corps commanders and a sound chief-of-staff to issue precise orders. The best corps commander Napoleon ever had, Davout, was right out of the running, behind an office desk in Paris. Soult, the man whose command of the centre corps had proved decisive at Austerlitz, was now chief-of-staff; and the right wing went to the Marquis de Grouchy, an undistinguished cavalry commander who would have been far better off commanding the central reserve under Napoleon's eye. In all three key appointments – the left wing, the chief-of-staff at the nerve-centre, and the right

wing – Napoleon showed his lack of judgement: each of the jobs went to an unknown quantity.

Despite all these hidden weaknesses, Napoleon's army was a powerful striking force with which he was confident of causing maximum grief to the scattered and multi-national allied forces.

Wellington and Blücher: the allies' dilemma

Ready to defend Belgium from the 'enemy of mankind', Wellington and Blücher seemed to have adequate troops for the purpose: 94,000 British, Dutch and Hanoverian, and 123,000 Prussians. But these were dotted right across Belgium from the Ardennes to the North Sea, weak everywhere and strong nowhere. Blücher held eastern Belgium from the Ardennes to Charleroi; Wellington the western zone of the country, with Brussels.

They had no choice but to let Napoleon show his hand, then concentrate their forces to beat him. While waiting for Napoleon to open the campaign, however, Wellington and Blücher did all they could to deploy their forces to the best advantage.

First, they agreed that neither would allow Napoleon to attack the other without coming immediately to the other's aid. Napoleon's desired strategy of piecemeal destruction was obvious and must be

Above: A British square repels Ney's cavalry at Quatre Bras on 16 June. Ney's failure to defeat Wellington at Quatre Bras, or impede the British retreat to the Mont St Jean ridge on the seventeenth, meant that the allied forces were still able to join hands at Waterloo on the eighteenth

frustrated by mutual trust and co-operation between the allied commanders. Second, it was equally obvious that Brussels was a natural objective for Napoleon, which must be denied him. But from these simple foundations a growing dilemma confronted the allies, for it was impossible to cover all the roads along which Napoleon might come at them.

There were four such roads, two in Wellington's sector and two in Blücher's. The westernmost came from Lille across the frontier through Tournai, Ath and Halle; the shortest of all came from Valenciennes through Mons and Soignies. Further east, in Blücher's sector, the Belgian town of Charleroi formed the crossroads of two other likely routes, one running Maubeuge-Beaumont-Charleroi and the other Rocroi-Philippeville-Charleroi. There were simply not enough allied troops to block all of these lines of possible French advance. If Napoleon moved fast enough to beat either Wellington or Blücher before the other could react in time, the second army could expect to be swallowed up in its turn.

Napoleon strikes: Ligny and Quatre Bras

Napoleon chose to take the Prussians first. He did so because he had routed their army in 1806, because they had broken free of their subservience to France in 1812, because they had marched with Austria and Russia to take Germany from him in 1813, and because they had spearheaded the allied drive on Paris in 1814. The Prussians were the old enemy, the beaten foe of Valmy, and another victory over them at the outset of the 1815 campaign would be the most promising of omens for the battle that would follow. In strictly practical terms the Prussians were a tougher nut than Wellington with his English-Dutch-German confection of an army. The Prussians once dealt with, Wellington would prove easy meat.

The River Sambre, which flows into the Meuse at Namur, formed the frontier at the outset of the campaign, and Napoleon crossed it on the night of 13 June. The southernmost Prussian corps fell back from Charleroi and Blücher ordered his entire army to concentrate at Sombreffe, telling Wellington that a powerful French force was coming up the road from Charleroi and that the Prussians would stand and fight it. But Wellington dared not assume that this was the main French army, and that Napoleon would not also attack up the direct road from Charleroi to Brussels, or even further west. The Emperor had pulled off far more ambitious manoeuvres in the past. With rumours flying in the capital, Wellington did what he could to stop Brussels panicking by ostentatiously attending the Duchess of Richmond's ball on the night of the fifteenth. During the ball a message from Blücher finally made it clear to Wellington what the French were up to: a lightning advance to split the allied armies apart. 'Napoleon has humbugged me, by God!' was his reaction. Determined to do all he could to support Blücher without exposing Brussels, Wellington immediately started packing off troops to hold Quatre Bras, a vital crossroads commanding the

Above : The battlefield seen from the French side, with Napoleon on his charger receiving yet another depressing report on the right of the picture. Wellington and his staff can be seen in the left background. Early in the battle an officer excitedly reported to Wellington that he had Napoleon within range of cannon-shot; should he open fire? Certainly not, was the Duke's sharp retort, it was no part of the business of commanders-in-chief to be firing at each other

roads running north to Brussels and east to Namur.

By early afternoon on the sixteenth, Napoleon was ready to fall on Blücher's army at Ligny, six miles east of Quatre Bras. He planned to send Ney up to Quatre Bras with 40,000 men to take the crossroads and block any attempt by Wellington to come to Blücher's aid. With this assured, Ney's two corps could be swung east to finish off the Prussians at Ligny. 'If Ney carries out his orders thoroughly', enthused Napoleon, 'not a man or gun of this army [the Prussians] in front of us will get away.'

But the orders Soult sent to Ney failed to spell out the master-plan, giving the impression instead that Ligny was not the crucial battle zone of the day. Ney was told to attack and smash everything in front of him, and then to 'join us to envelop this corps'. Ney started his assault on the afternoon of the sixteenth, his original target being the 7,000 Dutch and Belgians at Quatre Bras under the Duke of Orange; but as the day wore on he ran into tougher and tougher resistance as British regiments came marching down from Brussels. Then, at four in the afternoon, an order reached Ney from Imperial HQ that d'Erlon's First Corps was to switch from Ney's command and march to join the fray at Ligny. Convinced that *he* was facing the stronger allied army, Ney overrode the order and d'Erlon's corps started to march back to Quatre Bras when they had just reached the fringe of the Ligny battlefield. Ney's intervention therefore meant that d'Erlon's corps never got into action at all – either at Quatre Bras or at Ligny – and that both

Wellington and Blücher were spared from crushing defeat on 16 June.

The fatal twelve hours

Napoleon now turned his original plan inside out. If the French right wing kept the Prussians on the run, that would leave Wellington to face the music on the Quatre Bras-Waterloo-Brussels road. What Napoleon could not know was that he had done the Prussians a good deal less damage at Ligny than he thought. Nor had he ever encountered such an iron-hard opponent as Blücher: seventy-three years old, bruised and battered after falling and being ridden over during the retreat from Ligny, yet issuing orders for his corps to stand and rally at Wavre. Blücher kept in touch with Wellington throughout the night, and vital messages crossed between them. Wellington promised that he would stand and fight if Blücher could spare him a single corps, and Blücher guaranteed this.

Wellington knew precisely where he was going to fight. He had first seen the place twenty-one years before, in July 1794, when he was a colonel with the British expeditionary force fighting with the Austrians against the Republican French. He had heard his commander-in-chief, the Duke of York, plead with the Austrians to make a fight for Brussels along the ridge of Mont St Jean, which crosses the Quatre Bras-Brussels road just south of the village of Waterloo. In the aftermath of Ligny and Quatre Bras the Mont St Jean ridge stood out as ideal for a defensive stand, with Blücher rallying and promising to send up further reinforcements from Wavre, which was only eight miles away to the east.

Ney let the British get away from Quatre Bras and fall back on Mont St Jean. But Napoleon himself did not quit Ligny until shortly before noon on the seventeenth. As for the Prussians, Napoleon was equally laggard in bustling them safely out of touch with Wellington. He gave the job to Grouchy and the French right wing – some 33,000 men – only on the morning of the seventeenth, by which time Blücher was already in Wavre hauling his army back into fighting trim. By the time Grouchy finally approached Wavre on the eighteenth only the Prussian rear-guard was left there: Blücher's leading corps were already streaming west to the field of Waterloo.

Napoleon could not be blamed for the weather, which made life hell for everyone on the sixteenth and seventeenth: repeated violent thunderstorms and downpours which kept the open country saturated and forced both sides to struggle along the roads. But he can be blamed for not taking the weather into account, and for taking so long to get his forces on the move. The morning and early afternoon of the seventeenth was the fatal period when Napoleon let the allies off the hook. Wellington was given enough time to pull back to Mont St Jean; Blücher was given enough time to recover his balance at Wavre and get ready to come to Wellington's aid on the following day.

Waterloo: deployment of the armies

Wellington never thought that Napoleon would actually do him the favour of launching a frontal attack: he expected the French army to sidle round the west end of the Mont St Jean position. That was, in fact, what Soult had suggested, but Napoleon impatiently dismissed the idea – there was no time for the finesse of manoeuvre, he wanted to deal with Wellington at one blow. 'Damn it!' exclaimed Wellington, when he saw what was coming from Napoleon, 'he's a pounder after all!' But he missed acutely the 18,000 men he had placed at Halle, on the Mons road, in order to fend off any French encircling move; these played no part in the battle at all.

Second, Wellington himself indignantly denied that Mont St Jean was a 'last ditch' position – it was backed by a wood, the Forest of Soignes. 'It is not true that I could not have retreated. I could have got into the

wood and I would have denied the Devil to drive me out.' The Mont St Jean ridge straddled the Quatre Bras-Brussels road and was an ideal place for infantry to deploy in line and bring maximum fire-power to bear on an attacking army – Wellington's favourite ploy during his five years campaign against the French in Portugal and Spain. But in 1815 he did not have an all-British army. Against Napoleon's 48,950 infantrymen, Wellington had 49,608 – only 16,816 of which were British, and 12,806 Hanoverian. The rest were Dutch and

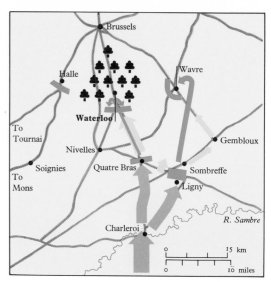

Right : The Waterloo campaign. Napoleon (*brown*) was trying, with two wings and a reserve, to split apart Wellington and Blücher (*blue*) and destroy them separately. At Quatre Bras and Ligny, on 16 June, Napoleon fondly believed that he had thrashed the Prussians into a headlong retreat, leaving Wellington's badly-mauled army an easy prey. But the Emperor had not bargained for the wonderful tenacity of Blücher, who treated Ligny as a temporary setback and refused to break faith or lose contact with Wellington. 'I have promised Wellington!', Blücher exhorted his weary gunners as they hauled their guns through the mud from Wavre to Waterloo; 'You would not have me break my word!'

Belgian. When he drew up his lines at Waterloo, Wellington studded his British regiments through the allied host like fence-posts. It was the best he could do to deny Napoleon any easy advantages by way of weak sections in the allied line, for Wellington dared not leave the uncertain allied units without close, reliable support on either side.

An interesting throwback to Naseby and the day of the pikeman was Wellington's use of the old 'forlorne hope', deployed forward to take the sting out of the enemy attack. He put small garrisons in the farm complexes with their substantial buildings that ran from Braine l'Alleud and Merbe Braine out on the allied right to Papelotte and Smohain on the left. By far the most important were the two closest to the Brussels road: Hougoumont and La Haye Sainte. These were vital, because as long as Wellington's men held them the French guns could not be pushed forward close enough to pound a breach in the allied line.

Waterloo: the long wait

Thus by the morning of 18 June the question was whether Napoleon – who had convinced himself that the Prussians were

out of the running after Ligny – could break Wellington before the Prussians came to the rescue. But a vital point about Waterloo, often overlooked, is that the French did nothing from first light (4–5 a.m.) to 11.30 a.m., during which time Blücher was hounding the bulk of his army west from Wavre. And the reason for the delay was all the rain of the last three days, the French deciding to wait as long as possible to let the ground dry out. No wonder the British are fond of talking about the weather. It helped them in many a campaign, but none more so than Waterloo.

Hougoumont holds out

At 11.30 a.m. Napoleon unleashed his first move: an attack on Hougoumont by Reille's Second Corps. This had a double purpose. It would clear the decks for an all-out attack on Wellington's line, but it was also an attempted repeat performance of Marlborough's tactic at Blenheim: jabbing at one enemy flank to make him strengthen it at the expense of the centre. Yet this time the ploy failed to work. Hougoumont's garrison held out, beating off three ever-increasing French attacks; Wellington fed in dribbles of reinforcement, only just enough to enable the Coldstreamers in Hougoumont to keep going, without weakening the rest of the line. As 1 p.m. approached Hougoumont was still resisting, drawing the attention of the entire French left-wing corps.

By 1 p.m. Napoleon was just about to order the main attack in the centre when distant troops were sighted approaching from the direction of Wavre. Wild hopes that this was Grouchy's corps, arriving on the scene after routing the Prussians again, were soon dashed. Those distant troops were Prussian, and Napoleon now had only three hours in which to destroy Wellington, re-group and face the new menace. He had concentrated a central battery of eighty guns with which to shred the allied line before punching it to pieces with infantry and heavy cavalry attacks; the French guns crashed out at 1 p.m. and hammered the allied centre for thirty minutes as a prelude to an attack by d'Erlon's First Corps.

D'Erlon's attack fails

At 1.30 p.m. d'Erlon's Corps rolled forward to the attack, bypassing furious resistance at La Haye Sainte but over-running Papelotte and Smohain. 8,000

Above : One of the most famous 'epic' paintings of the great cavalry charges during the afternoon of Waterloo. It shows the superb French *cuirassiers*; heavy cavalrymen in back-and-breast armour, boiling round a square of Highlanders. Wellington was later asked if the French cavalry 'had not come up very well'. 'Yes,' he replied, 'and they went down very well, too.'

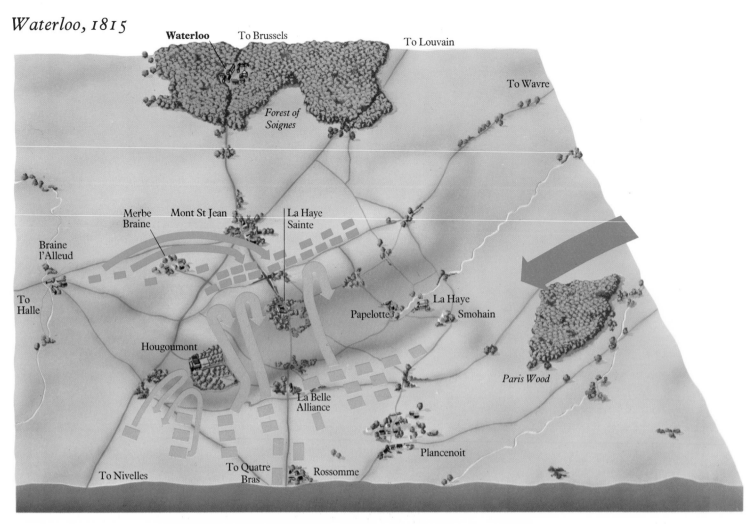

Waterloo, 1815

Waterloo
To Brussels
To Louvain

Forest of Soignes

To Wavre

Merbe Braine
Mont St Jean
La Haye Sainte

Braine l'Alleud

To Halle

La Haye
Papelotte
Smohain

Hougoumont

Paris Wood

La Belle Alliance

Plancenoit

To Nivelles
To Quatre Bras
Rossomme

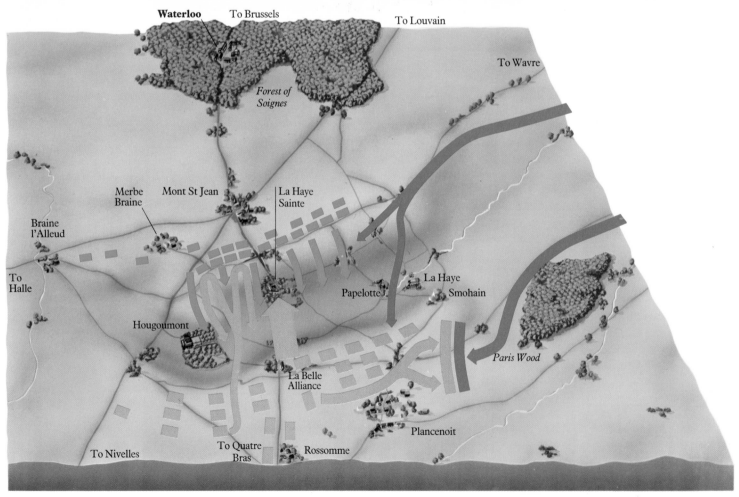

Waterloo
To Brussels
To Louvain

Forest of Soignes

To Wavre

Merbe Braine
Mont St Jean
La Haye Sainte

Braine l'Alleud

To Halle

La Haye
Papelotte
Smohain

Hougoumont

Paris Wood

La Belle Alliance

Plancenoit

To Nivelles
To Quatre Bras
Rossomme

confident French infantry headed for the allies on the ridge, panicking a Belgian brigade into flight, as Wellington had feared. But General Picton's brigade, all veterans of Spain, deployed in line as the triumphant French headed for the breach, staggered the attackers with a tremendous volley and charged with the bayonet, hurling the French back.

Further east along the ridge, however, the picture was black as two of d'Erlon's divisions, both unscarred, both at Quatre Bras and at Ligny two days before, crashed into Pack's brigade which had suffered badly at Quatre Bras. Heavily outnumbered, Pack's men had started to fall back when Lord Uxbridge, Wellington's cavalry commander, came charging to the rescue with two brigades of heavy cavalry.

Wellington's cavalry: triumph and disaster

It was all over in a couple of minutes. Still strung out in column for the attack, d'Erlon's corps had no chance against the British Household and Union Brigades. They broke and ran, with 2,000 exultant British troopers on their heels. But suddenly the picture changed. Instead of halting, regrouping and pulling back into reserve, Uxbridge drove the cavalry on in a wild fox-hunt, heading for the heart of the French position. It was Naseby all over again, with Uxbridge playing the reckless role of Prince Rupert, and with results that were far more dire. The cavalry had got in among the guns of the French battery when Napoleon's cuirassiers and lancers fell on them in a devastating counter-attack, turning the tables and effectively wiping out Wellington's only mobile reserve.

Ney intervenes: the great cavalry charges

The ruin of d'Erlon's charge and its tumultuous aftermath was followed by a lull from about 2.30 to 3 p.m., apart from the continuing fight for Hougoumont. Wellington put in his last packets of reserve British troops to patch the battered line; the French set up their battery again. After 3 p.m. the French bombardment reopened and was followed by the most spectacular phase of the battle: repeated charges by the massed French heavy cavalry, led in person by Ney.

The idea was all right – force Wellington's infantry into defensive squares, then swiftly draw off and let the gunners shoot the squares to pieces – but Ney's leadership and timing were hopeless. Seeing Wellington's men pulling back over the crest of the ridge to get some shelter from the French guns, Ney led the cavalry prematurely into action, thinking that Wellington was retreating. When the cavalry reached the squares the horses naturally refused to charge into the bristling hedges of bayonets waiting for them. Great seas of horsemen lapped about the squares, shielding the allies from the French guns before washing back down the hill with heavy loss. And each time the French cavalry retired the British gunners rushed out of the squares and opened fire again. These charges were mad and blind, like Ney himself, who was seen through the smoke, bareheaded and on foot, roaring mad and smashing at an abandoned gun with the flat of his sword. It was no way to lead an army. Above all, it wasted two precious hours. As Wellington's squares faced up to the last great charge at about 5 p.m., they heard at last the thud of the Prussian guns firing from the eastern edge of the battlefield.

Napoleon's last chance

From 5 p.m. Napoleon was forced out of the apathy which had induced him to leave the tactical control of the battle to Ney. Now the French were fighting on two fronts, for Lobau's Fourth Corps was desperately striving to hold off the advancing Prussians and give the main body a last chance of finishing off Wellington. At the same time Ney's battle fever slackened for just long enough to show him how to win the battle. In the next two hours, eleventh-hour French successes left Wellington staring defeat in the face.

At 6 p.m. Ney led 6,000 reserve infantry in a relentless attack on La Haye Sainte, which fell after half an hour. Now the French guns could be moved forward to gut Wellington's centre, but when Ney appealed to Napoleon for more infantry to finish the business the Emperor refused. His last reserve was the Imperial Guards corps; the regiments of the Young Guard were already fighting for their lives against the Prussians – and he shrank from committing the élite grenadiers of the Old Guard. Another half-hour passed – vital for Wellington, who could bring across units from the left now that the Prussians had arrived – before Napoleon agreed to release the Old Guard.

Opposite: The crucial highlights of the French assault at Waterloo. Wellington (*blue*) had never believed that Napoleon (*orange*) would be content with a head-on attack, but thought he would try an encircling move to the left. Hence the troops posted at Braine l'Alleud and Merbe Braine, on which Wellington was able to draw in order to feed meagre packets of reserves into his battered line. The French were repeatedly plagued by the ferocious defence of Hougoumont and La Haye Sainte, which held out like breakwaters. By the time La Haye Sainte eventually fell, the Prussians were already beating on the French right wing. Even so, the loss of La Haye Sainte immediately brought on the biggest crisis of the battle, for Wellington's centre was now wide open. The day was saved by Napoleon's further waste of time in agreeing to an all-out assault by the Old Guard, and the splendid way in which the charge was held and repulsed by the English Guards

Charge and defeat of the Old Guard

The Old Guard's attack, which Napoleon ordered at 7 p.m., was to be the supreme stroke, followed by an all-out advance by the French left and centre. To raise morale to fever-pitch Napoleon had it announced that Grouchy and his men were coming (though he had no idea where they were). The attack fell on Wellington's centre and right, which for the last half-hour was battered as never before by the French guns. But the charge was wretchedly led by Ney. One column prodded heavily at the allied centre and wavered uncertainly when its head was shredded by musketry from the English Guards; the other column slanted obliquely across the front of the allied line, suffering wicked losses by its un-

necessary exposure to heavy flanking fire.

The man who beat the Old Guard was Colonel Colborne, commanding the British 52nd Regiment. Totally on his own initiative, he wheeled his first battalion through ninety degrees, catching the Old Guard's second column in perfect enfilade and murdering it with the first volley. As the French column broke and took to its heels, Colborne's men gave the same treatment to the other column, which the English Guards had halted but not broken. Appalled, the French army watched the recoil of the Old Guard and the menacing advance of the entire allied line with Wellington urging them on.

Napoleon's army had been beaten before, but had never fled from a battlefield in total rout. Here and there, as the darkness descended, isolated French squares of infantry put up a brief resistance before being overwhelmed. Wellington's exhausted men

Above : Napoleon accepts defeat and turns in flight, with the faithful Roustam still at his side. The flowery French caption to this print states that 'Napoleon sought safety in a headlong flight; and the domination of the Conqueror of the World, with the glory of his arms, were shattered for ever by this single blow.'

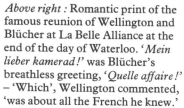
advanced as far as Napoleon's battle position before the Prussians took up the running, converting the French retreat to the Sambre into a rout. Here indeed was a battle without a morrow.

Assessment and losses

For such a short engagement (only eight hours from the first attack on Hougoumont to the defeat of the Old Guard) the casualties at Waterloo were frightful. Confined to an area under 4 miles by $2\frac{1}{4}$, they amounted to 25,000 French plus 8,000 prisoners, 15,000 of Wellington's men and 7,000 Prussians. Inevitably, Waterloo has always been remembered as the one-day battle in which Napoleon was beaten for good; but it was really a three-day, not a one-day battle, and it makes no sense to consider 18 June on its own.

It is easy – not to say traditional – to put all the blame on Grouchy for his absenteeism on the eighteenth. Grouchy was a stuffy, dim little man who thought he was doing what the Emperor wanted, and it was Napoleon's fault that the communications problem turned out so lamentably. The real problem was that Napoleon had never mastered the art of defensive warfare, and was up against a past master at it. As a former gunner officer, Napoleon should also have put his finger on artillery as the key to victory at Waterloo, instead of letting Ney waste so much time and so many fine troops. The teamwork on his own side was bad, and that was Napoleon's fault too; communications between Wellington and Blücher, and their understanding of each other, were the best seen since the days of Marlborough and Prince Eugene. Wellington and Blücher made plenty of mistakes during the Waterloo campaign. But their great opponent made even more.

Balaclava, 1854

Right and *opposite* : Two views of the gory curtain-raiser of the Crimean campaign: the charge of the English Guards on the heights above the Alma river on 20 September, which captured the powerful Russian positions blocking the road to Sevastopol. But all the gallantry expended at the Alma went for nothing; the leisurely allied pursuit gave the Russians plenty of time to retreat into Sevastopol and begin frantic work on building defences

Previous pages : Titled simply *Balaclava*, Lady Elizabeth Butler's superb painting captures the agonizing return of the survivors of the Light Brigade, limping, wounded and wild-eyed, from the notorious charge. Lord Cardigan, their arrogant commander, escaped without a scratch. 'It is no fault of mine,' he told a group of survivors. 'Never mind, my lord,' one of them was heard to reply; 'we are ready to go again.'

The amateurs meet the incompetents – a feckless battle in a pointless campaign

The war

IF wars are the grimmest accidents of history, the Crimean War of 1854–6 was a practical joke in the worst of taste. There is a pious platitude that wars are far too serious to be left to generals, but the Crimean War was, more than anything else, a terrible warning of what can come about through widespread civilian boredom, the power of warmongering journalism, and the weakness and stupidity of politicians.

The cause of the war, on both sides, was simple enough to define. Russia, posing as the champion of modern Christian civilization, was hoping to get a foothold in the Mediterranean at the expense of the feeble Turkish Empire, and therefore invaded Turkey's provinces in modern-day Romania (then the Danubian principalities). Britain and France, posing as the champions of the defenceless Turks, went to war as Turkey's allies and sent a Franco-British force to the Black Sea to expel the Russians.

This was the first action since the Crusades in which the French and English had fought on the same side. For both countries, this was also the first full-scale European war since Waterloo, which made their new association particularly odd. The military on both sides of the Channel had their heads full of memories of the Napoleonic Wars. France was an empire again, ruled by Napoleon's nephew; the British Army was commanded by Lord Raglan, who had lost an arm at Waterloo,

and who never did anything without wondering what Wellington would have done. He crippled all his allied hearers with embarrassment by constantly referring to the French as 'the enemy'.

Only the French had had any recent experience of war. They had conquered Algeria and Tunisia in 1830–1 and had marched to overthrow the Roman Republic and restore the Pope in 1848. The British, however, had recent fighting experiences only in India, and the careers of Indian Army officers were blighted by outrageous snobbery at home. 'Indian' officers were looked down on; birth and seniority on the Army List decided the key promotions. This prejudice against 'Indian' officers was particularly absurd because Wellington himself was the greatest commander the Indian Army had ever produced. Nevertheless it endured; and it meant that when the Crimean War broke out the top commanders of the British Army were either old, or totally inexperienced, or both.

By far the most splendid arm of the British Army was the cavalry, whose richest colonels poured out thousands of pounds on magnificent uniforms and thoroughbred horses. It was in the cavalry, too, that snobbery was most deeply entrenched, but events were to prove that this had not affected the fighting qualities of the light and heavy cavalry regiments. What it had done, however, was to make two disastrous promotions: the Earl of Lucan to command the Cavalry Division, and the Earl of Cardigan to command the Light

Cavalry Brigade. The fact that neither had ever commanded troops in action was typical, and the same applied to the commander of the Heavy Cavalry Brigade, Brigadier the Hon. James Scarlett. But Lucan and Cardigan were bitter personal enemies and their feud was to have a terrible outcome, which was to prove every bit as baneful as the total neglect of medical and supply services in the British Army.

The war did not boil up overnight, but simmered steadily throughout the second half of 1853, with Russia going to war with Turkey in October of that year. France and Britain went to war in March 1854. The main base was Scutari, just across the Bosphorus from Constantinople, where the first units arrived towards the end of April; but by June the French and British armies had moved up to the squalid Black Sea port of Varna. By this time the Russians were besieging Silistria on the lower Danube – but they were suffering so badly from cholera, and the Turks put up such a fight, that on 23 June the Russians raised the siege and retreated clean out of Turkish territory. All this time the British and French had done nothing but sit in Varna, ravaged by cholera and dysentery.

When the news reached home that the Turks had won their war without any help from the expeditionary force, and that the cost of sending out the troops was now a complete waste, it was not greeted with heartfelt thanks. On the contrary, popular opinion was very much that of a packed football stadium being told that there would be no game after all. The politicians were embarrassed; warmongering journalists bayed for blood. In London, *The Times*, echoing the general feeling that the army must do *something* before it came home, demanded the invasion of the Crimea and the capture of the strongest Russian naval base on the Black Sea: Sevastopol. As a way of bringing Russia to her knees, taking Sevastopol would be as useless as trying to kill an elephant with a pin; but as a way of appeasing popular clamour, and at the same time acquiring a bargaining counter that would undoubtedly come in handy when the time came for peace talks, taking Sevastopol was an easy way out for the politicians. What is shocking is the casual way in which the decision was taken – at a British Cabinet meeting on 28 June at which half those present were dozing off.

When Raglan got his marching orders for the Crimea he could hardly believe that he was to launch an invasion of a place about

which absolutely nothing was known, attacking a powerful fortress with little or no siege equipment, with the Russians holding all the cards when it came to reinforcement and counter-attack. For once there was no doubt what Wellington would have done: the Duke would have refused to have anything to do with the idea. But it was equally clear that the Cabinet was set on the Crimea/Sevastopol gamble and that if Raglan and his generals were to veto the idea they would be

Above : The British supply base at Balaclava on the south coast of the Crimea. Totally inadequate for the job, Balaclava was a pretty little holiday resort for rich Russians before the British descended on it and reduced it to a hell-hole of dirt, disease and chaotic supply arrangements

Right : The Balaclava campaign, one of the worst-ever examples of an army being ordered to 'do something' to satisfy public opinion back home. The British and French (*red*) went to war to save the Turks south of the Danube, but the Turks managed to do the job on their own. Despite the fact that the objective of the war had been achieved, the Crimean adventure went ahead

replaced by generals willing to tackle the job. The French commander, Marshal St Arnaud, was prepared to go along with the scheme (for similar reasons : his Emperor had also approved the plan); and so on 7 September, after weeks of frantic improvization and a chaotic embarkation, the allied armada set sail for the Crimea.

The Alma and after

They landed on the fourteenth in Calamita Bay, about twenty-five miles north of Sevastopol; but the British arrangements were so bad that it took four days before the two armies were ready to begin their march on Sevastopol : 24,000 French, 7,000 Turks and 27,000 British in all, with 128 guns. Waiting for them in a formidable position on the heights south of the River Alma was Prince Menschikov's army of 39,000 men and 96 guns. St Arnaud proposed a double outflanking attack, the French crossing the Alma at its mouth and the British enveloping the Russian right flank further inland, but Raglan would have none of it. He was determined not to expose his cavalry to unnecessary loss. Fortunately Menschikov was equally fearful of losing his guns, and a panic-stricken Russian withdrawal gave the allies undoubted victory in their clumsy, disjointed attack on the Alma position on the twentieth.

If a miracle were needed to give the Crimean expedition any hope of success, the allies had been granted one. The way to Sevastopol was open. A flat-out pursuit by the untouched British cavalry would have destroyed the retreating Russians and left Sevastopol to drop defenceless into the allies' laps. But the casualties had been severe : just under 2,000 British killed and

wounded, and 500 French, against about 5,500 Russian casualties, 1,800 of whom were killed. The wounded had to be gathered in, treated and evacuated by sea – a job that took two full days. By the twenty-third, when the march was resumed, Menschikov's troops had returned to Sevastopol, ships had been sunk to block the harbour, and there was no longer any chance of rushing the place.

Instead the allies embarked on a long flanking march round Sevastopol, ending up on the south coast of the Crimea at the tiny port of Balaclava, which Raglan selected as the new British base. Painfully, preparations were begun for the drawing of siege lines, with siege guns being landed from the fleet as from 29 September – but nothing was done to disrupt the frantic

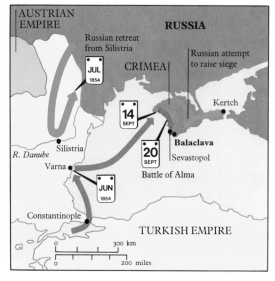

work going on in Sevastopol, where the first proper Russian defences were being built. These were still far from complete when the first feeble allied bombardment opened on 17 October. On the following day an alarming new threat began to materialize to the east : Russian reinforcements gathering to attack Balaclava and end the allied siege. By the twenty-fourth these forces had grown to an army of 25,000 men and 38 guns, commanded by General Liprandi.

Raglan's problem was the distance between Balaclava port and the allied siege lines round Sevastopol, six miles away to the north-west up on the Chersonese plateau. This plateau ended abruptly at the Sapoune Ridge apart from a spine of high ground, named by the British the 'Causeway Heights', running away to the east. North and south of the Causeway Heights, and named accordingly, were two shallow valleys, and it was on 25 October that Liprandi's attempt to take the Causeway Heights and wheel south to

Balaclava brought on the most notorious battle of the Crimean War.

Opening moves: the advance on the redoubts

To hold the Causeway Heights and dominate the North Valley a string of six redoubts had been dug by the allies, armed with twelve-pounder guns and garrisoned with Turks. These were the prime objectives for Liprandi early in the morning of the twenty-fifth. After a brisk and accurate artillery bombardment, No. 1 Redoubt was stormed by the Russians, and the garrisons of Nos. 2, 3 and 4 panicked and ran. Powerful Russian infantry and cavalry forces moved up onto the eastern end of the Causeway Heights. Between them and the port of Balaclava there was nothing but the British Heavy and Light Brigades in the South Valley and Sir Colin Campbell's 93rd Highland Regiment.

Russian shells were soon falling on the cavalry division, which had no choice but to fall back to the western end of the South Valley. This left Campbell's Highlanders virtually on their own apart from the doubtful aid of Turkish forces on their flanks. By 9.30 a.m. the situation could hardly have been worse for the allies. The initiative lay with the Russians, who had established themselves on the Causeway Heights. Covered by their comrades up on the Heights, the bulk of the Russian cavalry, over 3,000 strong, moved into the North Valley and began to advance. As they did so a force of about 400 peeled off to the south, crossed the Causeway Heights and prepared to charge down and eliminate Campbell's Highlanders.

Raglan had meanwhile established himself with his staff on the Sapoune, 600 feet above the plain. He had ordered the First and Fourth Infantry Divisions to come east to halt the Russian advance, and was determined to keep the cavalry safe until the infantry arrived – humiliating and frustrating for the cavalry, who resented Lord Lucan's rigid adherence to Raglan's orders. All this meant that Campbell's Highlanders were left to bear the brunt of the Russian charge without help from their own cavalry.

'The Thin Red Line'

'That thin red streak tipped with steel' was how war correspondent William Russell described the Highlanders as the Russian cavalry thundered down on them. As they came nearer the Turks on the Highlanders' flanks fired a panicky volley and fled for Balaclava – but the Highlanders shook the Russians with two good volleys, and the speed of the charge slackened. For a moment it seemed that the Russians, wheeling left, would sweep round the Highlanders' line, but this move only exposed them to another punishing volley in flank. Exultantly the Highlanders saw the Russian mass wheel left again, then trail back towards the Causeway Heights.

Charge of the Heavy Brigade

From his vantage-post up on the Sapoune, Raglan had seen the developing threat to Campbell and had ordered eight squadrons of dragoons from the Heavy Brigade to advance and support the wavering Turks on Campbell's flank in the South Valley. But the action of the 'Thin Red Line' was over before General Scarlett's troopers were fairly under way, picking their route

Left: One of the first-ever war photographs, taken by Roger Fenton: British light cavalrymen (a group of the 8th Hussars) by their revolting-looking 'cook-house' in camp at Balaclava

Balaclava, 1854

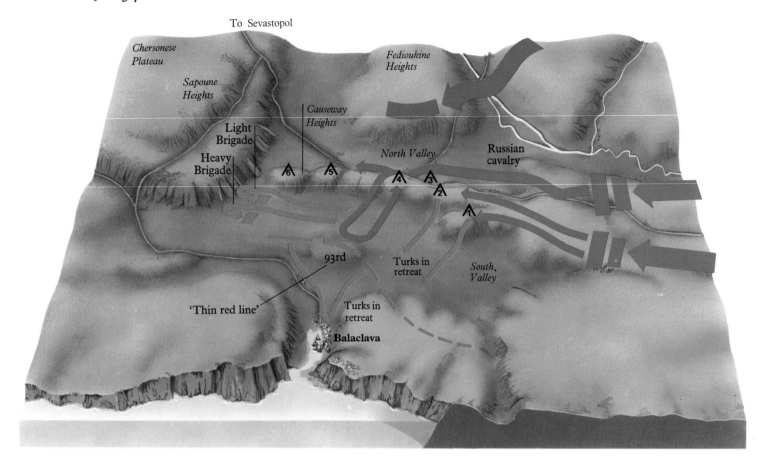

Chersonese Plateau

Sapoune Heights

To Sevastopol

Fedioukine Heights

Causeway Heights

Light Brigade

Heavy Brigade

North Valley

Russian cavalry

93rd

Turks in retreat

South Valley

'Thin red line'

Turks in retreat

Balaclava

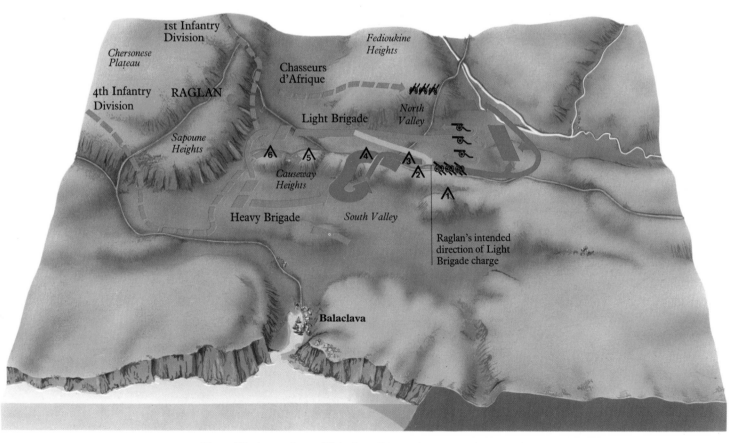

1st Infantry Division

Chersonese Plateau

4th Infantry Division

RAGLAN

Sapoune Heights

Fedioukine Heights

Chasseurs d'Afrique

Light Brigade

North Valley

Causeway Heights

Heavy Brigade

South Valley

Raglan's intended direction of Light Brigade charge

Balaclava

Above: The key actions of Balaclava. Liprandi, the Russian general, was let down by the lamentable performance of his cavalry (*blue*), beaten first by Campbell's Highlanders and again by Scarlett's charge with the Heavy Brigade (*red*). But Raglan, having had success handed back to him by these two actions, did nothing to follow up until the Russians began to pull out the captured guns up on the Causeway Heights. He sent the Light Brigade in to get the guns back – but they charged the wrong guns

Above : Colin Campbell's Highlanders open fire on the Russian cavalry, shortly to be immortalized in *The Times* as 'that thin red streak tipped with steel'. When the oncoming Russians panicked the Turks into headlong flight, Campbell's men were the only troops blocking the path to Balaclava. Exultant at their repulse of the Russian cavalry, some Highlanders made as if to charge after them. 'Ninety-Third!' bellowed Campbell. 'Damn all that eagerness!'

carefully through the Light Brigade's camp-site. As they came abreast of the captured No. 5 Redoubt, the leading squadrons of the Heavy Brigade passed right across the front of the advancing Russian cavalry, who chose this moment to appear on the crest of the Causeway Heights.

It seemed that all the Russians had to do was to roll down the slope and wipe the Heavy Brigade off the face of the earth. There were at least 3,000 of them and they had caught the British completely un-awares. Unaccountably, however, the Russians stayed on the ridge, and General Scarlett wheeled his force into an im-maculate line and prepared to charge.

For cavalry to meet hostile odds of nearly eight to one in an *uphill* charge was against all the rules, but the uncertain air of the Russian cavalry had already made itself obvious, quite apart from the defeat they had already suffered at the hands of the Highlanders. As Scarlett and his men went up the hill, right into the heart of the Russian mass, their blood was up and their sabres out. From the Sapoune the Russian mass was seen to sway and heave – then the rear two regiments of the Heavy Brigade, charging home in support, crashed into the fray at just the right psychological moment. The Russian mass broke, fragmented,

and streamed back across the crest of the Causeway Heights.

Scarlett's superb achievement had com-pletely reversed the course of the battle. After two resounding defeats, the Russian cavalry pulled back down the North Valley, their tails between their legs. Now was the time that the Light Brigade, which had been bursting with impatience at being kept immobile while the 'damned Heavies' got all the glory, should have swept forward and sabred the retreating Russians to bits – it was what light cavalry was for. But although his frantic officers almost went down on their knees to him, Cardigan stubbornly refused to move the Light Brigade from where his blood enemy, Lord Lucan, had ordered him to keep it. Circumstance had made the order absurdly out of date, but it made no difference to Cardigan. He stayed where he was, there-fore, and the fruits of the Heavy Brigade's triumph were not gathered in.

Charge of the Light Brigade

Having had the initiative handed back to him by the defeat of the Russian cavalry, Raglan now prepared to regain the Causeway Heights and the redoubts. But the Fourth Infantry Division had not yet arrived from the siege lines, and he was loth to send the cavalry into action again. Raglan had a simple choice: either wait for the infantry, or clear the Heights with cavalry alone.

What he did was to order Lucan to 'advance and take advantage of any oppor-tunity to recover the Heights', adding that the cavalry would be supported by in-fantry. Lucan, however, could see no opportunity whatsoever for cavalry alone, and read the order to mean that he was to advance only *when* supported by infantry.

Right : The Charge of the Heavy Brigade, made against all the rules of cavalry tactics: uphill and against vastly superior numbers. However, it was a total success, in ironic contrast to the fiasco soon to follow

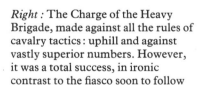

Balaclava, 1854

All he did was to move the Light Brigade up to the west end of the North Valley with the Heavy Brigade in support and follow the example of his commander-in-chief – wait.

After nearly an hour of inactivity, however, it was the Russians who decided to wait no longer. Liprandi ordered the guns in the redoubts to be harnessed up and brought back into the main Russian lines. It was obvious that the recapture of the guns had to be the next British objective; this move would at least see that all they recovered would be empty redoubts.

When the sudden new movement round the captured guns was spotted by Raglan's staff on the Sapoune, there could be no more waiting for the infantry. Raglan issued an immediate order: 'Lord Raglan wishes the cavalry to advance rapidly to the front – follow the enemy and try to prevent the enemy carrying away the guns.' It was fatally inadequate on two counts. First, Raglan was looking at the redoubts over the heads of the Light and Heavy Brigades down in the North Valley – but what was 'front' to him was not 'front' where they were, 600 feet below. It was, if anything, 'flank front' or to be precise, which that order most certainly should have been, 'right flank front': ahead and to the right. Second, Raglan could see the redoubts on the crest of the Causeway Heights – but the cavalry, down on the valley floor, could not. All they could see was the mass of Liprandi's army two miles away at the far end of the valley, shielded in front by artillery. Over to the left they could also see more Russian troops and guns up on the

slopes of the Fedioukine Hills.

When Captain Nolan galloped up to Lord Lucan with Raglan's order, therefore, Lucan could see no sense in it. He peered and puzzled while Nolan fumed with impatience and finally burst out 'Lord Raglan's orders are that the cavalry are to attack immediately!' 'Attack, sir?' barked Lucan, 'Attack what? What guns, sir?' This was when Nolan should have taken a deep breath, counted to ten, and spelled out in careful detail what Raglan wanted; but instead he lost his temper completely. Like an arrogant schoolmaster taunting a dim pupil, he pointed towards the Russians at the end of the North Valley. '*There*, my lord, is your enemy,' he jeered. '*There* are your guns!'

The fatal chain of events was complete, cemented by resentment of earlier bad orders and the mule-headed determination to carry them out at all costs. Even Lord Cardigan, whom Lucan now ordered to lead the attack at the head of the Light Brigade, protested that they would come under fire from three sides. 'I know it', shrugged Lucan, 'but Lord Raglan will have it.' Cardigan saluted without further commment, rode back to his brigade, drew it up in two lines, and gave the quiet order: 'Brigade will advance. Walk, march, trot.'

From the Sapoune, Raglan and his watchers expected to see the cavalry move forward past Redoubts 6 and 5 and work up to a full gallop before sweeping sharply to the right, up on to the crest of the Causeway Heights and straight into the Russian-held redoubts. What they actually saw, with

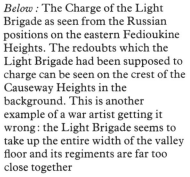

Below : The Charge of the Light Brigade as seen from the Russian positions on the eastern Fedioukine Heights. The redoubts which the Light Brigade had been supposed to charge can be seen on the crest of the Causeway Heights in the background. This is another example of a war artist getting it wrong: the Light Brigade seems to take up the entire width of the valley floor and its regiments are far too close together

Right : Another famous Fenton photograph from the Crimea: an after-the-battle shot of the 'Valley of the Shadow of Death', littered with roundshot

mounting horror, was Cardigan leading the Light Brigade, with impeccable discipline and precision, into the murderous crossfire from the Russian guns on the Causeway, at the end of the North Valley, and on the Fedioukine Heights. Smoke from the Russian guns gradually filled the valley like a pall, stabbed by tongues of fire from the guns, and into that smoke the Light Brigade charged and vanished.

Incredibly, Cardigan – who never once turned his head during the Charge to see the annihilation of his superb troopers – survived. He was first into the Russian battery and first out. He thought it no part of his duty to take command of the handful of survivors and bring them out. Theoretically, not a man of the Light Brigade should have survived, but the masses of Russian cavalry waiting behind the guns did not attack. Shrinking from hand-to-hand combat after their earlier defeats, the Russian troopers tried to fence off the Light Brigade survivors, most of whom, like Cardigan himself, managed to break through.

Only 195 out of some 700 men came back from the Charge of the Light Brigade; 500 horses had been killed. The casualties would have been made even worse during the withdrawal had it not been for the French *Chasseurs d'Afrique*, out on the British left, who made a brilliant charge of their own against the Russians on the Fedioukine Heights and silenced their guns.

The end of the battle

The disaster to the Light Brigade ended any chance Raglan had of inflicting a decisive defeat on Liprandi's relief army. When the infantry finally arrived it pushed cautiously along the Causeway Heights and recovered No. 4 Redoubt, thus securing the supply lifeline to Balaclava. The battle ended in virtual stalemate around 4 p.m., with the Russian relief army still in being and Balaclava still in British hands.

Aftermath

The Russians made only one more attempt to drive the allies away from Balaclava, at Inkerman ten days later. This time the British infantry had their chance and inflicted a decisive defeat on the Russians, who suffered 12,300 casualties. The siege dragged on through an appalling winter for the exposed allied forces in the trenches; by spring, both sides had put out peace feelers, and the Russians had begun to evacuate Sevastopol by the time of the final allied attacks, of August 1855, which broke the defensive ring. Peace was finally signed in March 1856.

Balaclava had been a stupid battle fought at the beginning of a particularly stupid war. Apart from the charge of the *Chasseurs d'Afrique* it was really an all-British affair, and for an army which prided itself on the achievements of the great Duke of Wellington its performance was lamentable. Rigidity of command and hopeless personality clashes were the real culprits. If Lucan and Cardigan had been able to work together, to talk things over sanely, they would have been able to unscramble Raglan's cryptic orders and win a decisive victory. Even had this come about, however, nothing would have prevented the siege of Sevastopol from running its miserable and unnecessary course.

Previous pages : Confederate high tide at Gettysburg – Pickett's infantry tears vainly at the centre of the Union Line

Both armies were looking for battle – but it began before either was ready

The war

GETTYSBURG is often cited as the decisive battle of the American Civil War of 1861–5, but this is not really true. The battle certainly did not bring the war to a rapid conclusion; it was fought in the high summer of 1863, and the last shots of the war were not fired until May 1865. In this sense, then, Gettysburg was no Waterloo. It was more like the battles of Blenheim, Alamein or Stalingrad: a clear-cut victory followed by several defeats for the victors which, in the end, failed to change the outcome of the war.

By the time the United States reached its seventieth anniversary in the late 1850s, the Northern states of the Republic were becoming seriously embarrassed by the successes of the international anti-slavery movement. Moderates wanted restrictions placed on slavery within the USA; abolitionists wanted to root it out altogether. But the Southern states, whose substantial tobacco- and cotton-growing ouput depended on slave labour, fiercely

resented and distrusted Northern criticisms. They were determined to resist any attempt by the Federal government to interfere with the 'peculiar institution' of American slavery.

Then, at the close of 1860, the Republican Abraham Lincoln became President-elect after a campaign in which slavery and states' rights were the central issue. The last thing Lincoln wanted was a crusade against slavery in the South: on the slavery issue he preached *laissez-faire* with no extension, not root-and-branch abolition. But the Southern states decided to bring the problem to a head by making the whole business an issue of states' rights to secede from the Union, and form their own independent Confederacy of slave-owning states.

Jefferson Davis, former Senator for Mississippi, became President of the Confederate States and immediately spelled out the new nation's watchword: 'All we ask is to be let alone.' But the prospect of the Southern states peacefully going their own way never stood a chance. Lincoln's

Below : Union and Confederate uniforms in 1861, at the outset of the American Civil War, the 'War of the Blue and the Grey'. Few of Lee's hard-case ragamuffins presented such a spotless appearance by the time of Gettysburg

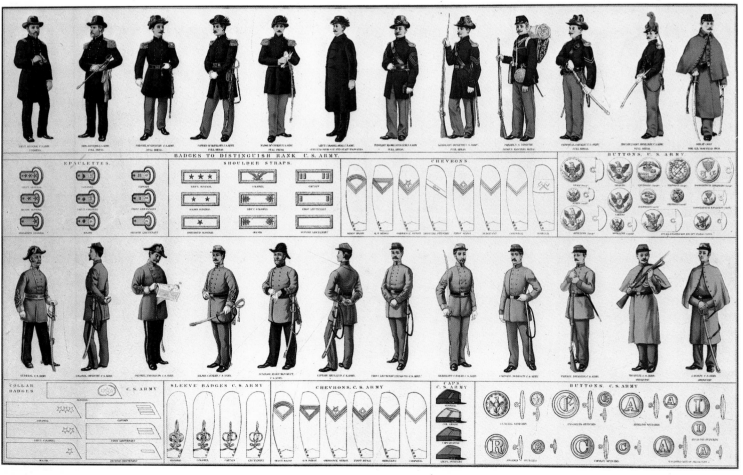

presidential oath bound him to preserve the Union, not to acquiesce in halving it. Faced with invasion, the mood of the South was militant defiance, very much like the white Rhodesians in 1966 when Ian Smith declared UDI. The fact that the North had all the factories and over double the manpower (population about twenty-two million, against the South's five million plus four million slaves) did not prevent the Confederacy from forming its own army and navy and getting ready to fight.

Davis had a lot more to rely on than the South's huntin' and shootin' aristocracy. Most of the Southern officers in the US armed forces resigned and came home to fight for the Confederacy, by far the most respected of whom was Colonel Robert E. Lee of Virginia, rapidly promoted general. Again, Davis was a former officer himself and Lincoln was not; Confederate generals were therefore not constantly bedevilled by political pressure to 'do something', while Lincoln's were.

Lee and his army

The war began with the Confederate shelling of Fort Sumter at Charleston, South Carolina, on 12 April 1861. It was fought on three main fronts: in Tennessee, along the line of the Mississippi, and in the east which was the most prominent theatre. Richmond, Virginia, was the Confederate capital and it stood less than 100 miles from Washington itself. As Winston Churchill put it in *History of the English-Speaking Peoples*: 'Thus the two capitals stood like queens at chess upon adjoining squares, and, sustained by their combinations of covering pieces, endured four years of grim play within a single move of capture.' Churchill might have extended the simile, and added that the war in the east soon became a matter of Washington vainly putting up challenger after challenger to take on the Confederate 'grand master': Robert E. Lee and his superb Army of Northern Virginia.

By the spring of 1863 Lee had beaten McClellan in the 'Battle of the Seven Days' (June 1862); Pope at Second Manassas or Bull Run (August 1862); McClellan again at Antietam, this time on Federal soil (September 1862); and Burnside at Fredericksburg (December 1982). These victories ran the full gamut of the general's art, from the dogged defensive on chosen ground to audacious flank marches and attacks from the rear, as well as beautifully executed attacks in strength against

carelessly-exposed sectors of the enemy force. Not once did Lee enjoy more than three-quarters of his opponent's strength, though it always seemed to the Northern generals that Lee had far more men than he actually did.

In May 1863 Lee did it again, with 60,000 men against 130,000. At Chancellorsville, close to the Fredericksburg battlefield, he daringly divided his dwarfed army, fell upon the flank of the Army of the Potomac (under the command of General 'Fighting Joe' Hooker) and drove it back in confusion. Yet again, Richmond was saved. But it was a victory hardly won, for Stonewall Jackson, who was to Lee what Prince Eugene had been to Marlborough, was shot by his own men in the confusion of the night action. For his follow-up, Lee decided to repeat his ploy of September 1862, and invade Northern territory for the second time.

By invading Pennsylvania, the very cradle of the Union, where the original Declaration of Independence from British rule had been made in July 1776, he would score an automatic propaganda victory. In strategic terms he would also force Washington to look to its own defences within weeks of the gory failure at Chancellorsville to take Richmond. The Army of the Potomac must follow Lee north and if necessary he would beat it again, this time on its home ground.

This time, however, Lee would not have Jackson with him, and Lee's style of generalship demanded a right-hand man on whom Lee could rely absolutely. Not that the other corps commanders of the Army of Northern Virginia – A. P. Hill, Ewell, and Longstreet – were incompetents, far from it; but a unique partnership had been broken with Jackson's death. Two other

Above: Primitive field hospital on the Gettysburg battlefield, with the surgeon operating in the open-sided shack on the right of the picture. Medical treatment had barely advanced since the Napoleonic Wars, though chloroform was occasionally available for the privileged few

Below: General George Meade, who took over the Army of the Potomac on 28 June, the latest in a long line of commanders for that brave but out-generalled army

Gettysburg, 1863

Right : The Gettysburg campaign. In his invasion of Pennsylvania Lee (*pink*) was sadly handicapped by the absence of his old and trusted lieutenant, Jackson – killed at Chancellorsville back in May – and by the lack of scouting intelligence normally supplied by 'Jeb' Stuart, his dashing cavalry commander

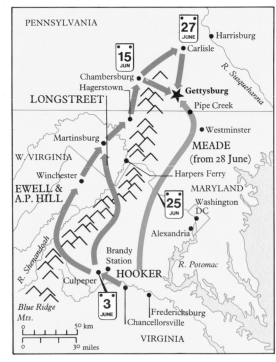

Below : Union guns thunder along Cemetery Ridge to strengthen Meade's centre at Gettysburg. By the third day of the battle Lee had no choice but to try the desperate expedient of an infantry assault on the strongest part of the Union line

things went wrong with Lee's plans. The Army of the Potomac followed him much faster than he thought it would; and his own cavalry lost touch with the Union army. The separate corps of the Army of Northern Virginia crossed the Potomac and passed through Maryland into Pennsylvania with Lee assuming that the Army of the Potomac had stayed put – simply because the brilliant 'Jeb' Stuart, Lee's cavalry commander, had not sent in any news to the contrary.

'Fighting Joe' Hooker resigned on 28 June and Major-General George Meade, former commander of the Fifth Corps, took over the Army of the Potomac. A dour man who did not believe in taking risks, Meade kept his army together. The result was that on 28 June, Lee suddenly discovered that the Army of the Potomac was already in Maryland while his own corps were strung out on a forty-five-mile arc. There was only one thing to do: concentrate, and fast. By 30 June the Confederate forces were duly converging on the nearest mutual road junction: the town of Gettysburg.

Meade was planning to make a stand at Pipe Creek, fifteen miles south of Gettysburg, where he intended to let Lee

come and get him, in a good defensive position. To cover the move of the army to Pipe Creek he sent J. F. Reynolds' First Corps up to Gettysburg, which was already screened by three cavalry brigades under John Buford.

Gettysburg: first day

Early on the morning of 1 July the first of Lee's corps to approach Gettysburg – A. P. Hill's – ran into Buford's cavalry outposts west of the town. Buford's logical move should have been to keep in touch with the approaching enemy and fall back, passing the word to Reynolds and Meade; cavalry alone could not hold a town against an attack in corps strength, even if Meade had issued any orders that Gettysburg was to be held. Instead, Buford got his men dismounted and started to fight a pugnacious delaying action, completely on his own initiative.

Pushing a cavalry screen out of the way was routine for the Confederates; when Reynolds arrived with the First Corps he immediately pitched in to support Buford, and Hill riposted by deploying his corps for a full-scale attack. Thus by noon on 1 July, Lee and Meade heard with surprise that their troops were already in action – a battle which neither general had had any idea of fighting where it had started, but from which it would be difficult if not impossible to disengage now it had.

When Lee arrived on the scene shortly after noon he saw every reason to keep the

pot boiling. Another Union corps – Howard's, which had taken a severe mauling at Chancellorsville – had come up to support Reynolds and Buford, only to be split wide open by the arrival of Ewell's Confederate corps from the north. Lee promptly ordered a general advance. By the middle of the afternoon the two Union corps had been broken and thrown out of Gettysburg by the exultant Confederates. Total disaster was averted only by Major-General W. S. Hancock's arrival with fresh troops. Like his C.-in-C. Meade, Hancock was a man who did not panic easily. He promptly seized all the high ground to the south of Gettysburg and formed a formidable new battle line. By nightfall on the first, Lee had won the first round but knew that he would have to start again, virtually from scratch, on the following day.

Gettysburg: second day

The armies had clashed by accident; Lee's men had taken Gettysburg by accident; but Hancock's instinctive grab at the high ground on the late afternoon of the first had given Meade's army an extremely strong position by accident. The Federal right flank rested on Culp's Hill, from where the ridge ran west to Cemetery Hill and then abruptly south along Cemetery Ridge to the heights of Little Round Top and Big Round Top, three miles away. Between the southern sector of Cemetery Ridge and the Gettysburg-Emmitsburg road, the slopes and lower ground were held by Sickles' Third Corps.

The tremendous fighting on 2 July saw the failure of Lee's attempt to dislodge Meade's army by smashing its flanks. The day began well, with Longstreet driving back Sickles' corps through locations known as 'the Peach Orchard', 'the Wheatfield', and on up through 'Devil's Den' to Little Round Top; the Confederates reached the high ground only to be flung off by point-blank cannon fire with hideous losses. But the absence of Jackson and Stuart was keenly felt: the Confederate attacks at the other end of the Federal line were sadly unco-ordinated. Everywhere the story was the same: at Culp's Hill, Cemetery Hill and Little Round Top the Confederate wave lapped into the Federal line, only to wash back in confusion before coming on again. It might have been Waterloo all over again, with Lee's splendid infantry taking the place of Napoleon's cavalry unable to panic Wellington's line.

By nightfall on the second Lee was forced to admit failure. All he had done was to hammer Meade's line into a tougher position. The only Confederate reserve left was General George Pickett's division,

Above : The Confederacy's grand master of the offensive-defensive; Robert E. Lee, commander of the Army of Northern Virginia

Below : Another depiction of the tense moment when the leading units of Pickett's Charge broke into the Union line. The bare, open slopes dropping westward from Cemetery Ridge stretch away to the woods fringing the Emmitsburg road, where Lee's guns continue to fire

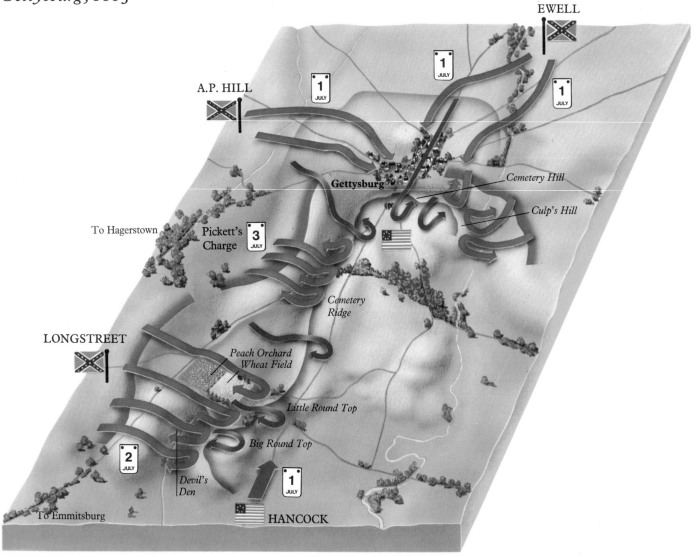

EWELL

A.P. HILL

1 JULY

1 JULY

1 JULY

To Hagerstown

Cemetery Hill

Gettysburg

Culp's Hill

Pickett's Charge

3 JULY

Cemetery Ridge

LONGSTREET

Peach Orchard
Wheat Field

Little Round Top

Big Round Top

2 JULY

Devil's Den

1 JULY

To Emmitsburg

HANCOCK

Above : Neither general chose the Gettysburg battlefield – the battle took shape as the two armies touched and instinctively clashed. All the Confederate advances of the first day (*red*) achieved was to hammer Meade's army (*blue*) into a position of great natural strength which Lee had no choice but to go on attacking

5,000 strong, untouched by the day's fighting. Having failed to shake the flanks of the Army of the Potomac on the second, Lee planned an all-out assault on the centre of the Army for the third with Pickett's division and two others drawn from A.P. Hill's corps.

Gettysburg: third day

Lee spent the morning of the third assembling an immense line of artillery, over 130 guns, along the Emmitsburg road; these were to soften up Meade's line ready for the infantry attack in the centre. At 12.30 p.m. an uneasy calm still brooded over the battlefield, and then, at about 1 p.m. two shots gave the signal for the Confederate bombardment to open.

Neither side had ever known artillery fire of such intensity, but it did a good deal more damage to the senses than it did to Hancock's men up on the heights. The noise was deafening, not just the roar of the Confederate guns and the replying fire from Cemetery Ridge, but the shriek and yowl of shell fragments ricocheting off the

stony ground of the heights. The smoke of the guns did not help the Confederate gunners, most of whose shells landed behind Hancock's line instead of on it. The replying fire of the Federal guns did a lot to steady the men on the ridge but Hunt, Hancock's artillery commander, had enough sense not to trade shot for shot and run out of ammunition; it was only too plain what was coming, and by about 2 p.m. most of the Federal guns had prudently fallen silent.

Then, around 3 p.m., the Confederate bombardment abruptly fell off, and out of the woods fringing the Emmitsburg road came Lee's infantry. They deployed outwards to form a line a mile wide – two divisions side by side and one in reserve – and surged forward up the bare slopes towards the heart of the Federal line.

As they did so they came under intense fire from the Federal guns which concentrated their fire on the left-flank division of General J. Pettigrew. Pickett kept coming in the Federal centre, but out on his right Hancock had pushed forward a brigade to inflict flanking fire – just like Colborne at

Waterloo during the charge of the Old Guard – and the right flank of the Confederate attacking line was forced in to the centre. Nothing stopped Pickett's men; the ranks re-formed, always closing in, enduring dense musketry fire and going on to get to grips with their enemies. But only a few hundred managed to break into the Federal line and get among the guns before being overwhelmed and driven back from each flank. As the smoke began to clear Lee could see that the Federal lines still held the heights – and only about half the men of Pickett's charge returned down the hill.

Lee had played his only remaining card, and it had failed him. He was deep in enemy territory at the head of a beaten army and there was nothing for it but retreat across the Potomac into Virginia. Meade, whose army was almost as stunned as the Army of Northern Virginia, was content to let Lee go and follow cautiously. The last offensive made by the Army of Northern Virginia was over.

Aftermath and losses

Considering that Lee's army was out-numbered by at least 20,000 and lost about the same number in the three days of Gettysburg, the North could well afford the 23,000 casualties who fell in the action. The effect of the battle was immense. Meade had broken not only the most serious offensive mounted by the South, but, far more important, the legend of Lee's invincibility.

The fatal third day of Gettysburg was a disastrous one for the Confederacy, for on the same day General U. S. Grant received the surrender of Vicksburg on the Mississippi River. The 'Father of Waters' was now entirely in Federal hands and the Confederacy had been split in half. The twin defeats of Vicksburg and Gettysburg marked the turning of the tide for the Confederacy within a month of its most splendid victory at Chancellorsville.

If Lee had been a Northern general he would almost certainly have been sacked after Gettysburg, but Davis never thought twice about keeping him. Lee was still commanding the pitiful remnants of the Army of Northern Virginia – a mere 8,000 effectives – when he surrendered to Grant at Appomattox Court House on 9 April 1865. Only six days before, Richmond, the Confederate capital, had finally fallen.

Below : Matthew Brady's sobering photograph of the dead on the Gettysburg battlefield

CHAPTER ELEVEN
SEDAN
5th JULY—2nd SEPTEMBER 1870

Previous pages : German infantry storm into the attack at St Privat on 18 August 1870, the battle which sent Bazaine's army reeling back into Metz and left MacMahon's army on its own. These are not Prussian troops but Hessians – members of the North German Confederation which Bismarck had brought into existence and which the tawdry Second Empire of Napoleon III had gone to war to destroy

Below : French infantry of the time of the Franco-Prussian War. The performance of the French troops was by no means a total disgrace, their excellent *chassepot* rifles being superior to the Prussian Dreyse. Unfortunately the Prussian artillery with its fine Krupp guns was the best in the world and the Prussians made full use of the fact

The terrible price to pay for starting a war with an unprepared army and a grimly efficient foe

The war

You, staring at your sword to find it brittle,
Surprised at the surprise that was your plan,
Who, shaking and breaking barriers not a little,
Find never more the death door of Sedan.

THIS poetic lament of G. K. Chesterton for *la débâcle* sums up all the dread symbolism of the French surrender at Sedan at the beginning of September 1870, after which the Prussians marched triumphantly on Paris. But calling Sedan a 'death door' is misleading, suggesting a frontier gateway through which the enemy came storming at the outset of the campaign. Chesterton would have done better to call Sedan a 'death trap', which closed on the last French army that could have kept the Prussians out of Paris.

For the French, the results of the Franco-Prussian War of 1870 were hardly less shameful than the way in which the war had broken out. French national arrogance and contempt for their opponent brought the war into being; it was deliberately engineered to cement Napoleon III's shaky, corrupt and justifiably unpopular regime with a helping of cheap and easy military victory. When the Spanish throne became vacant, the Hohenzollern ruling family of Prussia had put forward a candidate. France protested vehemently about naked ambition and blatant encirclement, and the Hohenzollern candidate was withdrawn. This should have been the end of the crisis but for France's malignant demands that Prussia should grovel and publish apologies to the world. When Prussia declined to oblige with such apologies, France declared war on 5 July 1870.

If, as a state with pretensions to military efficiency, you go starting wars with the neighbours, you should first make sure that your army is ready and that you know precisely what you want it to do. In 1870 the French were sure of neither. Mobilization hit the army like a scourge of God and the results were chaotic. Units in the south had to go north to mobilize, then deploy in the centre. Generals arrived at their new headquarters and had to start by searching frantically for their troops. In the key arsenals and depots, ammunition and stores were low and frequently non-existent. Nor was there any cohesive strategy behind the great crusade against the Prussians. '*A Berlin!*' was a popular but meaningless chant; there was no other concrete objective.

With frantic grindings of rusty gears and rampant confusion all round, two French armies took shape in Alsace-Lorraine, vaguely intended for a northerly drive, east of the Belgian frontier, to throw the Prussians off the west bank of the Rhine: Marshal MacMahon's at Strasbourg and Marshal Bazaine's at Metz. Their mobilization was still far from complete when Napoleon III assumed personal command

Left : The dour, spare figure of Moltke reports another Prussian victory to his king at Rezonville on 18 August 1870

of the 'Army of the Rhine' at Metz in France on 28 July. By this time the Prussian Field Marshal von Moltke already had 400,000 men, grouped in three armies, fully concentrated across the Franco-German frontier. Railways were the secret of this deployment: Prussia and her allied German states alone had a railway network designed specifically for the rapid movement of troops to strategic points on the frontiers of Germany. The Prussian Army was in magnificent trim, particularly with regard to its artillery, the arm in which the French had once led the field. Now the Prussians had breech-loading steel Krupp cannon against France's antique bronze muzzle-loaders.

They also had a thoroughly workmanlike plan of campaign. Once the gaseous French armies had solidified at Metz and Strasbourg, Moltke's first worry had been dispelled. He would not have to try to split up the French Army: the French had done if for him. The left-flank Prussian army on the upper Rhine would therefore contain MacMahon while the other two came driving in, fast and hard, between Bazaine and MacMahon. This would immediately wreck the vague French plans of campaign in Germany and seize any initiative from them. Once held, the Prussian initiative would be retained by constantly hustling the French off-balance.

Retreat from Alsace-Lorraine

On 2 August Napoleon led the 'Army of the Rhine' out of Metz to its only success in the war of 1870: the capture of Saarbrücken against lightweight Prussian resistance. While France celebrated a premature victory, the Prussians began to move; and on 4 August they hit the inner fringe of MacMahon's 'Army of the Vosges' at Wissembourg. On the sixth, then both MacMahon and Napoleon were shaken by Prussian attacks, at Woerth and Spicheren respectively. These were minor actions in which the French troops did not perform too badly, and certainly gave as good as they got as far as casualties were concerned; but, by proving to the French that they had already lost the initiative, the course of the campaign was affected almost from the outset. Certainly the heart was knocked out of Napoleon III, a tired and sick man in constant agony from a giant bladder stone. On 12 August Napoleon turned the 'Army of the Rhine' over to Marshal Bazaine, who promptly decided to retire to Metz.

Over half a century before, the Duke of Wellington had put his finger on the biggest flaw in the French manner of waging war.

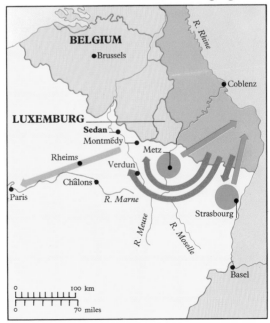

Left : The one-sided course of the 1870 Sedan campaign. Rarely if ever has a nation with pretensions to military efficiency provoked a war with its armed forces so unprepared for combat, and with such vague plans for the prosecution of the conflict. The French armies (*blue*) took shape with little more than the vague intention of crossing the Rhine and somehow repeating the fleeting triumphs of Napoleon I, and were thrown onto a paralysed – and permanent – defensive by the first aggressive Prussian attacks (*red*)

French generals, he said, planned their campaigns like a splendid set of harness, which worked all right until a single strap broke; after that the whole strategy was useless. 'I made my campaigns of rope. If something broke, I tied a knot and went on.' Nothing had changed by 1870. A resilient commander-in-chief would immediately have dropped his own offensive plans and ordered Bazaine and MacMahon to attack flat-out towards each other, forcing the Prussians onto the defensive to save themselves from being bitten in half. But on the French side, no such co-ordinating control existed. The two wings of the French Army, drifting into an utterly demoralizing retreat, fell back to the west, forced to endure the contempt and fury of their countrymen at every step of the way.

MacMahon and Bazaine

MacMahon's initial problem was where he should retreat to. The Prussians lay between him and Bazaine in Metz. Neither on the upper Moselle, upstream from Metz, nor on the upper Meuse, further west, could he see any obvious spot to halt and rally. In the end he retreated to Châlons-sur-Marne, stretching the gap between him and Bazaine hopelessly wide.

Through that gap came the Prussian First and Second Armies, sweeping south and west around Bazaine in Metz. Bazaine was completely out of his depth. He had never commanded more than 25,000 men in his life and was now responsible for nearly 200,000. Not once did he even try an aggressive push south to chop at the Prussian tentacles curling round his back. Instead he ordered another retreat, this time west to Verdun – precisely the worst thing he could have done, because instead of the Prussians exposing their flank to him, as they did in their sweep round Metz, a retreat to Verdun would expose *his* flank to the Prussians.

Thus offered tactical gifts on a plate, the Prussians did not miss their chance. They swung north and prepared to hack into Bazaine's vanguard. On 16 August came the first collision, an accidental clash of outposts, rapidly escalating, just like the first day at Gettysburg, and ending the same way in a stalemate. It was enough, however, to persuade Bazaine to head back to Metz, fighting a rearguard action against the Prussians as he went.

Moltke, with the First and Second Armies concentrated to hand, had as his

Below : Crown Prince Albert of Saxony watches his gunners pound the French line at St Privat. His opponent, Marshal Bazaine, had already made one bad mistake by allowing the Prussians to bypass Metz to the south without counter-attacking them. By attempting to retreat westward to Verdun, Bazaine merely exposed his own army to another vicious hammering on 18 August. He turned back to Metz, impudently claiming that all the enemy had done was to speed up the move

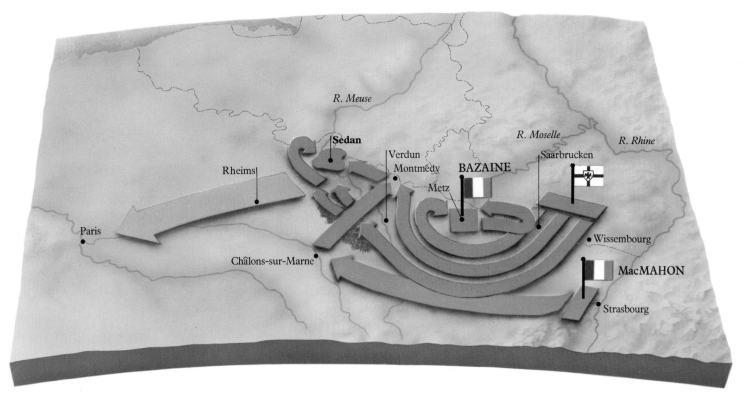

Rheims

Paris

Châlons-sur-Marne

R. Meuse

Sedan

Verdun
Montmédy

Metz

BAZAINE

R. Moselle

Saarbrucken

R. Rhine

Wissembourg

MacMAHON

Strasbourg

main objective the prevention of Bazaine from retreating any further west. By 17 August Moltke had about 188,000 men ready to attack Bazaine's 140,000 and push them back into Metz. The result, on the following day, was the double battle of Gravelotte-St Privat, the biggest field action of the entire war. Largely as a result of the slapdash handling of the First Army by General von Steinmetz at St Privat, it was a punishing day for the Prussians. They lost 20,000 men, the French only 13,000. By any standards it was an heroic day for the French, outnumbered as they were and with only 520 guns against 732. The French centre and left, anchored on the Moselle behind Gravelotte, stood up well, but by nightfall the French right at St Privat had been driven back. Unhesitatingly Bazaine ordered the continuation of the retreat to Metz; with a touch of 'whistling in the dark', he commented that all the Prussians had done was speed up the move.

French strategy: a masterpiece of errors

When Bazaine pulled back into Metz this left only MacMahon's army at Châlons in position to impede a Prussian move on Paris. It should have been obvious that MacMahon's first priority was to keep the route blocked, and preferably while

co-operating with Bazaine to throw the Prussian advance out of gear. Instead, political requirements intruded disastrously on any attempts of the generals to put matters to rights. Urged that the whole regime would totter and fall if he merely stood on the defensive before Paris, Napoleon listlessly agreed to a flashy piece of flank-marching by MacMahon's army, which looked masterly when drawn on a map with no regard to what the Prussians were doing. MacMahon was now to head north-west for the Belgian frontier at Montmédy, whence a junction with Bazaine could be made by the back door and the combined French armies could fall like a thunderbolt on the rear of the Prussians. It was a piece of pure showmanship, treating the French people like a magician's audience. Stunned by such sleight-of-hand at the eleventh hour, they would wildly applaud the Emperor and his Marshals as in older and happier days – assuming that the earlier disasters of the campaign could be forgotten. Worst of all, however, it assumed that the Prussians would be stupid enough to fall for it.

The march to the Meuse

By 20 August MacMahon's army was on its way through the Argonne, temporarily vanishing from view and leaving Moltke to wonder where on earth he could be going. Moltke had been expecting a decisive fight

After Bazaine had been locked up in Metz, MacMahon's army (*blue*) was the sole obstacle on the road to Paris. But MacMahon's advance through the Argonne to the Belgian frontier enabled the Prussians (*red*) to block him out of play with little trouble

with MacMahon on the direct route to Paris, and he could not believe that MacMahon was really marching out of the way, courting disaster from the superior Prussian forces now on his flank. But by 25 August there could be no further doubt. MacMahon was still heading for the Belgian frontier. If he could be contained and beaten there, Paris would drop like a ripe apple and the war would be won.

The last act

Moltke's reaction to MacMahon's flank march was to swing the Prussian Third Army north through ninety degrees and reach the Meuse between MacMahon and Bazaine in Metz. On 30 August contact was made at Beaumont-sur-Meuse, fifteen miles south-east of the frontier city of Sedan and sixty miles from Metz. Confounded by the speed of the Prussian reaction, MacMahon – accompanied on this march by the wretched Napoleon, like a skeleton at the feast – could think of nothing better to do than withdraw into Sedan. The great flank march was over. So far from magically producing victory like a rabbit out of a hat, it had left the last unfettered army of the Second Empire jammed up against the Belgian frontier, hopelessly blocked out of play, with two buoyant Prussian armies closing in for the kill. General Ducrot, one of MacMahon's most energetic corps commanders, summed up their position crudely but succinctly, '*Nous sommes dans un pot de chambre,*' he said, '*et nous y serons emmerdés!*'

True to form, the French gleaned a few tattered shreds of utterly useless glory on 1 September in the form of repeated cavalry charges out of Sedan, led by the dashing General de Gallifet (famed for his formidable moustache). Invariably broken up by the Prussian guns, these charges won nothing but a generous compliment of 'Ah! The brave fellows!' from the King of Prussia, who was watching the battle with Bismarck, the Prussian War Minister Roon, Moltke, and the American Civil War general Philip Sheridan. Shortly after first light on the first, MacMahon was wounded on the outskirts of Sedan and was replaced by General de Wimpffen, who presided over the last hours of the dying army.

With every break-out attempt shattered and beaten back the French were hopelessly penned inside Sedan; their transport, cannon and the emperor's baggage lay chaotically jammed together, wheel to wheel, under murderous shellfire from 400 Prussian guns. For the first time in modern warfare, a civilian population was deliberately made part of the battle zone to add to a defending army's problems. Sedan was, in fact, a watershed in military history – one of the last battles in which generals could stand on a hill and watch the action unroll before them, and one of the first in which terror tactics were used against civilians. All that was missing at Sedan in 1870 were the howling Stukas of the *Luftwaffe*, and they were only seventy years away.

It is at least to the credit of Napoleon III that he refused to prolong the agony into a total massacre. Pitiful figure though he cut at Sedan, his face plastered with rouge to conceal his pallor, he insisted on capitulation and at 6.30 p.m. he sent out a general under a flag of truce, with a personal note to the King of Prussia:

As I have not been able to die in the midst of my troops, it only remains for me to put my sword in Your Majesty's hands. I am Your Majesty's good brother.

The surrender was concluded on 2 September at Donchéry, five miles outside Sedan. Napoleon surrendered not only his own person but 104,000 French troops – not to his 'good brother' the Prussian king, but to the towering and contemptuous figure of Otto von Bismarck – and headed for captivity in Germany.

Aftermath and losses

The capitulation of Sedan not only removed the last field army which could have saved Paris: it brought down the Second Empire like a house of cards. As in France's first revolution, Paris now took the lead, proclaiming a republic, heroically fighting off the besieging Prussians from 20 September 1870 to 24 January 1871 – a resistance of over four months, when the opening campaign had been wrapped up at Sedan in six weeks.

Sedan is therefore one of the most *moral* campaign-battles in military history: the classic example of rough justice, of the inevitable punishing of hubris by nemesis. Napoleon and his regime set out to humiliate Prussia: instead Prussia not only humiliated them but swept them away. Apart from its most immediate after-effects – the siege and fall of Paris, followed by civil war and a second siege – Sedan is also a grim warning of what can happen when one state inflicts too much humiliation on a beaten enemy. For the French never forgot the shame of Sedan, while they remembered the siege of Paris with pride. A growing lust to wipe the slate clean on the battlefield was to bear terrible fruit in 1914.

When Bazaine surrendered in Metz with 179,000 officers and men on 29 October 1870 the grand total of *capitulards* rose to 281,000 men. In the war about 150,000 French were killed or died of wounds, and roughly the same number were wounded. Another 4,000 were killed and 24,450 wounded during the siege of Paris, in which civilian deaths from all causes came to 6,250. Prussian and allied German losses came to 28,208 killed and 88,488 wounded. If the war of Sedan and its aftermath is accounted the first of Europe's 'total' wars – in which civilian populations were deliberately rather than accidentally involved – then the French got off comparatively lightly. By comparison, during the terrible winter of 1941–2 over a million Leningraders – one-third of the city's entire population – were to freeze and starve to death.

Below : The last humiliation. The German host tramps through surrendered Paris after the four-month siege, a gallant but futile resistance after the conclusion of the six-week campaign at Sedan

CHAPTER TWELVE
FIRST MARNE
5th–8th SEPTEMBER 1914

Previous pages : British cavalry during the long retreat back to the Marne in August 1914. Amid the total collapse of the Allied strategy in the West, the British had scored the only clear-cut victory, savaging the clumsy attacks of Kluck's 1st Army at Mons on the twenty-fourth. But when their flanking partner, Lanrezac's French 5th Army, began to retreat, there was nothing for it but retreat for the British as well

Below : Joffre, Allied C.-in-C. during the crisis of the Marne. By no stretch of the imagination a dynamic leader of men, Joffre drew his strength from his sleepy refusal to panic – which is more than can be said for his opposite number, the younger Moltke

A somewhat dubious miracle: the chapter of accidents that ruined Germany's master-plan to knock out France in 1914

Background

THE defeat of France in 1871 was so complete and so humiliating that it could never be the basis of a lasting peace; the best modern parallel is the Israeli victory over the Arabs in 1967. France would never rest until she had got Alsace and Lorraine back *and* laid the outraged ghost of the great Napoleon by fighting a glorious offensive war. As for the Germans, the great Moltke had shown how instant, knockout wars could be conceived in detail, fought and won. However, as France became patched into a web of alliances hostile to Germany, German strategists had to face up to the likelihood of having to fight a war on two fronts. The results were the opposing master plans of 1914: France's 'Plan 17' and Germany's 'Schlieffen Plan'.

After the humiliations of 1870-1 the French looked forward greedily to *La Revanche* – The Revenge. To banish the awful memories of the inertia and sheeplike surrenders of 1870, Colonel de Grandmaison, Chief of the French General Staff's Operations Bureau, came up with a suicidal 'theory of attack' that a professional soldier should never have entertained. De Grandmaison preached that modern weapons and military technology were worthless: assault with the bayonet was all that mattered. The enemy's intentions were also irrelevant: all that was needed was to attack him. Giving ground under overwhelming pressure was out of the question: every inch of ground inadvertently yielded must be won back at once, no matter what the cost. Aircraft, heavy artillery, barbed-wire, machineguns – none of them had any significance compared to the all-out bayonet charge. Alas for France, de Grandmaison's ravings were just what the army wanted to hear. As for the plan for *La Revanche*, eventually drawn up as 'Plan 17', nothing could be simpler: four out of France's five armies would sweep forward *à la Grandmaison*, throw the Germans clean out of Alsace and Lorraine and drown the survivors in the Rhine. For after all, what the Germans intended to do did not matter.

The German planners, forced to worry about Russia in the East as well as France in the West, had a far more complex task. The solution of Graf von Schlieffen, Chief of General Staff until 1905, offered all the brutal effectiveness of a self-defence expert attacked by a couple of thugs: take one, flatten him quickly and make sure he won't get up, then concentrate on the other. Railways would mobilize the bulk of the German army for a huge wheeling march through neutral Belgium into France, smashing everything in its path, sweeping westward round Paris then east to catch the main French armies in the rear and annihilate them. This done, railways would whisk the victorious armies East to settle accounts with the Russians.

Schlieffen was happy to let the French advance into Alsace and Lorraine while the great flank march was under way; it would only make the encirclement of the French more certain. But Moltke, his successor, was frightened at the prospect of the French pushing too hard, and took eight divisions away from the wheeling right wing to strengthen the left. In the East he went to the other extreme and left too little to hold the Russians, which meant that when the crisis approached on the Marne two whole army corps were snatched away to be rushed to the Eastern Front just when they were most needed in the West.

Schlieffen's successor was the nephew of the great Moltke, and, the Kaiser hoped, a reincarnation as well as a namesake. But the two Moltkes could hardly have been less alike. In appearance they were quite different: Moltke the elder, hatchet-faced, the fierce hawk; Moltke the younger, the soft pouter pigeon, with his double chin and uncertain eyes. Moltke the younger turned out to be a panicker, a changer of plans, a vacillator. His opponent was Marshal Joffre, stolid and unflappable, lacking in imagination, let alone last-minute doubts about the wisdom of the last order.

The Archduke Francis Ferdinand, heir apparent to the Austro-Hungarian Empire, was shot in Sarajevo on 28 June 1914; ultimatums, vows of support, orders to mobilize and declarations of war flew about Europe all through July; and the war in the West got under way in the first week of August 1914.

The march through Belgium

The trouble with the Schlieffen Plan was that once the armies had been unleashed at maximum speed (thanks to the railways) they depended on marching feet to keep up the tempo. The right-wing armies had to get as far west as quickly as possible, which meant violating Belgian *and* Dutch territory. Moltke, however, shrank from alienating the Dutch: he wanted a neutral safety-valve preserved on Germany's western frontier in case things went badly wrong. This meant that the extreme right-wing army, instead of heading straight for Antwerp before wheeling south-west to Ghent, must struggle round the dangling bladder of Dutch territory enclosing Maastricht and Heerlen, then squeeze through a fifteen-mile bottleneck before breaking out to the west.

Another assumption of the Schlieffen scenario was that the Belgians would see sense and let the German armies through their country. Instead they decided to fight. King Albert's threadbare army never stood a chance of holding up two German armies, and German heavy howitzers smashed the Belgian forts at Liège to bits; but the British Expeditionary Force and the French 5th Army pushed into southern Belgium to help and pulled the two German right-wing armies, Kluck's 1st and Bülow's 2nd, south like magnets. Already forty-eight hours behind schedule, Kluck's 1st Army was held up for another day by furious British resistance at Mons on the twenty-fourth. But Bülow pushed back Lanrezac's 5th Army and there was nothing for it but retreat for the British, keeping pace with the 5th Army – a retreat that took them all the way to the Marne and beyond.

German forces were already deep into Belgium when Joffre's generals moved forward to execute 'Plan 17' in Alsace and Lorraine. As soon as they did so the folly of the Grandmaison strategy was replaced by reality: the terrain simply did not allow armies to sweep into the attack. Plain carelessness rather than battle frenzy brought disaster to the French 1st and 2nd Armies at Sarrebourg and Morhange (20–22 August). Over the next forty-eight hours, on the Ardennes sector, the French 3rd and 4th Armies were thrown back towards the Meuse. From 20 to 24 August the French lost an unbelievable total of 140,000 men, most of them to German artillery and machine-gun fire. 'Plan 17' was in ruins. But its collapse helped ruin Schlieffen's strategy as well.

The Germans swing east

The delays in penetrating Belgium limited the German westward sweep; the advance of the BEF and French 5th Army pulled the 1st and 2nd German Armies sharply southward. When the British and French fell back the German right-wing armies followed instead of edging westward again. This kept them out of the Somme valley long enough for Joffre to cobble together a new left-flank army, Maunoury's 6th, which began to form near Amiens from 25 August. If Kluck had detected this, left the British to retreat and smashed Maunoury's new army at birth, he would still have been able to encircle Paris from the west. But on the twenty-ninth Lanrezac attacked Bülow at Guise, Bülow called on Kluck for aid, Kluck swung the German 1st Army *east* – towards Lanrezac and away from Maunoury – and the pursuing German right-flank armies, now chasing the Allies on a line that would take them east of Paris, presented Moltke with an entirely new problem.

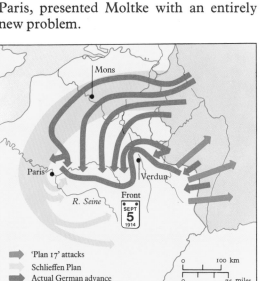

Above : Not a German secret weapon, but a bridging-train complete with pontoons and spans, briefly halted during the march into France. But there were few such respites for the German infantry in the forefront of the advance

Left : The original Schlieffen Plan for the defeat of France, and the actual course of the armies in August 1914. The southward swing of the German armies, instead of continuing their wide-reaching wheel to the west of Paris, was the result of the attempt by the British and French to come to the help of the Belgians. Long before the retreat to the Marne was fairly under way, the grandiose French offensives of Joffre's 'Plan 17', in Alsace and Lorraine, had already collapsed in utter ruin

Moltke plays for caution

By 30 August – the day Joffre ordered Maunoury's army south to cover the approaches to Paris – it seemed to the German headquarters far away in Coblenz that a total Allied collapse could only be a matter of days. The field armies were clearly winning a runaway victory, though not on the lines Schlieffen had envisaged. As the Allies continued to retreat their front was now sagging like an over-burdened tarpaulin in a cloudburst, between Paris and Verdun. Moltke seized on this: it offered the chance of a 'small solution' in which there would be no danger of the German armies attempting the impossible by swinging west of Paris. All Kluck and Bülow would have to do was to drive on to the south-east, slice in behind the French 5th and 4th Armies, and the whole Allied front could then be rolled up.

Galliéni sees his chance

According to the legend of the 'Miracle of the Marne', Kluck's bypassing of Paris prompted Joffre to order a general turn-about; to order Galliéni, the military governor of Paris, to fall upon Kluck's exposed right flank with the Paris garrison, rushed out of the capital in a fleet of taxi-cabs; to order the British Expeditionary Force and the French 5th Army to drive forward, splitting Kluck and Bülow apart, so throwing the Germans back in retreat. Certainly Joffre himself never went out of his way to correct this interpretation in later years. For Joffre was not the man who spotted the unique opportunity offered by Kluck's turning away from Paris; it was Galliéni, who cried exultantly: '*Ils nous offrent leur flanc!*' – 'They are presenting their flank to us!' And Galliéni practically had to blackmail Joffre into agreeing to attack. A captured German map was actually in Joffre's hands, showing Kluck's planned lines of advance – but Joffre had decided that the Allied armies were too jaded for a counter-attack at short notice, and had ordered a continued retreat to the Seine.

On 4 September, after further air and cavalry reconnaissance had confirmed that Kluck had not changed direction, Galliéni ordered Maunoury to prepare the 6th Army for an attack on Kluck's right flank and rear. And that evening, in one of the great unrecorded but clearly inspired telephone conversations of history, Galliéni persuaded Joffre to order a general counter-attack.

Joffre's contribution

When Joffre's orders for the attack went out on 5 September his greatest contribution had already been made. Despite the utter wreck of 'Plan 17', Joffre had kept his head. Amid the depression of retreat he sacked unduly pessimistic or obstructive generals – Lanrezac of the 5th Army, Ruffey of the 3rd Army – and replaced them with Franchet d'Espérey and Sarrail, men whose hearts were still in the fight. Above all Joffre managed to conjure up two new armies from the wreckage of 'Plan 17': Maunoury's 6th, which now spearheaded the Allied counter-blow, and Foch's 9th, which entered the line between the 4th and 5th Armies on 4 September.

Opposite : Not Joffre, but Galliéni from his unique vantage-point in Paris first spotted the exceptional opportunity offered by the German swing to bypass Paris from the east. The great turn-around of the retreating Allied armies took three days to set in motion; and when it got under way the crucial gap opened between the German 1st and 2nd Armies was penetrated not by design but by accident

Below :
'Very like a series of grouse-butts!' chortles the caption of this British drawing showing German troops making a stand during the retreat from the Marne. The attitude that scraping trenches was faintly comic and unsporting did not last long when the period of open manoeuvre ended and trench warfare began in earnest

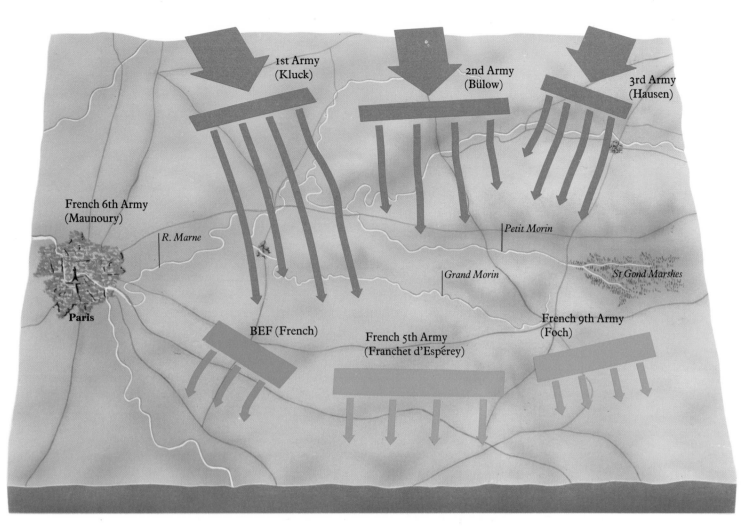

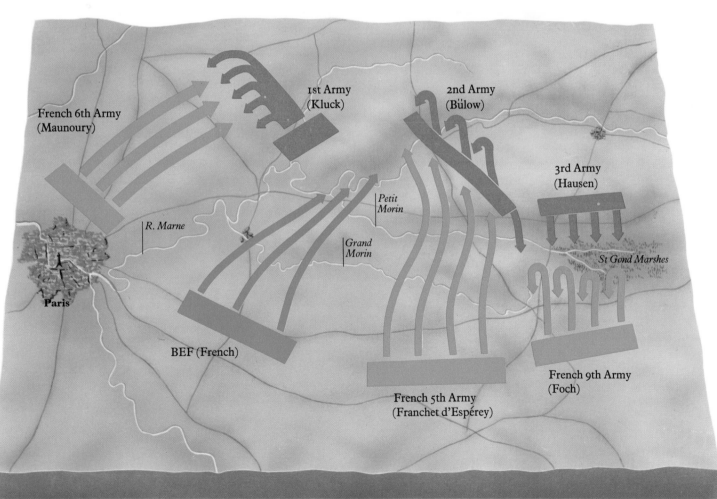

Above: A sight to gladden the heart of any German machine-gunner: massed French infantry, bayonets at the ready, doubling forward to the attack. Charges like this were bloodily repulsed during the initial 'Battle of the Frontiers', but – though remaining the ideal of French tacticians for many months – featured little in the cautious Allied advance back across the Marne. As the Allies probed the gap between the German 1st and 2nd Armies, there was general bewilderment over the apparent absence of Germans

Below : In the French sector. The shock and bewilderment on the *curé*'s face says it all. What had become of all the boasting of *La Revanche*?

Thus even if Joffre had followed his first instinct and ordered the retreat to continue, he would already have laid the building-blocks of victory – and in any case Kluck's men had very little fight left in them. The outermost flankers of the great German wheel, they had marched flat out from Germany to the outskirts of Paris at an average pace of twenty-four miles a day. By 2 September they were nearing the end of their tether, staggering along with eyes closed, singing in chorus to keep awake, getting increasingly drunk (with the connivance of their officers) to glean enough artificial energy to keep going – and all this amid the choking dust and baking heat of a torrid summer. Bülow's men, further east, had had less distance to cover; they were a little better off, but not much.

'Withdrawal is becoming inevitable'

On 5 September, the day his rear flank units first made contact with Maunoury's advancing 6th Army, Kluck received some deeply ominous news. Colonel Hentsch arrived from German headquarters with 'reports' that the British were landing troops 'continuously' on the Belgian coast; there was word of a Russian expeditionary force in the same area. It seemed that the Allies were preparing a decisive strike at the long German lines of comunication; in view of this, Hentsch concluded, 'withdrawal is becoming inevitable'.

In fact, British First Lord of the Admiralty Winston Churchill, ignoring the opposition and ridicule of his Cabinet colleagues, had landed a force of 3,000 Royal Marines at Ostend on 27 August, only to pull them out again on the thirty-first. Wild rumour in Moltke's headquarters inflated this abortive move into a full-blooded invasion by 40,000 British, while the Russian force never existed at all. But it was all real enough to Moltke, always ready to dread the unseen threat; and it meant that Kluck and Bülow faced the Allied counter-offensive of 5–8 September half-prepared in advance to order a retreat, on totally spurious grounds.

Faltering steps to victory

It took the Allies three days of faltering, unco-ordinated moves, gradually gaining confidence, to nudge the Germans into making the decision to retreat.

On the 6th, Kluck faced about to cope with the increasing menace from Maunoury and held the French 6th Army's advance with little trouble. But Kluck's about-face opened a gap of about thirty miles between Kluck and Bülow, and into this gap the BEF and the 5th Army – halted at last the day before – prepared unknowingly to advance.

The night of the 7 September saw the exploit with the Paris taxi-cabs, commandeered by Galliéni, rushing forward every reserve soldier that could be found, 6,000 in all (five to a cab), to reinforce Maunoury. Meanwhile, Franchet d'Espérey's advance against Bülow had been distracted by a needless and unauthorized attack by Foch's 9th Army. Foch was supposed to be masking the right flank of the 5th Army during its advance against Bülow, but – a fanatical 'Grandmaisonite' – he indulged in repeated attacks across the St Gond marshes, all of them repelled. On 8 September – a supreme irony – Bülow's men counter-attacked Foch with a bayonet charge, driving him back until Franchet d'Espérey sent a corps to the 9th Army's aid.

Foch's stupidity took the pressure off Bülow on the eighth, and Kluck continued to hold off Maunoury, but nothing could be done to plug the gap between the German 1st and 2nd Armies. This was skinned over by nothing more than a cavalry screen – and advancing straight into the gap were the five columns of the BEF. On 8 September, virtually unopposed, the leading British units became the first Allied forces to recross the Marne. When confirmation reached German headquaters, Colonel Bauer, one of the Staff officers, recalled that 'Moltke completely collapsed. He sat with a pallid face gazing at the map, dead to all feeling, a broken man.' Hentsch was sent back to the front with full powers to co-ordinate the retreat, if it had begun. He got there just before Kluck and Bülow ordered a withdrawal north to the Aisne.

Aftermath and losses

The four days of First Marne were only the climax of an extraordinary campaign, the like of which had never been seen before and would never be seen again. The next time such an ambitious offensive was attempted, mechanized transport and swarming air cover would take the load off the infantry. But at First Marne everything was being tried for the first time. Generals were learning to command armies by telephone and wireless (the Eiffel Tower caused terrible interference) instead of by telescope and note-pad; airborne observers were learning how to distinguish enemy forces on the ground; cavalry commanders were learning that their troops and squadrons had a very short life expectancy indeed in the age of the machine-gun.

When the Germans fell back from the Marne the Allies followed shakily and managed to prevent the formation of a German front along the Aisne. Both sides edged off to the north and west, each trying to find a way round the other's flank, ending up on the Channel coast in the third week of October. This marked the end of a war of movement in open country, and the start of four years of carnage in the trenches.

The most horrific losses, thanks largely to de Grandmaison and his doctrine, were suffered by the French, who announced killed, missing, captured and died of wounds as 329,000 for the period 6 August-13 September. German *Reichsarchiv* figures for this period never attempted more than general estimates – 224,390 killed, missing and captured between August and November, plus 453,050 wounded (these figures combine the losses of the Marne campaign, the Aisne, and the first battle of Ypres in October-November). The diminutive BEF recorded losses in killed, wounded and missing of 15,000 up to 5 September. And it was with regard to casualties that the First Marne campaign had its grimmest significance: soldier's lives were already regarded as mere corpuscles in the huge body of the war.

Below : The only losers – a huddle of German dead in a French field, overtaken by the recoil of their armies from the Marne

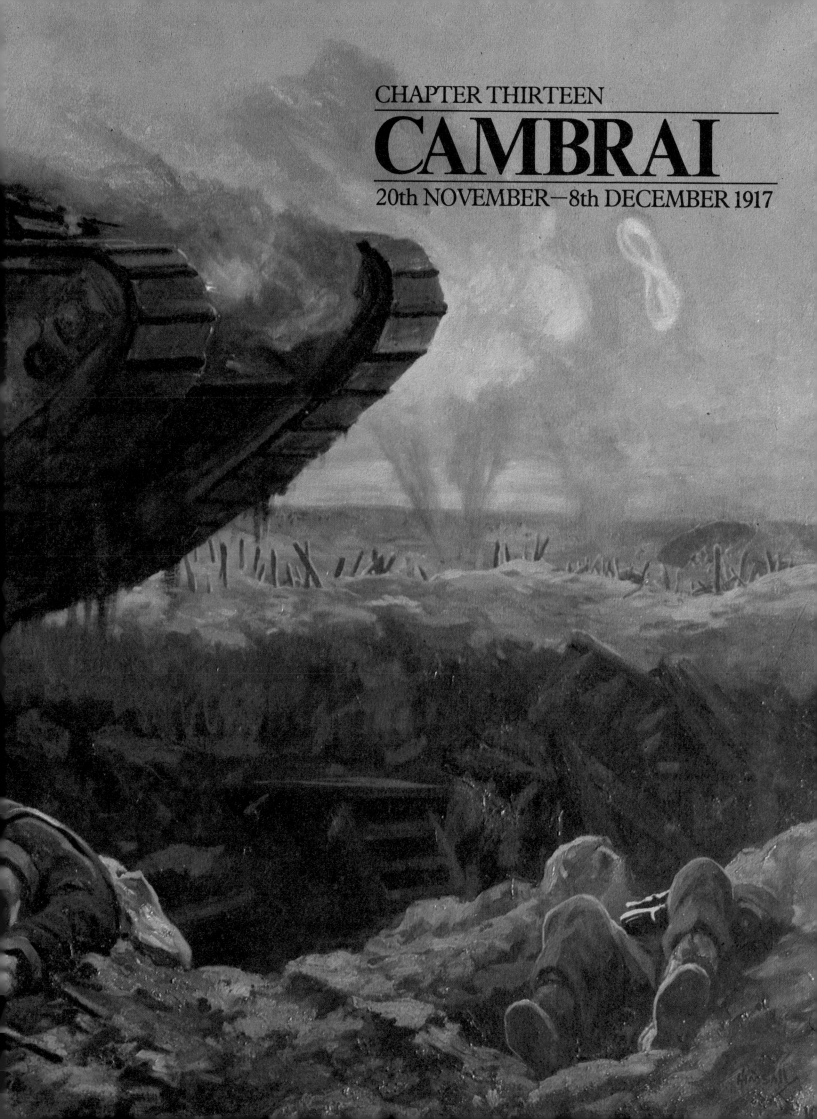

CHAPTER THIRTEEN
CAMBRAI
20th NOVEMBER—8th DECEMBER 1917

After the slaughter of the Somme and Passchendale, the first demonstration of what massed tanks can do

Above:
'We are the guns!
Saw you our work by the road?'
Until the coming of the tank, Allied commanders had tried to win victories by pitting flesh and blood against barbed-wire and fire-power. Heretical though it seemed, tanks were to prove the only way of giving flesh and blood a chance

Previous pages: The shape of things to come – lunging for the far bank of a German trench, a British tank demonstrates the ultimate reply to three years of murderous deadlock on the Western Front

The Western Front

THE fighting on the Western Front in 1914 petered out in mutual exhaustion with both sides accepting that, for the moment, it was stalemate; neither was going to break through the other's trench lines and start a war of movement again without a good deal of reinforcement and preparation. Germany had no choice but to yield the initiative to the Allies because of her war with Russia: she simply lacked the resources to fight offensive campaigns in the West and the East simultaneously. That was the conundrum the Schlieffen Plan had hoped to solve.

The German armies in the West dug themselves into their trenches to hold the considerable gains made in August and September 1914: practically the whole of Belgium and the industrial regions of north-eastern France. To win these back, the Allies would have to break through the German trench lines. They spent the next three years trying to do this while the German armies in the East strove to knock out Russia so that a full effort could be made in the West.

In theory the problem was simple. Any general accepted that troops on a good defensive position, given adequate fire-power, could murder any attacks sent at them across open terrain, especially if the attackers had to struggle through barbed-wire defences on the way. The correct answer seemed to lie in massive artillery bombardments which would cut the wire to shreds, kill large numbers of Germans in their forward trenches, and stop them moving reinforcements up to their front line. There was little or no chance of mounting a surprise assault, because the Germans would see the large numbers of troops being crammed into the Allied forward trenches before the attack. The guns, then, must bulldoze the way to victory for the attacking infantry, while cavalry

waited in the rear to sweep through the breach and develop the pursuit – their traditional role. But this never seemed to happen. Bombardments that often removed whole villages from the map did not eliminate belts of barbed wire; instead, by churning up the ground, they only made the tangle more effective. Nor did bombardments kill all the Germans in their trenches; the German infantry either hid in deep dug-outs or pulled clean out of the forward trenches until the bombardment lifted for the attack, rushing back to their original positions and opening fire on men who had been told that they would encounter only dazed survivors.

Ninety per cent of the efforts of the Allied troops normally went into reaching the German first-line trench, only to find that the defenders had pulled back to the zigzag of further trenches leading into the German rear areas. For the handful of attackers who actually got into the first-line trench there was, inevitably, an instant German counter-attack, sealing off the breach as soon as it was made and bundling the survivors back across no-man's-land into the Allied trenches. Yet the agonizing experiments went on. British monthly casualties on the Western Front in 1915 averaged about 25,000, in no single month going below 9,000 and peaking horrifically with each new 'push': 65,730 in May, the month of Festubert and Aubers Ridge; and 59,615 for September, the month of Loos – an offensive which began on the twenty-fifth of that month.

The French did even worse. During their offensives in Artois and Champagne they lost 55,000 in February and March; 121,000 from April to June; and 115,000 from September to November – and those figures do not include the total of men who died of their wound in the three offensives, 55,000 in all. Like the statistics for the extermination of the Jews by the Third Reich, Western Front casualty figures, studied for long enough, become so appalling that they are difficult to grasp. The worst thing about the troop losses is that nothing like them had ever been envisaged before August 1914 – yet, within months, they were accepted as a fact of life by the generals and their planning staffs.

By the summer of 1915 a small group of enthusiasts in Britain – officers and civilians, all far removed from the inner circle of the General Staff – thought otherwise. They believed in the concept of an armoured fighting vehicle, able to cross the churned-up soil of no-man's-land, getting right up to the German trenches, wiping out the defenders, and pushing on into the German rear areas, with their crews fighting all the while from behind armour. The official attitude of both the British and French High commands was that this was pure science fiction. (H.G. Wells had, in fact, written a short story envisaging armoured fighting vehicles, *The Land Ironclads*, as early as 1903.) They would believe it when they saw it, and in the meantime would try to win the war as best they knew.

It is grossly unfair to blame the generals for blinkered stupidity in refusing to adopt new ideas. The technological breakthrough of the early twentieth century was only just getting under way in 1915 and nobody could imagine how fast it would move. Efficient motor cars were barely ten years old, and the best of them could operate only on firm ground; it was only six years since the first aeroplane had staggered across the Channel, after repeated failures, to crash-land at Dover. Even those with the greatest enthusiasm for the wonders of science and technology had to admit that for every idea that had proved workable some other crackpot scheme had been put forward by yet another wild-eyed inventor; and it was with thoroughly justified scepticism that Lord Kitchener, Britain's Secretary of State for War, went out to Hatfield Park on 2 January 1916 to see a prototype armoured fighting vehicle go through its paces.

A squat box, parallelogram-shaped, it ran on tracks to spread out its weight and avoid getting bogged down on muddy ground. Two box-like sponsons on the sides carried long six-pounder guns, manned by a gunner and loader apiece. The other four members of the crew of eight were all needed to drive the thing, braking the tracks to change direction, engaging

Above: In training for the Cambrai offensive, a Mark IV tank grinds up a slope at the Tank Driving School at Wailly. The object strapped to its back is a ditching-beam; if the tank bogged down, the beam could be hitched to the tracks and dragged forward and under the machine, providing a firm foothold over which – it was hoped – the tank could struggle clear

Above : At dawn on 20 November, without the traditional warning of an advance bombardment, the British guns crashed out on the Cambrai front and the tanks rolled into the attack, closely followed by the infantry

Right : The point of attack. After all the empty promises and agonizing losses of the preceding attacks, all Haig (*red*) looked for at Cambrai was some form of definite success. But though this attack was never intended to be a runaway victory, it was the one which stood the best chance of becoming just that

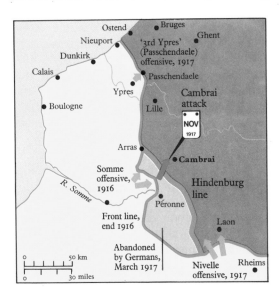

and disengaging the gears. It was the most futuristic, ungainly and thoroughly unlikely-looking object ever built for a battlefield – but it worked. It crawled forward, steered left and right; it crossed a convincing-looking trench prepared by the demonstrators. Kitchener was impressed, and when Kitchener was impressed things happened: within ten days of the Hatfield Park trial 100 were ordered to be built. No better name could be found for the new machine than the one coined for security purposes during development: 'tank'.

Debut of the tank

The premature committal of the tank to action in the Battle of the Somme, revealing the new weapon before the difficulties had been ironed out, has been scathingly criticized, again unfairly. Battle conditions on the Western Front were hideously unique; there was no way of duplicating them for realistic battle trials. Fifty tanks had arrived in France by the end of August 1916, by which time the Somme battle had already cost the British over 260,000 casualties. Ordered into action with the second phase of the offensive of 15 September, thirty-four made it to their starting-lines without breaking down, and fourteen reached the German lines on the Flers-Courcelette sector, operating at most in twos and threes and ripping open a four-mile gap in the German front. As there were no reserves to follow up the success, the Germans sealed the breach with little trouble, but the tank's debut had proved conclusively that here was a weapon with a significant future.

Naturally there were improvements to be made, fresh crews to be trained, proper tactics to be worked out from the lessons gained on the Somme. None of this had had time to bear fruit when in March 1917 the Germans sprang a surprise on the Allies. They evacuated their most forward trenches and pulled back to the massive trench system of the Hindenburg Line, shortening their front by twenty-five miles. The Allies followed up and winced when they saw what was waiting for them. Then, in July, General Nivelle's disastrous offensive on the Chemin des Dames, coming after six

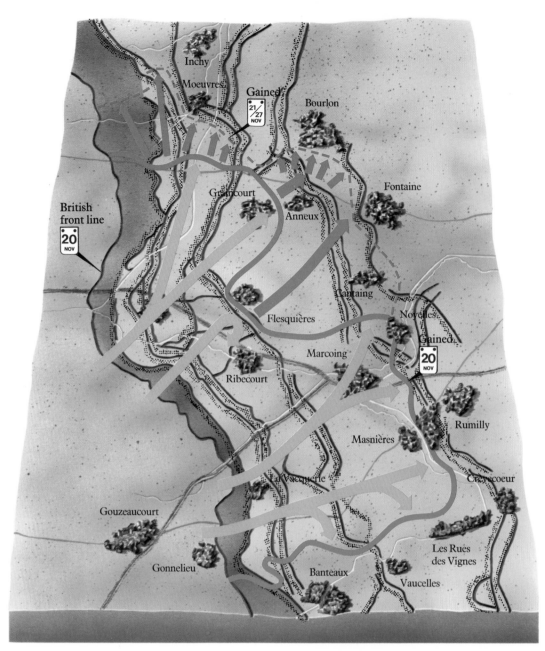

Inchy
Moeuvres
Gained
21/27 NOV
Bourlon
Graincourt
Fontaine
Anneux
British front line
20 NOV
Cantaing
Flesquières
Noyelles
Gained
20 NOV
Marcoing
Ribecourt
Rumilly
Masnières
Crèvecoeur
La Vacquerie
Gouzeaucourt
Les Rues des Vignes
Gonnelieu
Banteaux
Vaucelles

months of butchery at Verdun, all but broke the French Army; the British launched a relief offensive up in the Ypres salient, another fiasco in the liquid mud around Passchendaele village. At last, in November of an utterly disastrous year, desperate for success, the British commander-in-chief General Haig turned to the leaders of the new Tank Corps and gave them their chance to show what they could do.

The Cambrai plan

General Elles of the Tank Corps and his chief-of-staff, Lieutenant-Colonel Fuller, had taken a long hard look at the tank and what they knew it could do. The first essential was firm going, not liquid mud as at Passchendaele; and the plain of Cambrai was chalkland, firm and dry – the same type of ground on which the first tanks in action had done so well back in September 1916. Moreover, Cambrai had not been a heavily-contested sector of the Western Front, which meant that the ground had not been churned to a morass by shells.

Fuller had worked out a promising drill for overcoming the Hindenburg Line defences. Spearhead tanks, trailing grapnels to rip gaps in the outer wire, would swing left and rake the forward German trench with fire. The next tank through the gap would drop a huge brushwood bundle or 'fascine' into the trench, crawl over it and move on to rake the next trench, and so on through the entire system. 'Ditching beams' were carried to help 'ditched' or bogged-down tanks get themselves out.

There was to be no frittering away of tanks in penny-packets of twos and threes:

this was to be a full-blooded attack by 216 tanks, with 96 in close support and 54 in reserve. And – a revolutionary experiment indeed – there would be no drawn-out preliminary bombardment to broadcast the news that an attack was on its way.

The irony was that, for the first time ever, Haig did not want this attack to yield a runaway victory. After all the other disasters of 1917, all he wanted was a clear-cut local success to show for all the wasted efforts on the Western Front. He looked no further than Bourlon Ridge, six miles back from the German front line; if no breakthrough were made in the first forty-eight hours he was prepared to call off the whole attack. There were no reserves for anything more ambitious.

After three years of learning the power of numerically weak defensive forces to hold apparently overwhelming numbers of attackers, Haig was attacking at Cambrai with only five divisions against four – far too little margin to achieve anything worthwhile. And he placed far too much reliance on cavalry – five divisions in all – to follow up any substantial breakthrough made by the tanks. Only infantry can hold ground, and there were no infantry reserves at all.

First day

At 6.20 p.m. on 20 November, General Elles led the Tank Corps against the Hindenburg Line with his flag flying over his own machine, 'Hilda'. The results were spectacular. The squat monsters roaring out of the morning mist terrified the Germans in the forward trenches, which fell all along the six-mile assault sector. Within the first hour the tanks had surged forward to take all their key objectives on schedule. There was one exception: the 51st Highland Division, attacking towards Flesquières, whose commander had scrapped Fuller's tank drill and substituted his own, with the leading tanks pushing on 100 yards ahead of the infantry. As a result the tanks became isolated while the infantry remained uncovered – and Flesquières turned out to be the toughest sector of the entire German front. It held out like a breakwater on the first day of the Cambrai attack, while the British forces on either flank pushed forward an unbelievable four miles into the Hindenburg Line. By the end of the first day the British had taken over 4,200 shaken German prisoners for their own casualty rate of 4,000.

Second day

Once they had recovered from the shock, however, the Germans reacted with all their customary energy. They had an invaluable bonus in the form of the 107th Division, which had arrived at Cambrai from the Eastern Front on the nineteenth and proved a useful 'fire brigade' in plugging the most dangerous points of the breach. But the tank crews were soon suffering from the strain and fatigue caused by the shattering vibration, heat and noise in the confined interiors of those primitive machines. They were flagging severely as Haig's forty-eight hour deadline came and went with Bourlon still in German hands.

High tide

The last successes won by the tanks of Cambrai came on 23 November, by which time the German build-up was mounting rapidly. They already had 200 guns defending Bourlon: three days later they had 500, and their strength on the Cambrai front had risen from four divisions to seven. Haig finally accepted that no more could be done on the twenty-eighth, after a week in which the superb achievements of the first two days had been followed by a reversion to the ineffective bludgeon-work of Loos, the Somme and Passchendaele. Worse was to follow. On the thirtieth the Germans went over to the offensive at Cambrai, pushing the British over half-way back to the starting-line of 20 November before resuming the defensive on 8 December.

Aftermath and losses

The British had deployed a grand total of 476 fighting and supply tanks at Cambrai; 179 of these were lost – 65 from direct hits, 71 from mechanical failure and 43 from ditching. From 20 November to 8 December, the British lost 44,207 men; the Germans admitted to 41,000. By virtue of their counter-attack the Germans claimed a victory – 'since 1914 the first withdrawal of the proud Briton'. Liddell Hart, the great theorist of armoured warfare, called Cambrai 'a sombre sunset after a brilliant dawn'.

For the Allies, there could be no looking forward to a second attempt in the immediate future – only apprehensive preparations for a defensive battle, as the Germans fed division after division into the Western Front after the Russian

Below : The new image of offensive warfare – *A Tank* by Sir William Orpen. In reality conditions inside the lurching, roaring monsters were hellish – the first tanks lacked any kind of suspension. Special helmets with chain-mail visors were issued to protect the crews' eyes from fragments of hot metal sent flying by enemy bullets and shells hitting the armour

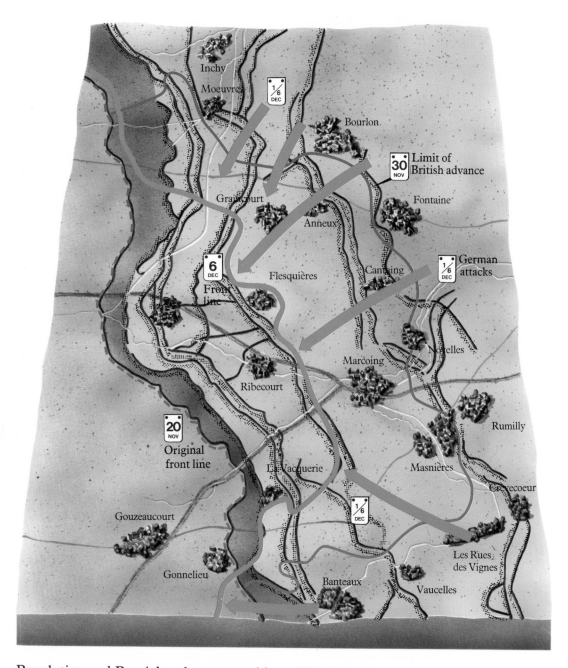

Labels on map:
Inchy
Moeuvres
Bourlon
1/6 DEC
30 NOV — Limit of British advance
Graincourt
Fontaine
Anneux
6 DEC — Front line
Flesquières
Cantaing
1/6 DEC — German attacks
Noyelles
Marcoing
Ribecourt
20 NOV — Original front line
Rumilly
La Vacquerie
Masnières
Crèvecoeur
Gouzeaucourt
1/6 DEC
Les Rues des Vignes
Gonnelieu
Banteaux
Vaucelles

Left: The German counter-attack at Cambrai exploited the limited resources of the British attack to the full. Aided by the arrival of a whole division from the Eastern Front, the Germans showed great imagination and energy, attacking in small but highly efficient assault teams. The experience gained in these shock tactics at Cambrai proved invaluable for the great German offensive on the Western Front in March 1918

Below: First of the many – the surviving tanks of Cambrai are shipped back from the front by rail to fight another day

Revolution and Russia's subsequent with-drawal from the war, declared on 26 November 1917. But after the German offensive of 1918 had petered out and the second battle of the Marne had been won by the Allies, there was to be no reversion to the former offensive tactics. Tanks spear-headed the great Allied advances of the last six months of the war. By rights it should have been Haig, and not Ludendorff, who wrote after Cambrai that: 'Our action has given us valuable hints for an offensive battle in the west if we wished to undertake one in 1918.' For the tanks of Cambrai had done far more than show the Allies the true road to victory: they had proved beyond all doubt that a new arbiter of land warfare had come to stay.

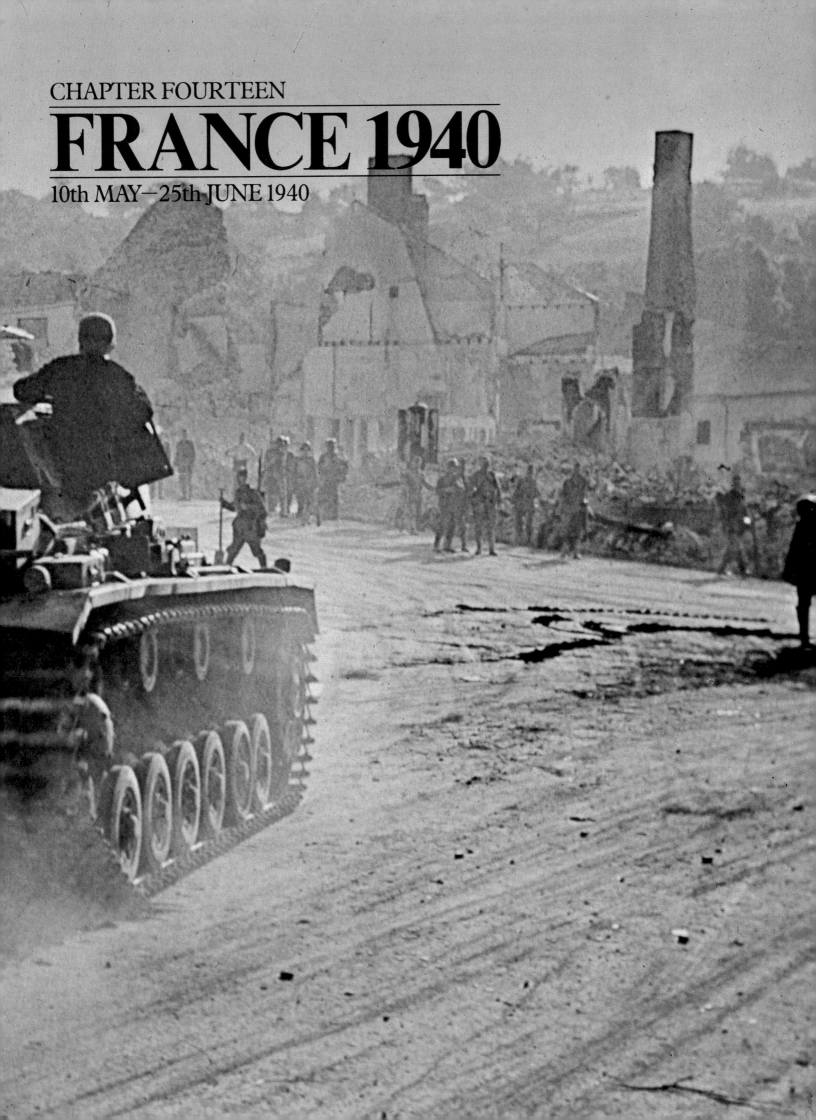

CHAPTER FOURTEEN

FRANCE 1940

10th MAY—25th JUNE 1940

Background to the campaign

'I am all for using aeroplanes and tanks, but these are only accessories to the man and the horse, and I feel sure that as time goes on you will find just as much use for the horse – the well-bred horse – as you have ever done in the past.'

EIGHT years after the spectacular debut of massed tanks at Cambrai, this deathless comment was made by Field Marshal Earl Haig in 1925. It was not, as it happened, a reference to official British policy as far as the armed forces were concerned, but it might as well have been. In 1919 Britain had the biggest and best air force and tank force in the world. In 1939, after twenty years of complacency and peacetime run-down, she was only just starting to renovate her tiny air force in the face of German military might and naked ambition. These restoration efforts with the RAF proved just enough to save the country from outright defeat in 1940, but nothing at all could be done that year with the withered and totally obsolete tank force.

It was even worse in France, which in 1940 resembled a once-powerful giant, running to fat, with totally shattered nerves. After the appalling losses of the First World War there was every excuse in the world for shattered nerves. In 1914 France had gone exultantly to war, believing that the hour of revenge had struck; in 1939 she went glumly, muttering *'Il faut en finir'* ('Time to stop it'). France and Britain went to war in 1939 ostensibly to help save Poland from conquest by Hitler's Germany, but were quite unable to do anything to save Poland. What they were really planning to do was to fight a defensive war when – not if – Hitler turned west. Remembering their joint failures against the German line of defence in the First World War, they were confident of winning such a battle. But they had forgotten Cambrai and what tanks could do when used *en masse*.

Both in France and in Britain, officers and theorists had pleaded the case for powerful tank units in the 1920s and 1930s, but the terrible stimulus of the Western Front no longer existed. Tanks reverted from being used as an offensive weapon in their own right, to the uninspired role of mobile fire support for the infantry, and – in the case of lighter machines – replacing horsed cavalry for reconnaissance and pursuit. The latter role was sound enough – and still is – but the former was plain disastrous. It meant spreading out tank units along the entire front, weak everywhere, strong nowhere, with no chance at all of holding and breaking a concentrated thrust by enemy tanks used *en masse*.

The Germans, on the other hand, were the ones who had been on the receiving end of tanks in the First World War; they had been faced with scattered tank attacks and concentrated tank attacks and had experienced the terrible difference between the two methods. Contrary to popular myth, the German Army between the wars contained just as many reactionaries as the French and British Armies. Six years after Haig made his fatuous prophecy about the 'well-bred horse', the German Inspector of motorized troops told Heinz Guderian, Germany's foremost tank theorist in the inter-war years: 'You're too impetuous. Believe me, neither of us will ever see German tanks in operation in our lifetime'. But in 1933, Adolf Hitler, Germany's new chancellor, watched a demonstration by one of Guderian's armoured teams and burst out: 'That's what I need! That's what I want to have!' And in October 1935 the first three German armoured or 'Panzer' divisions were formed. By September 1939 the German Army had five Panzer divisions deployed for battle against Poland.

The Panzer divisions were not invincible from birth: they had to learn their trade the hard way, and they learned a lot in Poland even though they had no serious opposition (the Poles had only 600 elderly tanks against 3,200 German). Guderian admitted in his memoirs that the first time one of his units came up against Polish cavalry the panicky German troops at the front asked for permission to withdraw – a fact somehow remembered a lot less readily than the popular stories of Polish cavalry charging to their doom against German tanks. Above all, it was in Poland that the Germans began to learn the art of tying-in deep advances by armoured and mechanized troops with accurate air strikes by the *Luftwaffe* – blowing up bridges in the

Above:
French anti-aircraft gunners 'ready', according to the boastful caption to this picture, 'to give Nazi armies a hot reception'. But in 1940 the Allied armies in the West had nothing like enough guns to challenge the *Luftwaffe*'s near-total command of the air. By contrast, the German ground forces advanced under the umbrella provided by excellent mobile AA batteries

Previous pages: Over a street already ripped and ground to dust by preceding caterpillar tracks, a German Panzer Mark III roars through a French town

rear of enemy troops, wiping out dangerous enemy columns and hard knots of resistance in the path of the advance. For the essence of *blitzkrieg* – 'lightning war' – was and still is swift penetration to cause maximum uproar in the enemy's rear.

The armoured line-up, 1940

Another popular myth is that the Germans had far more tanks than the Allies in 1940. In fact, on 10 May the Allies had about 3,310 – 3,000 French and 310 British – to the Germans' 2,690. It was the *concentration* of German tanks that mattered, not the overall numbers. The massing of tanks in self-contained divisions meant that whenever the Germans put in a tank attack they *did* have superiority where it mattered: at the point of the attack. Nor were the German tanks all invincible juggernauts. The best French and British heavy tanks were far better armoured than the heaviest German machines, but slower. And all the French tanks suffered from a ludicrous design flaw: the one-man turret. This meant that the wretched tank commander was busier than the proverbial one-armed paper-hanger, having to load, aim and fire the turret gun as well as look out for the enemy and tell his own driver what to do.

The rival plans

The plans under which the Germans and Allies went to war as from 10 May 1940 were entirely different from those of August 1914. The Allies had totally renounced the initiative to the German Army. In 1914 they had relied on the French to carry the main weight of the offensive. In 1940 they relied on the French to carry the main weight of the *defensive* in the form of the mighty Maginot Line, which ran along the frontier with Germany from Switzerland to the Belgian frontier. There, absurdly, the Line ended. Admittedly the Germans had shown, in August 1914, how little time it took to *march* through Belgium, let alone drive through with mechanized and armoured forces. But this time everything was expected to be different. The Belgians had converted the Albert Canal, connecting Antwerp to the Meuse, into the most formidable anti-tank ditch in western Europe. Belgium, like Holland, insisted on clinging to an ostrich-like neutrality for as long as possible – but if the Germans invaded Belgium again the Albert Canal

would hold them up long enough for the British and French to charge forward into Belgium, hinged on to the western end of the Maginot Line, and then form an unbreakable front.

This was precisely what the German planners wanted the Allies to do. The first plan served up in 1939 by the General Staff, who hated the idea of an early campaign in the West, was little more than the old Schlieffen Plan with tanks and air cover, extended to take in Holland as well as Belgium. But it seemed only too likely that however slowly the French and British reacted to this, there would be some kind of eventual deadlock between the Maginot Line and the sea, as in 1914. The brainchild of General von Manstein, a revised plan called *Sichelschnitt* – 'Sweep of the Sickle' – concentrated the bulk of the German armour in the middle of the three German army groups deployed against the West from the upper Rhine to the Dutch frontier. Enough of a demonstration would be made against Holland and Belgium to get the British and French to charge forward. Meanwhile the world's first tank army, the *Panzergruppe* of seven Panzer divi-

Above: Sweating under the glorious sun of summer 1940, German artillerymen struggle to haul one of their guns to its new position

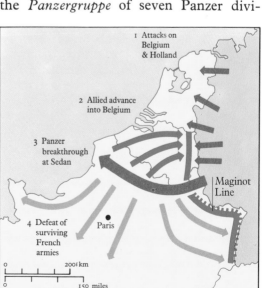

Left: The rival plans in 1940. Forced to respect the desire of the Dutch and Belgians to retain their neutrality, all the French and British (*blue*) could guarantee was a wheeling move forward into Belgium to block the German advance. (*red*). But Manstein's 'Sickle' plan was aimed at cutting off the advancing Allies by a concentrated blow against the 'hinge' of their line, through the Ardennes and across the Meuse around Sedan

Above: How the Germans crossed the Meuse and other 'impassable' river barriers: small groups and loads on rubber pontoon-rafts, under skies swept clean of all marauding Allied aircraft

Below:
French soldiers man an observation post set up in a barn. At first totally disconcerted by the speed of the German advance, the French put up a very different performance under Weygand's leadership, fighting with great tenacity on the Somme and the Aisne

sions, would sweep through Luxemburg and the Belgian Ardennes to arrive at the hinge of the Allied line, at the western end of the Maginot Line opposite Sedan and Dinant on the Meuse. They would then force a crossing, break clean through the Allied hinge, and drive westward, cleaving the Allied front in two. A continued advance to the West would thus slice off the northern third of the Allied line-up and leave France weakened and exposed to the final assault.

This concentration of the armour in the German Army Group 'A' left only three Panzer divisions for Army Group 'B', entrusted with the assault on Holland and Belgium. But Army Group 'B' had the cream of the German Army's other 'secret weapon', the crack paratroops and glider-borne troops of the German airborne forces, the like of which did not exist in either the French or British Armies. Their main task was to seize bridges across the Meuse in Holland and Belgium. Another group was to land on the airfields outside The Hague, hoping to catch the entire Dutch Government at the outset, while a special detachment of airborne assault pioneers was to land on top of the strongest fortress on the Albert Canal, Fort Eben-Emael, and knock it out.

10 May. Holland and Belgium: the first shock

The German airborne attacks on Holland early on 10 May met with mixed success; the landings at The Hague were a complete disaster, but the airborne troops took the Maas bridges at Rotterdam and Moerdijk. By noon on the eleventh, the fortress of Eben-Emael and the Albert Canal crossings had been forced, and the main Belgian defence-line cracked – but the British and French, advancing according to plan, were fast coming into the line. By the thirteenth

things were going well for the Allies: they had a unified front running from the western end of the Maginot Line north along the Meuse, picking up the line of the Dyle (or Antwerp-Namur line) and continuing north to cover Antwerp. Initial German attacks on this line, by General von Reichenau's 6th Army, were given rough handling – but within forty-eight hours all hell had broken loose down on the Sedan sector, where the *Panzergruppe* tanks had not only arrived on the Meuse but were streaming across it.

The Sedan breakthrough

The amazing feature of the German master-stroke of invading France through the Belgian Ardennes and across the Meuse was the way in which the nominal Panzer commander, General von Kleist of the *Panzergruppe*, persistently tried to pluck defeat out of the jaws of victory. He had never been a 'Panzer fanatic' and had no instinctive feel for *blitzkrieg* tactics; time after time he tried to slow down the Panzer spearheads to allow the infantry to catch up, or to guard against non-existent French threats from the flank.

The French had confidently believed the mountainous roads through the Ardennes to be impassable, and so they well might have been if defended in strength; but by the evening of the twelfth the seven *Panzergruppe* divisions had closed up to the Meuse with little or no trouble. First across was Lieutenant-General Erwin Rommel's 7th Panzer Division; the main crossings, ably assisted by precision attacks on the far bank of the Meuse by the *Luftwaffe*, took place on the thirteenth. On the fourteenth, the three Panzer divisions of Guderian's corps were happily widening their bridge-head when Kleist abruptly ordered Guderian to halt and let the infantry come up. The wily Guderian told Kleist that the bridgehead was too small for the moment, and told his men to keep going. By the sixteenth the foremost units were already twenty miles west of the Meuse and still driving forwards.

Kleist was furious when he found out how far the Panzers had advanced, and again ordered Guderian to halt. Guderian offered to resign instead, and a full-scale row ensued which reverberated all the way up to the headquarters of Army Group 'B'. Kleist's rage was not diminished when Guderian reminded him how timidity at the top had contributed greatly to the

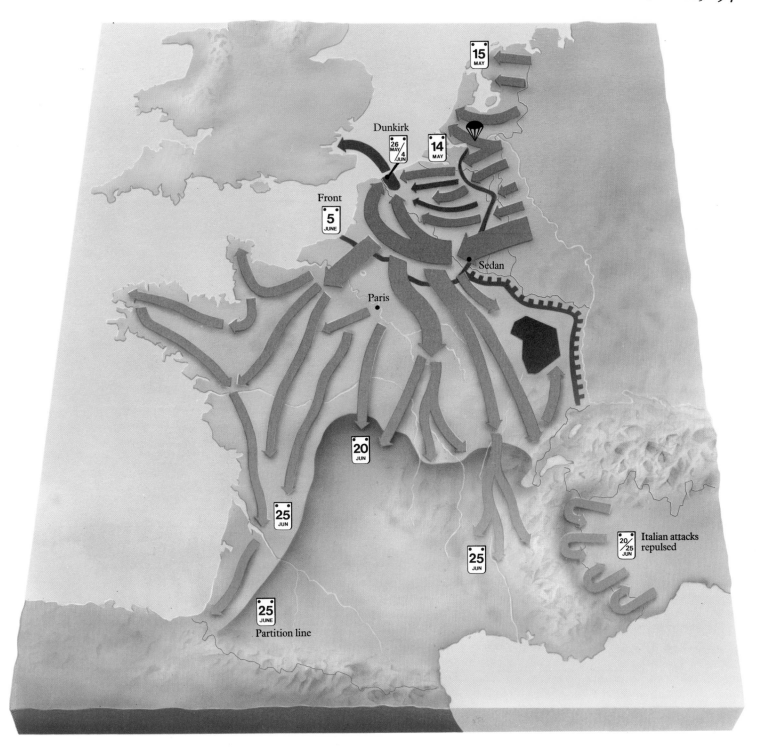

Dunkirk

Front

Sedan

Paris

Italian attacks
repulsed

Partition line

Above: The German conquest of France. First they punched through the Allied front on the Meuse and drove to the Channel; then they rounded on the exhausted French troops south of the Somme and Aisne rivers, pushing south past others trapped to the west of the Maginot Line

German failure on the Marne in 1914. In the end the Army Group C.-in-C., General von Rundstedt, overruled Kleist but by then the Army High Command and Hitler himself wanted to call a halt, too. Guderian was limited to 'reconnaissance in force' – which he interpreted his own way, once again telling the Panzer commanders to keep going.

And all this happened forty-eight hours *after* French Premier Reynaud had telephoned Churchill to stammer 'We have been defeated; we have lost the battle'; twenty-four hours *after* Churchill had gone to Paris and heard from the Allied C.-in-C., France's General Gamelin, that there were no mobile reserves at all with which to halt the German breakthrough. Allied consternation over what had happened on the Meuse was almost exactly matched on the German side; and the scale was tipped only by the expertise and dash of the Panzer commanders, who continued to stack up success after success, until even their reluctant superiors could not fail to see the immense possibilities which lay so close to hand. On the eighteenth and nineteenth Guderian's spearheads roared in forty-

eight breathtaking hours right across the Somme battlefield of the First World War; on the twentieth they took Amiens, Albert and Abbeville, pushed through Noyelles and arrived, hardly able to believe it, at the Channel. On the twentieth the first Germans at the Channel had come sixty-five miles in twenty-four hours; only twenty-five years previously armies of 200,000 men could count themselves lucky if they managed one mile a day.

In the trap

North of the 'Panzer corridor', some thirty-five French, British and Belgian divisions now lay between the narrowing jaws of a huge vice. Holland had surrendered on the 15 May, after a gallant fight and the savage bombing of Rotterdam, and the German Army Group 'B' was closing in for the kill from the north-east. It was obvious what the Allies must do now: counter-attack north and south of the corridor, slice it wide open and break out to the south. This was what the new Allied C.-in-C., General Weygand (who replaced Gamelin on the twentieth), tried to do, but few of the orders he issued to this effect made sense by the time they had reached the army commanders inside the pocket. The Germans refused to hold still so that they could be counter-attacked; the trapped Allied forces, retreating steadily west towards the coast, had no secure flanks or rear; all roads leading away from the Germans were clogged with columns of terrified refugees, urged on by the whip of the *Luftwaffe*.

At Arras on the twenty-first the British tried a clumsy counter-attack to the south, which was broken up, after initial success, by Rommel's 7th Panzer Division using

anti-aircraft guns against the British tanks. But Guderian's Panzers were already swarming north, under orders now to take Channel ports. By the twenty-fourth Boulogne had gone, Calais was besieged, and Dunkirk seemed to be the next to go – but on that day the Panzers were again ordered to halt, this time definitively, on the line of the Aa Canal west of Dunkirk. This decision to spare the Panzers more heavy fighting before the final battle for France was joined was one of the most controversial decisions of the war. It was not one of Hitler's whims; in fact this was one of the few occasions when he listened to professional advice. Rundstedt asked for the halt; and Göring promised that 'his *Luftwaffe*' would seal off Dunkirk from the air.

Dunkirk: the quarry escapes

In any event the Allied evacuation through Dunkirk (28 May–4 June) would never have been possible at all without the fanatical resistance of the French 1st Army at Lille, which fought on, totally surrounded, until nightfall on 31 May, pinning down seven German divisions which would otherwise have been free to attack Dunkirk. General Molinié's gallant Lille garrison was allowed to march out with the full honours of war, saluted by a German honour guard – a startling throwback, in the midst of total war, to the chivalrous military gentility of the seventeenth and eighteenth centuries.

By 4 June 225,200 British and 113,000 French troops had been evacuated from Dunkirk, having lost all their artillery,

armour, transport and heavy equipment. The battle in the north was over; within twenty-four hours the battle for France would begin.

Weygand's defence plan

So often overshadowed by the dramas of Sedan and Dunkirk, the last fight of the French between 5 and 25 June was in total contrast to their initially lamentable performance between 10 and 28 May. It also shows how very different the whole campaign could have been. Weygand was not afraid of Panzer attacks; he knew how to deal with them. There must not be a solid front line; the troops must bunch into 'hedgehog' positions. When the Panzers duly bypassed the 'hedgehogs' they must be lured into deadly corridors of artillery fire. The tragedy was that by the time Weygand took the helm there was no time to rehearse the troops in these novel tactics, and no reserves to make the tactics work in the face of repeated attacks. All he could do was to hold a frail 'crash barrier' along the line of the Somme and the Aisne – only 71 French divisions facing 143 German divisions.

For forty-eight hours the French beat off General von Bock's Army Group 'B', inflicting unheard-of casualties. (Between 10 May and 3 June the Germans lost 2,448 killed, wounded and missing per day; between 4 and 25 June, facing 64 fewer divisions, they lost 4,332 per day.) But by nightfall on the seventh the Panzers had broken through on the Somme; two days later Rundstedt's Army Group 'A' crashed into action on the Aisne, and after a two-day battle no less bruising than the one on the Somme, Guderian's Panzers were also out in open country. There was nothing to stop them, and after another runaway advance as spectacular as the drive to the Channel his leading units arrived at Pontarlier on the Swiss frontier, trapping over 40 French divisions sitting in and behind the useless Maginot Line.

On the night of 16–17 June Marshal Pétain replaced Reynaud as Prime Minister, determined that the fighting must be stopped; an armistice was signed at Rethondes on the twenty-second. By this time the southernmost German spearheads were well on the way to Bordeaux – where the French government had fled after Paris fell without a shot on the fourteenth – and to Limoges, Valence and Grenoble.

Aftermath and losses

The campaign in the West of May-June 1940 remains the biggest triumph in German military history. Allied killed and wounded came to 105,850 killed and 278,590 wounded, with a grand total of about 1,450,000 prisoners for the French alone. Official German losses were announced as 27,074 killed, 111,034 wounded and 18,384 missing – most of the latter presumably dead, as the Germans naturally got their prisoners back. Compared with First World War bloodbaths (the British lost 60,000 men on the first day of the Somme alone) it was an amazingly low price to pay for the conquest of Holland, Belgium and France in just over six weeks.

Yet it was an empty victory. The campaign had been intended to shatter the Western alliance and bring peace to a conquered Europe. To do that, the German High Command should have had their plans all cut and dried for the invasion and conquest of Britain as well as mainland Europe – and such plans did not yet exist. The totally unforeseen continued resistance of the British was more than an annoying blemish on the German victory of June 1940: it was a fatal flaw.

Above:
The last retreat begins; French troops fall back through a town already savaged by German bombing. The flimsy 'tankette' and tracked trailer in the foreground reflect the woeful inadequacy of French and British tank thinking during the period of neglect and stagnation between the wars. In 1918 the French and British had fielded the best armoured forces in the world

Below : When German tanks reached the shores of the Channel in late May 1940 their exultant crews thought that the war was over in all but name – but as Churchill said of another and later occasion, their achievement was only 'the end of the beginning'.

Above : Symbolic of the Anglo-American mix of tanks with which the 8th Army tackled Rommel's outnumbered Panzers at Alamein – American-built Shermans led by a British Crusader

Previous pages : After the long, grinding battle to clear corridors through Rommel's minefields, the leading Shermans of the 8th Army roar clear of the last minefield Montgomery had warned his men to 'organize ahead', forecasting 'whole affair about twelve days'. It took all of that

Before Rommel's army could be broken, he had to be fought to a halt and thrown back on the defensive – then ground down in a relentless battle of attrition

Background

ALAMEIN has a unique place in the hearts of the British, and justly so; it was a great and heartening victory, and it helped turn the tide of the war. But when Winston Churchill claimed that 'Before Alamein we never had a victory. After Alamein we never had a defeat', he should have known better. The British forces in North Africa had won several victories there; and if Churchill himself had been less keen to sack any general who displeased him, he could well have had his victory at Alamein a lot earlier than he did.

The real victor over Field-Marshal Rommel at Alamein was not Montgomery, the lucky man who had the job of administering the *coup de grâce* with double

Rommel's resources and the comfortable knowledge that an Allied invasion was due to go in behind Rommel's back. It was the man who, three-and-a-half months before, had picked up the pieces of a broken and demoralized army to fight Rommel to a standstill at Alamein and force him on to the defensive: General Sir Claude Auchinleck. What was more, Auchinleck's all-important first victory over Rommel at Alamein was the second defeat he had inflicted on Rommel in twelve tense but splendid months as Commander-in-Chief, Middle East.

The war in North Africa began almost by accident and was a thorough nuisance to the Germans, who had never intended to go there at all. But Mussolini wanted a cheap victory to put him on a par with Hitler, so he invaded Egypt from the Italian colony of Libya in September 1940. Starting in

December 1940, the British under General Wavell started to hit back, and much to their own surprise threw the Italians not only out of Egypt but out of eastern Libya as well. By late January 1941 it seemed that they would keep going and take Tripoli. It was to avert such a setback to the Italo-German war effort that Hitler sent an under-strength Panzer corps out to Libya under the command of the most successful Panzer divisional commander in the French campaign: Erwin Rommel. Such was the birth of the *Afrika Korps* and such was its mission: to save Tripoli for Mussolini and the Axis powers.

When Rommel got to Tripoli in February 1941, however, he immediately sensed that Tripoli was safe: all the steam had gone out of the British, who were holding their forward positions. (In fact their best divisions had all been taken away to be sent in a vain attempt to save Greece from conquest.) To the fury of the German Army High Command, Rommel disobeyed his orders to wait until more reinforcements had been spared him and launched an offensive of his own which pushed the British right back into Egypt. This made excellent propaganda but little or no sense from the military point of view, for there was no way of sending Rommel enough supplies for this unwanted new front. (German Army High Command was putting the finishing touches to the preparations for the invasion of Russia.) Not only that, but a garrison had withdrawn into Tobruk, the only decent port between Alexandria and Benghazi in Libya, which meant that Rommel had a tricky siege on his hands as well as an over-extended front to hold.

Rommel's failure to take Tobruk was his first defeat in North Africa. Instead of holding off, sizing up the garrison's weakest sector and attacking that, he battered wildly at the first sector of the defences he came up against, which also happened to be one of

the strongest. In June 1941, however, with the siege over a month old, he chalked up his second desert victory by defeating a relief attempt (Operation 'Battleaxe') on which Churchill had set his heart. Incensed at the failure, Churchill sacked Wavell, the brains behind the first desert triumph, and replaced him with Auchinleck.

Rommel's second North African defeat came in November-December 1942, a long, bruising battle in which Auchinleck came at him with the newly formed 8th Army, wore him down, exploited all his mistakes, and forced him to retreat into Tripolitania. Precisely at that moment, however, the 8th Army was milked of forces for the relentless demands of other fronts; Rommel got a timely reinforcement of tanks and fuel; and he bounced back half-way to Tobruk in January-February 1942. Both sides settled down to prepare for a showdown on the Gazala Line in May.

By this time the 8th Army was painfully learning how to cope with Panzer tactics in the desert. For a start it was getting some tanks which had a real chance of standing up to the Panzers in a fight – tanks which did not break down, shed their tracks, or burst instantly into flames and incinerate their crews when hit. These new tanks came from America: lightweight 'Stuarts' and heavyweight 'Grants'. A new model, the 'Sherman', was about to enter production in the USA, and this was better than anything the Germans had in 1942. But new tanks were not enough: the British still had to learn not to split their armoured divisions up into small, self-contained brigade groups, but keep them together, This, despite Auchinleck's urgings, was precisely what the 8th Army commander General Ritchie failed to do when Rommel attacked him at Gazala on 25 May 1942. By 14 June, aided by the 8th Army's inept tank tactics, Rommel had broken up the armoured opposition and was clamouring to be let loose in a dash on Tobruk

Above: Afrika Korps soldiers sweating out a desert sandstorm, which, at its worst, could reduce visibility to zero

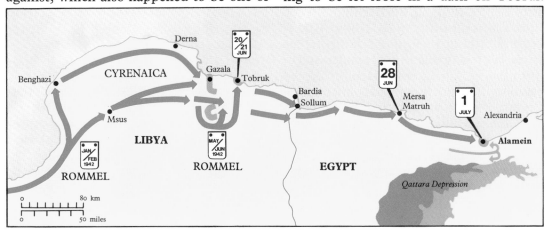

Opposite: Rommel with his men. His off-the-cuff invasion of Egypt (*left, shown in blue*) after the fall of Tobruk was a gamble, and Auchinleck (*green*) out-thought and out-fought him at Alamein in July. After his last breakthrough attempt failed at the beginning of September all he could do was to hang on, starved of supplies, and hope that his minefields would beat off the 8th Army's inevitable offensive

131

Above: German heavy artillery in action during the hard summer of 1942. Rommel's breakthrough offensive at Gazala began on 25 May and from then on his forces were almost constantly in action until the end of July. By the middle of that month Auchinleck had forced Rommel on to the defensive and the victors of Tobruk were having to fight for their lives

the Egyptian frontier – and the Nile.

Once again, as in February 1942, Rommel was under orders. If he managed to take Tobruk he must halt, while the Italian and German forces in southern Italy conquered Malta. With Malta out of the way enough supplies could be passed across the Mediterranean to enable Rommel to invade Egypt and try for the glittering strategic prizes of Alexandria, Cairo and the Suez Canal. But when he stormed Tobruk on 25 June he persuaded Hitler and Mussolini to overrule the strategists and let him storm on into Egypt with what he had. On the surface this was the natural choice for such an exponent of *blitzkrieg*: keep the enemy on the run, never let him stand and rally. But in practice the decision took too many liberties with the problem of supply, the arbiter of all long-distance advances into hostile territory. Beaten though it was, the 8th Army was falling steadily back on its supply bases while Rommel was advancing further and further from his own; soon he would be relying on captured fuel dumps just to keep going, while any serious setback could be fatal.

Egypt's defences

Rommel did have one natural ally: the difficulty of forming a solid front in the open desert inland from the North African coast. It was easy to pin one flank on the coast, but the other inevitably had to end in open desert. The British had tackled the problem by evolving a chain of wired-in defensive positions called 'boxes', which were the direct descendant of the squares of Waterloo. When sited correctly and manned with determination, these boxes could not be ignored; they had to be taken. At Gazala, Rommel had had no trouble in sweeping round the inland flank of the 8th Army's line of boxes, but he could not win

until he had punched a hole in the line through which to supply his armour on the other side.

Once past the Egyptian frontier there were only two places where the 8th Army had a hope of making a stand west of Alexandria: Mersa Matruh and El Alamein. Auchinleck, who took personal command of the 8th Army after the fall of Tobruk, tried to hold Rommel at Matruh from 26–28 June but Rommel repeated his favourite tactic and swept round the desert flank, forcing the 8th Army's 10th and 13th Corps to break out eastwards in total confusion. That left only Alamein – and at Alamein the lie of the land was unique. A coastal box had been built at Alamein on the coast; low-lying ridges, running east and west some ten miles inland, acted as natural channels for an advance from the west; and twenty-five miles further inland the desert dropped abruptly away to the treacherous floor of the Qattara Depression, an enormous natural feature bitten out of the desert floor. As the tired and depleted *Afrika Korps* and its accompanying Italian units sped towards the Alamein Gap on 29–30 June, therefore, Rommel lacked the elbow-room for another wide encircling sweep. Like a wasp entering a killing-bottle, he headed for the gap between the Alamein box and the inland ridges of Miteirya and Ruweisat.

First Alamein: halting Rommel's advance

What should always be, and seldom is, remembered as the First Battle of Alamein began on 1 July. Rommel planned to drive past the Alamein box on either side of the Miteirya Ridge, then curl northwards to the coast to cut off the Alamein garrison (3rd South African Brigade). At the same time the surviving armour of the *Afrika Korps* and the Italian 10th Corps would curl south to cut off the forward brigades of the 8th Army Corps skimpily plugging the Alamein Gap.

It was an elegant plan, and, judging by what had happened at Gazala and Matruh, should have succeeded; but it was let down by Rommel's failure to secure adequate reconnaissance reports of what was waiting for him. The left-hand tentacle was blocked and driven back by furious artillery fire from the 1st and 2nd South African Brigades; the right-hand tentacle suffered a similar fate at the hands of the 18th Indian Brigade, occupying a hastily-constructed box at Deir el Shein, south of the Miteirya Ridge, which Rommel had no idea was there and which fought to the death before it went under. Rommel's attempt to rush the Alamein defences had failed.

On 2 July he tried again, diverting the *Afrika Korps* to the northern flank; while Auchinleck tried to launch an effective counter-attack north and west from the western end of the Ruweisat Ridge. Neither attempt succeeded; and it was Auchinleck who first realized the folly of squandering his weak forces on tasks beyond their means. Keeping both his artillery and his armour concentrated, he began from 3 July to launch a series of limited attacks deliberately aimed at the weakest parts of Rommel's army: the Italian divisions. These attacks, switched from sector to sector, kept the *Afrika Korps* at full stretch, converting it from an offensive force to a fire-brigade forced to run hither and thither in order to save its allies from destruction. By the ninth Rommel had been manoeuvred into spreading his forces right across the Alamein Gap from the Qattara Depression to the sea. Then Auchinleck launched his most effective stroke yet: a smashing blow at the Italian 'Sabratha' and 'Brescia' Divisions on the coastal sector, pulverizing them and advancing west to take the hill of Tell el Eisa. He followed this up with another series of attacks further south, back on the Deir el Shein sector.

With these tactics Auchinleck not only halted the drive on Cairo that had seemed so irresistible at the end of June, but forced Rommel into a desperate defensive battle. The July fighting, however, was exhausting for both sides and by the end of the month Auchinleck was content to call a halt. Certainly there was no further immediate danger from Rommel, who wrote to his wife on 2 August that: 'Holding on to our Alamein positions has given us the severest fighting we've yet seen in Africa.'

The new brooms: Alexander and Montgomery

None of this formidable achievement was anything like enough for Churchill, who flew into Cairo on 4 August hell-bent on finding new brooms who would sweep the desert clear of Rommel for good. Great decisions had been made since the fall of Tobruk. The Americans were not only sending the 8th Army 300 Sherman tanks

before they had been issued to the US Army: they had agreed to 'Torch', a joint Anglo-American invasion of Algeria and Morocco, to go in at the end of October. By then Rommel must be soundly beaten, by new commanders in which the 'brave but baffled' 8th Army, as Churchill called it, had complete faith. Hence the brusque dismissal of Auchinleck on 8 August and his replacement by Alexander. Gott, by far the most experienced corps commander, was to take command of the 8th Army. But within forty-eight hours of agreeing to take on the job Gott was shot down and killed; and Montgomery, formerly earmarked to command the British 1st Army in 'Torch', took his place. The changeover became effective as from 15 August.

Alam Halfa: Rommel's last throw

First, Montgomery's personal 'battle' had to be won fast: getting himself accepted by the 8th Army as an eccentric but dynamic new commander with a firm grasp on the essentials under whom defeat was unthinkable. This he achieved, swiftly and brilliantly, with his prickly but stimulating 'personal touch'. Far less attractive was the way in which he claimed, for the rest of his life, that he alone was responsible for the dispositions that broke Rommel's last attack at Alamein: the so-called 'Battle of Alam Halfa' (31 August-2 September).

Rommel would have to attack, and attack

Below: A 25-pounder gun crew in action. The 25-pounder was an extremely versatile weapon: a 'gun-howitzer', it could either lob shells against unseen targets or fire in flat trajectory like an orthodox gun; it threw a shell as big as the dreaded German 88-mm. South African 25-pounders were instrumental in blocking Rommel's attempt to bypass Alamein on 1 July

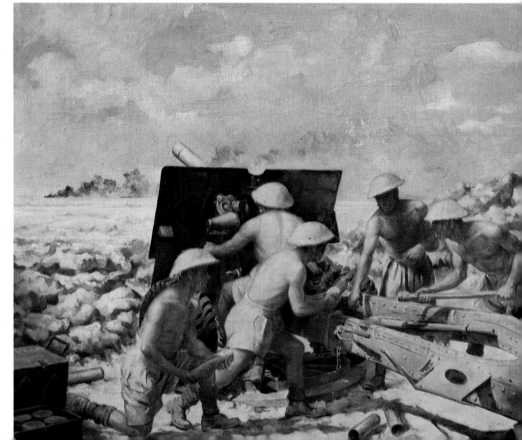

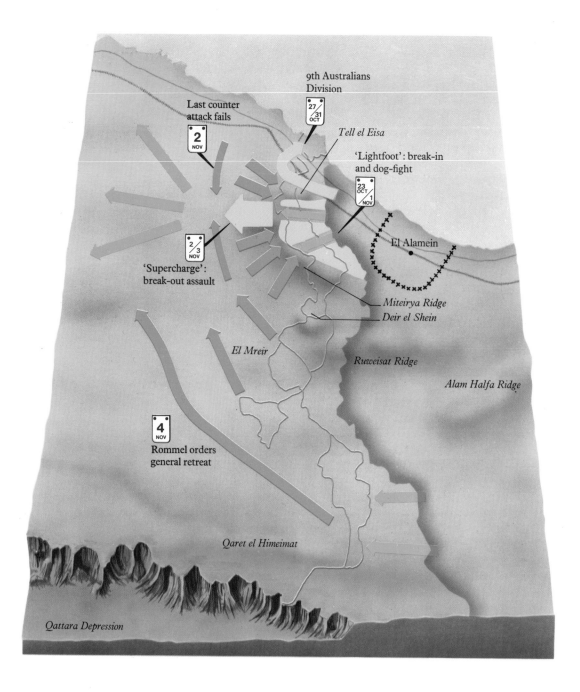

9th Australians
Division

Last counter
attack fails

2
NOV

Tell el Eisa

'Lightfoot': break-in
and dog-fight

27
31
OCT

23
OCT
1
NOV

2
3
NOV

El Alamein

'Supercharge':
break-out assault

Miteirya Ridge

Deir el Shein

El Mreir

Ruweisat Ridge

Alam Halfa Ridge

4
NOV

Rommel orders
general retreat

Qaret el Himeimat

Qattara Depression

Above : 'First Alamein', in which Rommel (*blue*), against all expectations after the loss of Tobruk and Mersa Matruh, was stopped in his tracks by Auchinleck (*green*). By the end of August, when Rommel tried his last attack at Alamein (*bottom of map*), British minefields and unceasing air attacks had proved far too strong for him

soon, before the 8th Army's vastly superior supply position made it too strong to be safely attacked. Equally obvious was the sector and manner in which Rommel would attack: in the south, with an encircling move to get in behind the now formidable 8th Army positions and minefields, for the coastal sector was far too heavily defended. Once into the British rear there was only one place at which he could be stopped: the ridge of Alam Halfa, which Auchinleck had already marked down as the decisive sector of such an attack. Montgomery always denied the latter fact, claiming that Alam Halfa had been totally overlooked until he came on the scene. He also claimed to be an innovator in keeping the British armour

static and concentrated, letting the *Afrika Korps* charge to its doom against a hedge of 8th Army anti-tank guns with the armour waiting behind. Auchinleck, however, had seen all this, but had lacked the hardware; Montgomery had the hardware in abundance. By 31 August, when Rommel attacked, Montgomery had about 700 tanks, while Rommel had only 443 (Italian and German combined).

Forty-eight hours' painful crawl through dense minefields, under incessant air attack, convinced Rommel that he must abandon the battle. The real problem was fuel, of which not enough had got through to enable him to fight a protracted action without his armour getting stranded.

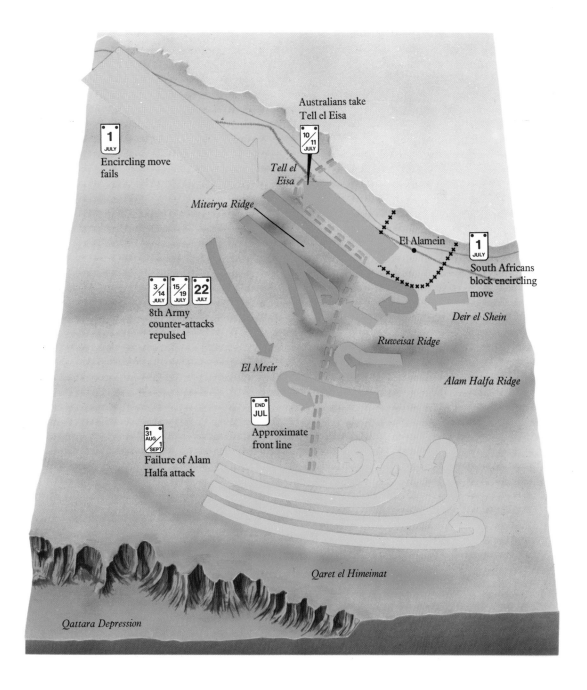

Australians take
Tell el Eisa

1 JULY
Encircling move
fails

10/11 JULY

*Tell el
Eisa*

Miteirya Ridge

El Alamein

1 JULY
South Africans
block encircling
move

Deir el Shein

3/14 JULY **15/19** JULY **22** JULY
8th Army
counter-attacks
repulsed

Ruweisat Ridge

Alam Halfa Ridge

El Mreir

END JUL
Approximate
front line

31 AUG/1 SEPT
Failure of Alam
Halfa attack

Qaret el Himeimat

Qattara Depression

Montgomery, for his part, kept a firm hand on the battle from start to finish, giving the 8th Army an inestimable morale boost: a battle won just the way in which the general had said it would be won. Now the 8th Army could look forward with ever-mounting confidence to the decisive offensive of the desert war.

Second Alamein: the balance of forces

By 23 October, when Montgomery attacked at Alamein, the 8th Army had been built up to an unprecedented superiority in manpower and weapons. Its manpower was 195,000, the Germans' and Italians' 104,000. It had 1,209 tanks against 496 German and Italian, double the number of field and medium guns, not to mention the 1,200 aircraft of the Desert Air Force. Yet it would all be needed; this was to be a battle the like of which had never been seen in the desert. In the Alamein Gap, two dense systems of minefields, strongpoints, and wire belts now confronted each other. This was not the mobile war of the desert theatre: it was nothing less than a direct throwback to the painful trench warfare of the First World War. Montgomery had planned to: 'Organize ahead for a "dog-fight" of a week. Whole affair about 10 days (which he amended to '12 days').'

Above : 'Second Alamein'. By October 1942 the Alamein front resembled a First World War battlefield, with the two armies facing each other across dense belts of minefields. Superior in manpower, tanks and guns, Montgomery (*green*) also held the trump card of air power over the battlefield and planned a remorseless battle of attrition to grind Rommel's army (*blue*) to breaking-point

Above : Tracer bullets and shells slash the night sky over Alamein. On 27 October during a desperate German air attack on the forward British positions, the British pushed ever deeper into the German-Italian defence complex

The first phase (23–25 October) was the 'break-in', and during it Rommel was not in Africa at all but in Germany on sick leave. His successor, General Stumme, died of a heart attack early on the morning of the twenty-fourth and Rommel flew back to Africa to pick up the pieces. It was not as bad as it might have been, for Montgomery's infantry had failed to carve the planned corridors through which the tanks were to pour. Montgomery was unmoved. He refused to change his plan. He was fighting a battle of attrition in which – for once – the German defence was not going to be good enough.

On the twenty-sixth Rommel learned that the last two tankers which could have brought him fuel in time to keep his armour moving had both been sunk; and he decided to drop the original dispersion of the German armour among the Italian divisions and concentrate what was left of his armour. However, by moving the 21st Panzer Division north of the Ruweisat Ridge he allowed Montgomery to pull out the 10th Armoured and 2nd New Zealand Division, while all the time, hammered by

the Desert Air Force, the German and Italian tank force continued to dwindle.

In night attacks on the 28–29 October and 30–31 October, the 9th Australian Division took up the running, attacking to the north-west, pinning the German 90th Light Division up against the coast. Now Montgomery put in the New Zealanders again, attacking westward this time, once more forcing Rommel to switch his last reserves to cover the Tel el Aqqaqir Ridge. 'Supercharge' was the code-name of this decisive assault, which went in at 6.15 a.m. on 2 November. At first, like every other phase of the offensive, severe losses were suffered but the New Zealanders soon began to sense that the German front was cracking. Rommel was in fact down to 35 tanks, while Montgomery's tank strength was still numbered in hundreds. It was time for Rommel to go, while he still had an army left – and his decision was confirmed by a typically outrageous telegram from Hitler, saying that Rommel had no choice but to show his troops the way 'to victory or death'.

On the night of 3 November, the 5th

Indian Brigade turned the flank of Rommel's last position, and three armoured divisions and two armoured brigades went racing through the gap. General von Thoma, commanding the *Afrika Korps*, was captured under Rommel's eyes. It was the end of any hopes of an orderly, staged withdrawal; without further hesitation, Rommel ordered an all-out retreat. He was saved from total annihilation by the constant improvization of the previous twelve days, which had made a thorough mess out of the 8th Army. By the seventh Rommel's survivors were already into a staged retreat down the coast road, which he intended to make as slow as possible, but on the following day came the stunning news of the 'Torch' landings in Morocco and Algeria. Now he had no choice but to retreat right across Libya to Tunisia and try to hold a last bridgehead there.

Aftermath and losses

The Germans lost 9,000 killed and wounded at Alamein, the Italians 17,000; total Allied casualties were 13,560, plus 600

tanks destroyed against 320. This reflects the heavy fighting needed to bulldoze the armour through; and this could only have been completed with such a heavy advantage in numbers. Apart from the mixture of persistence and flexibility with which Montgomery fought, the most obvious feature of the battle is the similarity to Auchinleck's constant switching of targets during First Alamein. Montgomery certainly did not invent what he liked to call 'wet hen' tactics: making the enemy chase to and fro until worn out.

One of the most striking features of so telling a victory was the 8th Army's cautious pursuit, which arrived at Mersa Matruh too late to trap Rommel and annihilate him. For all his claims to have mastered the lessons of mobile war in the desert, Montgomery never once attempted a surprise knockout during the long pursuit through Tripoli to the Tunisian frontier. Nearly six months of painful fighting in Tunisia was the result.

Above : Highland troops tramp forward along a corridor cleared through the minefields to take up a new position, led by their piper

The six-month ordeal on the Volga that sacrificed the toughest army on the Eastern Front

Background

IF anyone writes a book of rules for prospective warlords, Rule Number One will surely be 'Never invade Russia'. It is not that the Russian soldier is invincible, the Russian winter fatal, and the Russian terrain impossible – it is simply that there is far too much of all three for any nation to tackle single-handed. And that was precisley what Hitler's Germany did in June 1941, attacking with 153 of the German Army's 208 divisions. The thirty-odd Finnish, Romanian, Hungarian and Slovakian divisions which marched into Russia with the German Army were scant compensation for the 55 German divisions left behind to police Poland and the West.

Operation 'Barbarossa', the German invasion plan, was Germany's supreme land offensive of the Second World War and its objective was precisely the same as the German war plan of 1914: to win the war by Christmas. But Rule Number Two in our warlords' handbook should be that campaigns intended to win wars by Christmas hardly ever do. On its highest plane, that of grand strategy, 'Barbarossa' is a perfect example of how foggy Hitler's thinking really was. Constantly raising his stake, he was now hoping that this grandest of all his campaigns would turn out 'third time lucky' after two previous failures. Conquering Poland in 1939 had not made his enemies make peace. Nor had the breathtaking defeat of Holland, Belgium and France in 1940. By 1941 the Soviet Union was the only continental power able to join Britain; but why Hitler thought that the conquest of the Soviet Union would make Britain give up is a mystery. What is certain is that he believed he could do it.

Coming down to the level of campaign strategy, the German plan was to wipe out the Red Army in a series of huge encirclement battles, all fought as far west as possible. Once the Red Army had been swept out of existence in multiple repetitions of the Dunkirk encirclement (though without the evacuation facilities), the German Army could march where it liked in Russia. Where exactly the Germans would stop, was a point on which the 'Barbarossa' directive of 18 December 1940 was suspiciously vague: 'The enemy will be energetically pursued and a line will be reached from which the Russian Air Force can no longer attack German territory. The final objective of the operation is to erect a barrier against Asiatic Russia on the general line Volga-Archangel. The last surviving industrial area of Russia in the Urals can then, if necessary, be eliminated by the *Luftwaffe*.'

Here, spelled out in admirably brief terms, was the blueprint for the failure of the whole venture. It bristled with contradictions and false assumptions, and left no question unbegged. If the Russian Army were destroyed in western Russia before it could withdraw into the vastness of the country, what was 'the enemy' to be so 'energetically pursued'? As for the 'A-A' (Astrakhan-Archangel) stop-line, where precisely was this to run? If it truly followed the lines of the Volga and Dvina it would form a giant zig-zag with three monstrous salients poking westward into the German front – a nightmare 'barrier' from the defender's viewpoint. And the prospect of the *Lutwaffe* wiping out Soviet war industries in the Urals, which would lie at least 300 miles east of the remotest German airfields inside the 'barrier' – this seemed the most wishful thinking of all. In 1940 the *Luftwaffe* had totally failed to

Above:
Fighting in the ruins of Stalingrad at −40°C: a Russian assault party advances through what remains of the 'Red Barricade' ordnance factory. Nearly all the major strategic buildings in the ravaged city changed hands several times during the battle

Previous pages : Russian troops press home another attack on the Germans in the ruins of Stalingrad. 'Every German soldier', decreed Chuikov, the Russian commander, 'must be made to feel that he is living under the muzzle of a Russian gun.'

Right : The peaks of the Caucasus beckon Kleist's 1st Panzer Army. These *panzergrenadiers* are pushing through a maize field under Russian fire. The drive to the Caucasus was originally scheduled to begin *after* Stalingrad had fallen and the line of the Volga had been cleared, but Hitler jumped the gun and sent his two southern army groups marching steadily further and further away from each other

prevent the escape of the Allied armies from Dunkirk and to wipe out the grossly outnumbered RAF Fighter Command, and had no experience at all of strategic bombing to destroy enemy industries.

But the biggest and most fatal false assumption, however, was the bland belief that all the serious fighting would be over by the autumn because there would be no Red Army left. When Guderian first heard of 'Barbarossa' he thought the whole thing was a monstrous bluff to confound the British, and was horrified when he discovered that not only Hitler but the Army General Staff were perfectly serious. The triumph of 1940 had come home to roost with a vengeance. 'Our successes to date, and in particular the surprising speed of our victory in the West, had so befuddled the minds of our supreme commanders that they had eliminated the word "impossible" from their vocabulary. [All] evinced an unshakeable optimism and were quite impervious to criticism or objections', Guderian later admitted in his memoirs.

From the point of view of the Panzer generals, once more expected to spearhead the way to rapid victory, it all came down to space and distance. Every country in which the German Army had so far campaigned had its limits – natural limits like mountain ranges or coasts, or the political limits of friendly or neutral countries. But to take on Russia was like advancing into outer space. As the German armies drove ever eastward they would be advancing out of the neck of a huge territorial funnel, spreading out wider and wider and wider like the separate fingers of a hand clutching for the moon. The demands on men and machines were unimaginable – until too late.

'Barbarossa's' failure

For all these fundamental flaws in the plan it is difficult to see how Hitler's armies could have done much better in 1941. Army Group North drove to the suburbs of Leningrad, Army Group Centre to the suburbs of Moscow, and Army Group South as far as Rostov. By October they had destroyed two-thirds of the Red Army's peacetime strength, and by the climax of the assault on Moscow the Germans had actually attained numerical superiority in manpower – for the first and only time. But the German troops in the field died by the thousand from the winter cold while their winter equipment remained aboard railway trucks back in Warsaw, thanks to the complacency and inefficiency of the General Staff. And out of the snow came the fresh, well-equipped Soviet divisions from Siberia, battering Army Group Centre to within an ace of destruction.

'Plan Blue' – Stalingrad-Caucasus

When the winter crisis had passed and the armies in Russia were brought up to strength for the 1942 campaign, two points were clear. Although the stated objectives for the 'Barbarossa' directives still remained out of reach, there could be no question of a resumed offensive by all three army groups. But by standing on the defensive in the centre and north and advancing with a reinforced Army Group South, reverberating successes could be

Above left :
A ruined wall in Stalingrad serves as a breastwork for a Russian combat team, with the tommy-gunner getting ready to follow up his comrade's grenade with a quick burst of fire

Above right : German machine-gunners in a dramatically-posed shot for the cover of the German forces magazine *Wehrmacht.* The Stalingrad *débâcle* was represented as an epic feat of German arms by Goebbels' propaganda machine

Above: Panzer Mark IV with its improved 'long' 75-mm gun. In his attacks on Stalingrad General Paulus grossly misused his armoured forces, constantly getting them stuck in the forefront of the halting advance where Russian guns could knock them out

Right: The all-too-vague objectives of the Germans during their invasion of Russia. The basic problem was that there was no natural line on which they could stop. Invading Russia from eastern Europe means advancing over huge distances into an ever-expanding void. In 1941 the German Army did all that could have been expected of it. It achieved its primary objective – destroying the massive Red Army concentrations in western Russia – but failed to take Moscow and Leningrad, and was then forced to fight for its life against a counter-offensive launched by the armies rushed west from Siberia. The right-hand map shows how the Germans changed their tune in 1942, standing on the defensive in the north and centre and concentrating on a drive in the south to capture the lower Volga and the oilfields of southern Russia

Below: A 20-mm AA gun on the open steppe, pressed into action against a Russian attack. The soldier on the extreme left is squinting through a stereoscopic range-finder

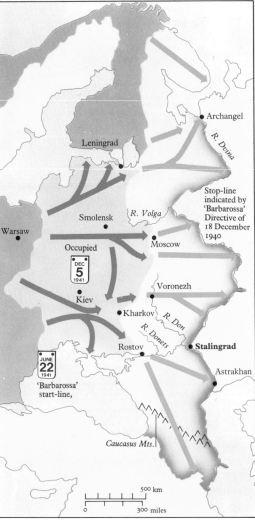

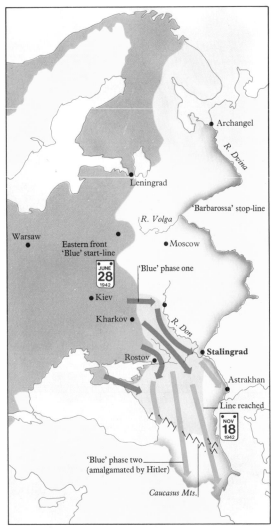

won on the southern sector. Between the Black Sea and the Caspian lay the pick of Russia's oilfields, vital strategic prizes in the era of mechanized war. And if the Germans could take the line of the Caucasus they would be able to break into the Middle East from the north.

Hence evolved 'Plan Blue', a two-stage offensive originally to be launched one stage at a time. The northern half of Army Group South, now designated Army Group 'B' (6th Army and 4th Panzer Army), was to drive east to take Voronezh and the line of the Don river, then cross and push on to take and hold Stalingrad on the Volga. Thus protected from the north, Army Group 'A' (17th and 1st Panzer Army) would break south-east across the Don, sweep through the oil-fields and on to the Caucasus.

A significant feature of the 'Blue' directive was an admission that the offensive could not be undertaken by German troops alone – in short, that the Russian war was already too big for Germany to handle. 'Units of our allies will be used to hold the Don front, which will become longer and longer as the attack proceeds ... Allied troops will be mainly disposed so that the Hungarians are furthest north, then the Italians, and the Romanians furthest to the south-east.' This flanking of the spearhead German armies with allied units of doubtful quality was to have the direst results in the months ahead.

The first four weeks

The spearhead of Army Group 'B' was the 4th Panzer Army, commanded by Colonel-General Hoth. He was originally intended to blaze the way to Stalingrad for Colonel-General Paulus and the 6th Army, the strongest individual army deployed in Russia. The 6th Army had been 'souped up' to a massive strength of eighteen divisions – including two Panzer and one motorized. Once Paulus had arrived before Stalingrad, Hoth was to hand over and head south to assist Colonel-General von Kleist's 1st Panzer Army in the second phrase of the offensive: the drive south-east from the Don.

But in the month that followed the

opening of 'Blue' on 28 July, Hitler's meddling fingers prised the original plan apart like a paper cup and produced a shapeless, spread-out mess. On 23 July his directive 45 replaced 'Blue' with 'Brunswick', which would send Army Group 'A' into simultaneous motions with 'B' *before* the Volga had been secured at Stalingrad. This meant that the two army groups would be advancing steadily away from each other, opening a gap that would eventually gape over 200 miles wide. The reason for the change of plan was the amount the Russians had learned since their disasters of the previous year. This time they declined to stand and be wiped out by the hundred thousand; they pulled swiftly back from between the oncoming German prongs, and so few Russian prisoners were taken that Hitler leaped to the conclusion that the Russians were down to their last reserves.

As a result the 4th Panzer Army, which could have drilled its way through the feeble Russian screen in front of Stalingrad at the end of July, was sent off to get in Kleist's way on the Don; by the time the 6th Army came toiling up the Russians had managed to reinforce their 62nd Army; and Paulus' divisions, attacking piecemeal as they arrived, got such rough handling that Paulus halted until the 4th Panzer Army could come up from the Don.

Into Stalingrad

Paulus and Hoth began their first joint assault on the Russian cordon in front of Stalingrad on 19 August, and by the evening of the twenty-third a narrow corridor had been forced through to the Volga north of the city. Hoth, however, was unable to match this to the south, and only succeeded in forcing the Soviet 64th Army slowly back into the city itself.

What should have been a deft *coup de main*, capturing Stalingrad with minimum fuss and bother in order to release the mobile units of the 6th Army for a cleaning-up dash down to the right bank of the Volga, now turned into a nightmare battle of house-to-house fighting. Over the next two months Paulus revealed himself as one of the worst tacticians ever entrusted with an army.

He was faced with an extended strip of a city, over ten miles long, strung out along the Volga, across which the Russians brought reinforcements night after night. The most economical technique would have been to seize two wide footholds on

the Volga north and south of the city, from which guns could help the *Luftwaffe* – the Germans had total air superiority over Stalingrad during the assault – stopping the flow of Russian reinforcements. From these footholds a pincer movement could have been closed inwards along the Volga bank, rolling up the shallow Russian line. Instead Paulus opted for a head-on, steam-roller approach through the ruins of the city, every block of which was constantly contested by General Chuikov's 62nd Army. It was a hand-to-hand death grapple with an enemy who refused to give up, the most horrible battle the German Army had had to fight in the entire war. It continued without a break for two-and-a-half months.

Zhukov's trap

Meanwhile Stalin's High Command, recognizing that in Stalingrad there was an anchor with which to bring the whole German offensive to a halt, had set up

Above : Russian tommy-gunners clear a ruined building in Stalingrad. The Russians made the 6th Army fight for the city block by block, building by building

Below : Weariness stamps the faces of these German infantrymen as they prepare for yet another advance into the ruined city

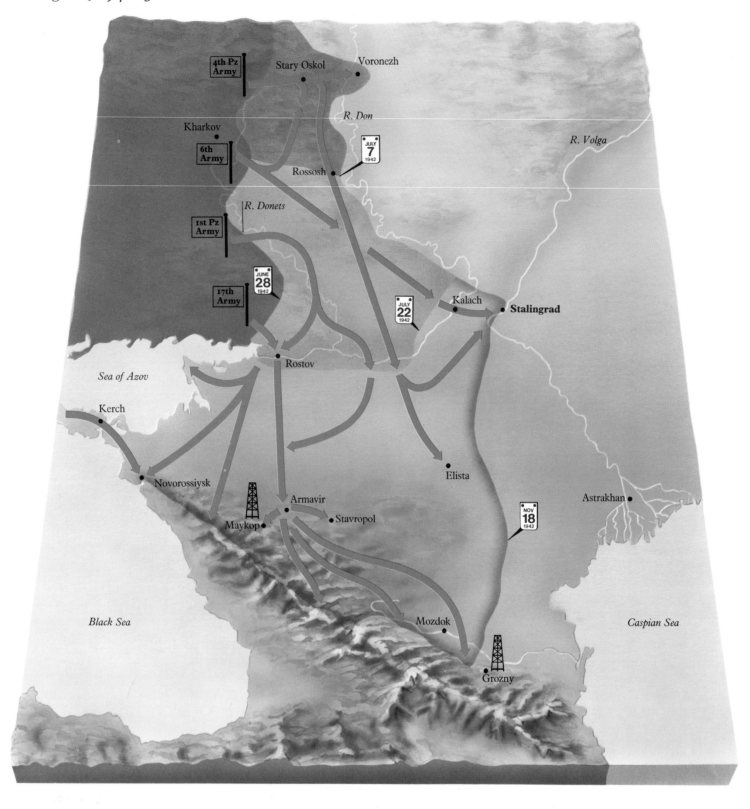

The following labels appear on the map: 4th Pz Army, Stary Oskol, Voronezh, R. Don, Kharkov, R. Volga, 6th Army, JULY 7 1942, Rossosh, R. Donets, 1st Pz Army, JUNE 28 1942, 17th Army, JULY 22 1942, Kalach, Stalingrad, Rostov, Sea of Azov, Kerch, Elista, Astrakhan, Novorossiysk, Armavir, Stavropol, NOV 18 1942, Maykop, Black Sea, Mozdok, Caspian Sea, Grozny

Above : The Stalingrad-Caucasus offensive. Had the 4th Panzer Army not been switched south to get in Kleist's way on the Don, Stalingrad would have been in German hands by the end of August

'Stalingrad Army Group' on 25 August under the command of General Georgi Zhukov who had master-minded the winter counter-offensive at Moscow, the only Russian general who had never lost a battle.

While feeding just enough men and supplies into Stalingrad to keep Chuikov's resistance alight, Zhukov looked greedily at the Romanian armies lying far out in the steppe on each flank of the 6th Army. Throughout October and the first half of

November, all unseen, Zhukov stealthily built up two overwhelming concentrations of striking-power opposite the static Romanians. To the north and west he prepared the Russian 5th Tank Army and 21st Army of 'South-West Army Group', with the 65th Army of 'Don Army Group'. South of the city he built up the two left-wing armies of 'Stalingrad Army Group': the 51st and 57th Armies. At last, on 18 November – when the German 6th Army

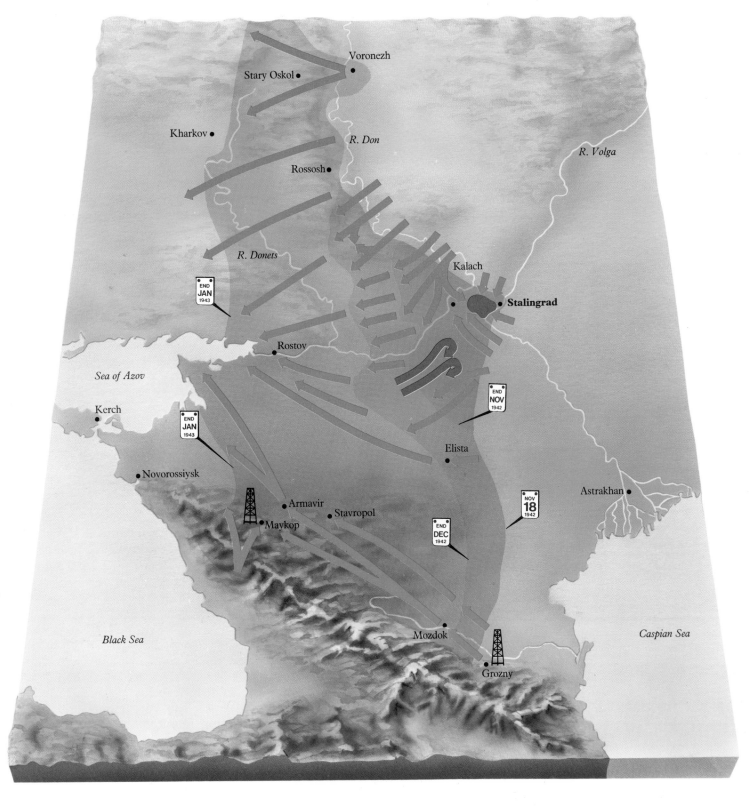

Voronezh

Stary Oskol

Kharkov

R. Don

R. Volga

Rossosh

R. Donets

Kalach

END JAN 1943

Stalingrad

Rostov

Sea of Azov

Kerch

END JAN 1943

END NOV 1942

Novorossiysk

Elista

Astrakhan

Armavir

Stavropol

NOV 18 1942

Maykop

END DEC 1942

Black Sea

Mozdok

Caspian Sea

Grozny

was preparing for its final drive to force the last scattered pockets of Soviet resistance into the Volga and clean out Stalingrad for good – Zhukov unleashed his blow.

Closing the trap

The massed Russian assaults of 18 November completely shattered the flanking Romanian 3rd and 4th Armies. (Some of their tanks had been lying idle for so long

that mice had got in and eaten the insulation off the wires, so that when the frantic crews leaped aboard and tried to start up, all they got were sparks and short-circuits.) A true pupil of *blitzkrieg*, Zhukov had set his sights on objectives fifty miles in the 6th Army's rear: the crossings over the great bend of the Don at Kalach and Nizhne Chirskaya. On 23 November the Russian jaws met at Sovetskiy, about twenty miles south-east of Kalach; and

Above: Zhukov's counter-offensive. He did exactly what Auchinleck had done at 'First Alamein', aiming his heaviest blows at the down-at-heel allied contingents operating on the Germans' flanks

Above: A Russian patrol moves cautiously through the rubble, with the tommy-gunner poised to give covering fire. Both sides at Stalingrad discovered that ruined terrain is the defender's dream and the attacker's nightmare

Below: Coming after the American naval victory over the Japanese at Midway and the 8th Army's breakthrough at Alamein in North Africa, Stalingrad completed the trio of Allied victories in 1942 which turned the tide of the war. 'We'll cut the wicked enemy's path; he won't get out of the noose', boasts this Russian poster

Zhukov wasted no time in hounding them on to the south-west, heaping the soil as high as he could on the grave in which the German 6th Army now lay buried alive.

Hitler's order: no breakout

At first there was little serious concern for the fate of the 6th Army; large German forces had been cut off before in the winter fighting, and had been successfully supplied by air until relief columns could fight through and enable them to break out. Even so, nothing on this scale had ever been attempted: the *Luftwaffe* simply lacked the resources with which to supply a trapped army of a quarter-of-a-million. No matter:

the 6th Army had all the fire-power and manpower it needed to fight its way out and help patch up the front. But Hitler refused. It was barely three weeks since he had ordered Rommel to fight on 'to victory or death' at Alamein and he still insisted that not an inch of unnecessary ground must be given up. The man who sealed the 6th Army's fate was Göring, who curried favour by assuring Hitler that the *Luftwaffe* could drop and air-land the 700 tons of supplies per day needed by the 6th Army. Top of the list of priorities was 6th Army's winter clothing and stores, which had not been issued by the time of Zhukov's breakthrough and never would arrive now.

The tremendous hole ripped in the German front on either side of Stalingrad threatened disaster not only to the 6th Army but to the whole of Army Group 'A' as well. The latter had done wonders, pushing south-east as far as the Terek river, but had been halted there at its last gasp by 13 November, the oilfields tantalizingly beyond its grasp. Now the Stalingrad breakthrough, should the Russians exploit it to the full, threatened Army Group 'A' with encirclement, too.

The relief march fails

This was obvious even to Hitler, who appointed Field-Marshal von Manstein to the command of a new 'Army Group Don'. Manstein arrived at his new headquarters on 26 November and immediately set about preparing a drive to break through to the 6th Army. Commanded by Hoth with the rump of the 4th Panzer Army, this started on 12–13 November and by the fifteenth had forced its way to within thirty miles of the Stalingrad pocket. Had Paulus now emulated Rommel at Alamein, ignored Hitler's stand-fast order and commanded a break-out himself, a fair proportion of the 6th Army probably would have escaped. Instead he shied away from the decision, claiming that the 6th Army could not move for lack of fuel.

Then, on the sixteenth, Zhukov aimed a masterstroke at Army Group 'B', launching the Voronezh and South-West Army Groups against the Italian 8th Army and the Romanian 3rd Army. By the eighteenth, five Soviet armoured corps were streaming through a huge breach in the Italian front. Manstein was forced to withdraw the 48th Panzer Corps and 6th Panzer Division – the last units that could have gone to the 6th Army's aid – to save the rest of the front.

Last stand in Stalingrad

Paulus and his doomed army had one last role to play: to hold out and pin down as many Russian armies as they could between the Volga and the Don, for as long as they could. Zhukov's offensive successively took all the forward airfields which the *Luftwaffe* would have needed for anything like an effective airlift. Starving, freezing, with ever-dwindling ammunition supplies, the 6th Army fought to the bitter end. On 9 January, Paulus rejected a Russian offer of surrender terms and the last act began with a murderous, concentric series of attacks on the tenth. Pitomnik airfield fell on 14 January, ending German air supplies and casualty evacuation. By the thirty-first the starvation rations had to be reserved for fighting troops alone, not the sick and wounded. Still refusing to let Paulus surrender, Hitler made him a field-marshal because no German field-marshal had ever

surrendered. This one had no choice: he surrendered within twenty-four hours. By 3 February the last flickers of resistance were over.

Aftermath and losses

In its scope, its duration, and its ferocity, Stalingrad was one of the most appalling battles of all time. Only 24,000 casualties and 18,000 irreplaceable specialists were flown out of the pocket; the Russians buried 147,200 dead and took 91,000 prisoners. The Russians themselves admitted to losing 46,700 men in the final battle. They had ringed the pocket with no fewer than seven armies.

Manstein patched up the southern front in an amazing series of flyweight counter-attacks while Army Group 'A' beat a fighting retreat from the Caucasus. By the spring of 1943 the Eastern Front was once more intact – but after the Stalingrad disaster the German Army never mounted such an ambitious offensive again.

Above : After the ordeal, the triumph: the Red Flag flies again over the centre of Stalingrad

CHAPTER SEVENTEEN
IWO JIMA
19th FEBRUARY—26th MARCH 1945

Previous pages : Marines shield their ears from the roar of mobile rocket batteries hammering Japanese positions on Iwo Jima

On Japan's doorstep: five weeks of agony for ten square miles of rock and dust

Background

O N 7 August 1942 American Marines landed on the island of Guadalcanal in the South-West Pacific and one of the most extraordinary phases of the Second World War began: the 'island-hopping' advance across the Pacific Ocean to the very shores of Japan. It was to end just over three years later, when Japan surrendered rather than fight on and face certain invasion.

Nothing on the scale of this gigantic campaign had ever been known in war, and is not likely to be seen again. It spanned distances and posed problems that were both unique in their immensity. In a sense the Pacific campaign was an enormous *blitzkrieg,* the pace of which was naturally slower than that of a land *blitzkrieg* because it was projected onto an area of over nine million square miles. For all that, the American re-conquest of the Pacific was very like a land *blitzkrieg.* The Americans did not solemnly besiege every fleck of land between Pearl Harbour and Tokyo, any more than an advancing armoured division mounts a set-piece attack on every village and hamlet in its path.

Just as, in a land *blitzkrieg*, unnecessary bastions of resistance are bypassed while the main attack plunges deep into the enemy's vitals, so vast areas of the Japanese Empire of May 1942 – Malaya, the whole of the Dutch East Indies, the Caroline Archipelago, Formosa – were left untouched to 'wither on the vine' until the end of the war. But other islands and island groups – the Solomons, the Gilberts and Marshals, the Marianas, the Philippines – became the scenes of savage fighting. Either the Americans needed these places as new bases to speed their own advance, or they would have posed too much of a threat if left in Japanese hands. Such a place was the barren lava hump of Iwo Jima in the Bonin Islands, 660 miles south-east of the Japanese mainland, which the Americans were preparing to take in the New Year of 1945.

They knew they were in for a hard and vicious fight, for the long road across the Pacific was studded with blood-soaked milestones testifying to the ferocity of Japanese resistance. At Tarawa in the Gilberts only 176 prisoners had been taken out of a Japanese garrison of 4,836, and most of those prisoners had been Korean labourers. At Saipan in the Marianas, the entire Japanese garrison of 31,629 was wiped out, together with hundreds of Japanese civilians who hurled themselves over the cliffs rather than surrender. On neighbouring Tinian the whole Japanese garrison also died fighting, 9,000 of them. Guam, the third American objective in the Marianas, yielded 1,250 prisoners out of a garrison of 19,500 – but scores of Japanese took to the jungle rather than surrender, and some of them were still coming out over

Below : Hitting the beach. The tortoise hump of Mount Suribachi smokes like a volcano under the American bombardment as the Marines begin their long and weary acquaintanceship with Iwo's barren lava soil

twenty years after the war had finished.

Whatever might happen on Iwo Jima there were no illusions among the attackers: a murderous battle lay ahead, and they knew it. It was the British Field-Marshal Slim who best summed up the unique experience of fighting the Japanese: 'We all talk of fighting to the last man and the last round,' he said. 'The Japanese soldier actually did it.'

Yet the Americans had to have Iwo Jima. They were building up the Marianas as the main base for an all-out bombing offensive against the Japanese homeland, and Iwo, lying squarely on the flight path the bombers would be taking, was needed both as a staging-post for the bombers and as an advanced field for land-based fighter planes. In American hands, Iwo would also complete the security of the Marianas against Japanese air attack.

Iwo's most obvious characteristic seemed to promise the invaders some natural aid. Nearly every Japanese-held island attacked before Iwo had boasted some kind of vegetation beneath which the Japanese, pastmasters of camouflage, cunningly concealed their pillboxes, coastal gun batteries and machine-gun nests; but Iwo was as bald as an egg, a rocky cinder cloaked in black lava dust, with little more than scrubby grass that gave little or no cover.

Shaped like a battered tear-drop five miles long and just over two miles wide at its widest point, Iwo was dominated at its narrow end by the craggy hump of Mount Suribachi, on whose slopes the Americans expected to meet the toughest resistance. For this reason the three US Marine Divisions of Lieutenant-General Holland

M. ('Howling Mad') Smith's assault force were to land side-by-side, as close to Suribachi as the unpromising beaches permitted; push across Iwo's tapering neck to the west coast; take Suribachi, then wheel north and east to comb out the rest of the island.

The Japanese defences

Taken completely unawares by the audacious American forward leap to the Marianas in June 1944, the Japanese had expected the place to fall then and there. 'It was as hazardous as being on a pile of eggs', recalled a staff officer. 'If American forces had invaded Iwo Jima at that time, it could have been occupied in one or two days.' But after the Marianas the American Pacific offensive switched to the liberation of the Philippines, and the Japanese threw themselves into the task of giving Iwo Jima a garrison, weapons, defensive positions – and a totally new defensive strategy.

The Japanese plan to defend Iwo was a startling throw-back to, of all things, First World War trench fighting – as seen from the German, defending, side. As there was no place to hide on the surface from the crushing American fire-power (naval, air and ground weapons), the defenders had to operate underground. A maze of narrow tunnels was dug, connecting hundreds of strong points and foxholes. As the attackers spotted, say, a sniper and moved in to deal with him, the sniper could vanish down the appropriate tunnel, scuttle *forward* beneath the oncoming attackers, then pop up from an unobserved foxhole and shoot them down from the rear. By the end of January 1945 this system was nearing completion

Above : 'Devil's breath on hell's island' is the sonorous caption to this US Marine Corps picture, showing a brace of flame-throwers burning out a Japanese strong point at Suribachi's foot

Left : Not dead, just sleeping – a war dog handler takes a nap on Iwo in a scraped-out trench. War dogs were one way of detecting Japanese infiltrating the American positions

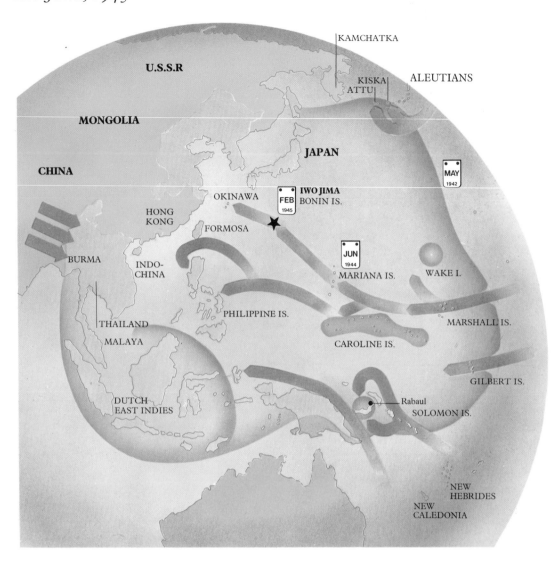

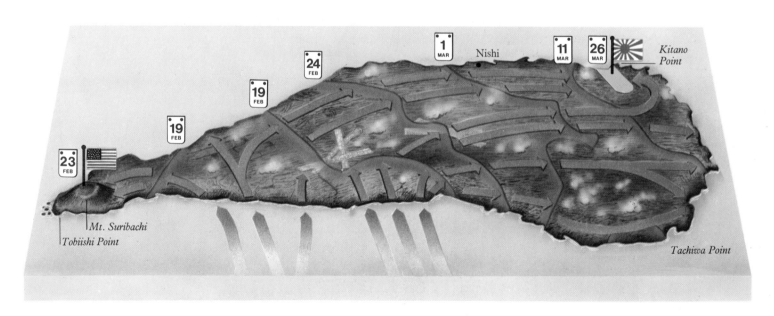

Top :
How Iwo Jima fitted into the America strategy in the Pacific. After the fall of the Marianas there was a pause while new airfields were built there for the bombing of Japan. The Philippines were the next big American objective, and by the time they turned on Iwo in February 1945 the Japanese were ready

Above : How the Marines took Iwo Jima – a long, bloody struggle for a fly-speck of land

and Major-General Kuribayashi's garrison had been reinforced to a strength of 21,000: 15,500 army and 5,500 navy troops. By D-Day – 19 February 1945 – this had been raised slightly to 23,000.

Assault

Beginning in November and December 1944, the Americans had carried out seventy-two days of air and naval bombardment to soften up Iwo – the longest and heaviest air bombardment of the entire Pacific War – culminating in three days' non-stop bombardment by the warships of the Pacific Fleet. On the morning of D-Day, the bombardment ships moved to 1,000 yards offshore and opened fire, laying down a classic advancing or 'creeping' barrage of the best First World War vintage to precede the waves of landing-craft as they headed inshore. Waiting for them, deliberately silent, were over 120 guns of over 75-mm, 300 anti-aircraft guns of over 35-mm, 20,000 rifles and machine-guns (with more than twenty-two million rounds), 130 howitzers, 20 mortars, 70 rocket-guns and 60 anti-tank guns.

The Japanese plan was to hold fire until just after the leading troops had landed on the beach, which they did at 9.02 a.m., the object being not to open fire too early and call down American counter-bombardment on the Japanese positions. By waiting until the Marines were virtually on top of them, the Japanese hoped to inhibit the American counter-bombardment plan and wipe out the troops in the first wave anyway. Unfortunately for the Japanese, this stratagem only allowed the Marines to land all the vital equipment and weapons they needed to move straight into action against the nearest Japanese positions. Within an hour-and-a-half of the first landing all eight assault battalions had secured their foothold, the tanks and artillery were coming ashore, and the drive across the neck of the island had begun. By nightfall on 19 February 1945 30,000 Marines had fought their way ashore and inland off the beaches and the leading elements had even reached the sea on Iwo's west coast.

Suribachi falls . . .

On the twentieth, the left-flanking fifth Marine Division wheeled left and ground its way towards the foot of Mount Suribachi, the first objective. In the bitter fighting over the next three days

Suribachi's squat hump smoked like a volcano as the battle raged ever upwards across its slopes; but at 10.20 a.m. on 23 February the first American patrol fought their way onto the summit and raised the American flag. (Shortly afterwards they had to do it again for the camera and one of the most famous, if slightly bogus, photographs of the war resulted.) But the fall of Suribachi was only the prelude to the most agonizing phase of the battle: the Marines' step-by-step clearance of the island's termite-like defences.

Above : Casualty evacuation – a 'walking wounded' is brought aboard a landing-craft for the trip out to the hospital ship. The Japanese garrison, totally isolated, enjoyed no such facilities

. . . and the real battle begins

None of the Marines had ever seen anything like it: in one sector, measuring no more than 1,000 yards by 200 yards, they counted no fewer than 800 separate strong points. Hills had been hollowed out to accommodate the defenders; the front of a dusty hummock would slide away to reveal a black hole and a blazing gun muzzle. Time and again the Japanese deliberately let the Marines walk straight onto their positions, or even straight past. Japanese morale was sky high and most of the garrison had cheerfully sworn to kill ten

Marines apiece before dying themselves.

The agonizing drive to the north was concisely if ruefully summed up by an Intelligence officer of the 4th Marine Division, which was advancing on the right-flank sector:

The enemy remains below ground in his maze of tunnels throughout our preliminary artillery fire. When the fire ceases he pushes OPs [observation posts] out of the entrances not demolished by our fire. Then, choosing a suitable exit, he moves as many men and weapons to the surface as he can, often as close as 75 yards from our front. As our troops advance toward this point he delivers all the fire at his disposal, rifle, machine-gun and mortar. When he has inflicted sufficient casualties to pin down our advance he then withdraws through his underground tunnels most of his forces, possibly leaving a few machine-gunners and mortars. . . . When the hot spot is overrun we find a handful of dead Japs and few if any enemy weapons. While this is happening, the enemy has repeated the process and another sector of our advance is engaged in a vicious fire fight. And so the cycle continues. . . .

On the Japanese side

With any other troops but Japanese, the slow but relentless American advance, inevitably breaking up the defenders' cohesion, would have caused growing confusion among them and accelerated the inevitable result. Necessarily out of touch with an increasing number of his units, General Kuribayashi never had to worry about this: his men continued to fight superbly. He kept up a stream of signal bulletins to the staff on Chichi Jima, recording the course of the gruelling battle as best he could.

'Troops at Tamanayama and northern districts still holding positions', he reported buoyantly on 8 March. 'Fighting spirit, believing in country's victory, looks god-like.' Two hours later: 'Am very sorry I have let the enemy occupy one part of Japanese territory, but am taking comfort in inflicting great damage on enemy.' Ten days later, with the writing clearly on the wall, Kuribayashi issued an Order of the Day to 'all surviving officers and men'. 'Battle situation come to last moment. I want surviving officers and men to go out and attack enemy until the last. You have devoted yourselves to the Emperor. Do not think of yourselves. I am always at the head of you all.'

Kuribayashi was as good as his word. At the head of a group of 400 Army and Navy troops he moved from cave to cave, keeping his flow of signals to Chichi Jima as constant as he could. On 17 March, the listeners on Chichi Jima thought he had gone and were delighted when he came through again on the twenty-first. 'Are continuing to fight. Have 400 men under my control. Enemy besieged us and on eighteenth and nineteenth approached us by shelling and flamethrowers from tanks. Are trying to approach entrance to cave with explosives.' At last, on the twenty-third, came the last flicker of communication from Iwo's commander: 'To all officers and men of Chichi Jima. Good-bye. . . .'

The last days

The Marines had broken through to the north-east coast of the island on 9 March – eighteen days after the first landing – but so intense was the resistance that the island was not officially declared secure until 16 March. Kuribayashi's last messages to Chichi Jima over the next week were coming from a shrinking pocket, barely one mile square, at the island's northern tip. Three days after his final farewell to Chichi Jima the last burst of resistance was made in the form of a suicide *Banzai* charge, 300 men strong. The Marines did not finish mopping up until the twenty-seventh.

Aftermath and losses

The Marines took only 1,083 survivors of Iwo Jima's garrison of 23,000, most of them too badly wounded to continue fighting or preferring to take their own lives rather than surrender. The Marines' own casualties came to a horrific 6,821 killed – losses that made the casualties of 'Bloody Tarawa' in the Gilberts, back in November 1943, look almost insignificant.

The fact that so many good troops had been killed in taking a mere eight square miles of Japanese homeland had the most resounding effects on world history. The casualties suffered on Iwo, the bloodiest battle of the Pacific war, made the Allied strategists wince at the prospect of what would happen when the time came to land on the Japanese mainland. Any alternative prospect of bringing the war to a speedy end seemed preferable. The fall of Iwo Jima pointed the first invisible finger at Hiroshima and Nagasaki.

Below : 'Old Glory' is raised on Suribachi's summit. One of the most famous photographs of the century, it was in fact taken just after the first flag was raised. But instead of signifying American victory on Iwo, the capture of Suribachi only ushered in the most bitter phase of the conflict

The French paras were dropped as live bait, confident in their fire-power – but the Viet Minh had more

Background

THE French defeat at Dien Bien Phu in May 1954 is one of the most notorious single failures of twentieth-century regular troops to defeat irregular nationalist insurgents. But it is also one of the most misunderstood battles of the post-war era, cloaked with vague but sinister overtones.

Like Saratoga in the American War of Independence, the strategy behind Dien Bien Phu was an attempt to pin down and destroy patriot insurgents – not, this time, by marching through the insurgents' territory, but by air-landing a force so far from friendly territory that the insurgents would be 'lured to the honeypot' to meet their doom. This plan did not fail because the opposition came up with a brilliant counterstroke; it failed because the opposition did precisely what it was supposed to do, only in overwhelming strength.

When French forces returned to Indo-China in 1946 after France's resumption of colonial powers, the Vietnamese nationalists were already an organized force under their leader, Ho Chi Minh, thanks to their guerrilla operations against the Japanese in the war. Ho rejected France's recognition of Vietnam as a 'free state' with the other members of the Indo-Chinese Federation (Laos and Cambodia) while remaining within the French Union; he

held out for nothing less than the total independence of Vietnam, and, in practice, the extension of Vietnamese authority over the rest of French Indo-China. His politico-military communist army, the Viet Minh, was led by a man now accepted as the Moltke of guerrilla warfare, Vo Nguyen Giap, who commanded about 50,000 men in 1946. To break the Viet Minh the French originally sent 40,000 regular troops, all seasoned veterans.

The French dilemma was that they could never increase their forces to match the pace at which Giap built up the Viet Minh, with extensive military aid from Communist China and the USSR, from early 1950; but at the same time the strategies used against the Viet Minh demanded extremely high manpower on the part of the French. The overall strategy was simple: to make it impossible for the Viet Minh to operate at will in Indo-China. The two main bases were Hanoi in the north and Saigon in the south. From these two bases the French would have regularly and minutely to comb thousands of square miles of mountain and jungle if they were to achieve their aim of keeping the Viet Minh as permanent fugitives, and they simply lacked the manpower to do it.

Lacking manpower, the French relied on mobility and fire-power as substitutes – the mobility being provided by control of the air, and the fire-power by weaponry that was superior to that of the Viet Minh only until Giap's men started receiving aid from China and the USSR. When the Viet Minh added fire-power to their superiority in manpower the French stood little chance – but the French had no way of discovering this without enduring a head-on conflict.

Limited airborne operations against specific targets – reported Viet Minh concentration areas and supply dumps – had given the French a string of extremely promising successes by 1953. A good example was Operation 'Lorraine' in November 1952, in which 2,354 French paratroops dropped at Phu Doan and cleaned out all the supply dumps that Giap was building up for a large-scale operation in Laos. 'Hirondelle', in July 1953, was even more successful, the French paratroops seizing and destroying stocks of

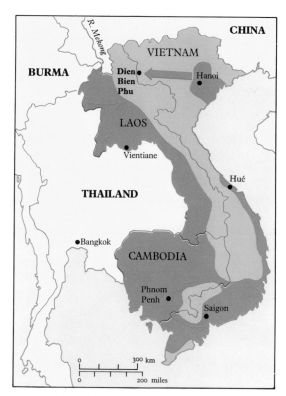

accumulated Viet Minh stores and ammunition north of Lang Son and Loc Binh.

But the success of operations like 'Lorraine' and 'Hirondelle' had a most baneful effect on French strategic thinking. They left an impression that the Viet Minh could be kept perpetually off balance by the use of airborne forces which, coupled with Giap's refusal to engage in a stand-up fight after earlier localized defeats, eventually produced the strategy for the disastrous experiment of Dien Bien Phu.

The 'Castor' plan

'Castor' was the joint brainchild of General René Cogny, C.-in-C. Tongking province, and General Henri Navarre, C.-in-C. Indo-China. They agreed that the main objective for 1953-4 must be to prevent Giap from extending Viet Minh operations into Laos. 'Lorraine' and 'Hirondelle', short-term in-and-out airborne attacks, had yielded only temporary relief. Now the French would implant an airborne army deep into Giap's supply lines, a powerful irritant which he could not ignore. This, it was hoped, would bring on the longed-for direct confrontation in which French fire-power would win hands down and open 1954 with a crushing defeat of the Viet Minh.

The location selected for this 'land/air base' was Dien Bien Phu, a small village on the Nam Youm river only eighty miles from the Chinese border. The village lay in a long valley some ten miles long, the floor of which was studded with bumps of high ground suitable for conversion into strong points. Just to the north of Dien Bien Phu itself was a mouldering airstrip of Second World War vintage which, once cleared, would make for easy supply. The whole valley was ringed with hills between 1,400 and 1,800 feet high.

The 'Castor' plan was flawed by several fatal oversights and assumptions. It failed to take note of the fact that every French success had been won with hit-and-run tactics, not hit-and-stay tactics. It overlooked the mist and rains of the Nam Youm valley that could make accurate and regular delivery of supplies and reinforcements extremely problematical. Above all it assumed that when the Viet Minh took the bait, they would lack anti-aircraft guns with which to savage French supply flights, and artillery with which to hammer the French strong points from the surrounding hills.

The trap is laid

The 'Castor' plan was put into operation on 20 November 1953, three French paratroop battalions landing on the old airfield and chasing off the two Viet Minh companies training in the area. The Viet Minh predictably melted away before the impressive fire-power dropped to support the paratroops: two batteries of 75-mm recoilless guns and a platoon of 81-mm mortars; the paratroops pushed north and south, meeting no opposition; and from 24 November the airfield was fit to receive air-landed reinforcements to bring the air base up to full strength.

The build-up went on through December, January and February – four battalions

Left : The strategy behind the Dien Bien Phu drop was to stop the Viet Minh from extending their operations into Laos. The French (*blue*) at Dien Bien Phu were to lure the Viet Minh to destruction by the French superiority in fire-power – but it was the Viet Minh, not the French, who turned out to have the superiority

Below : Vietnamese colonial troops take shelter from Viet Minh mortar fire north of Dien Bien Phu

Dien Bien Phu, 1953–4

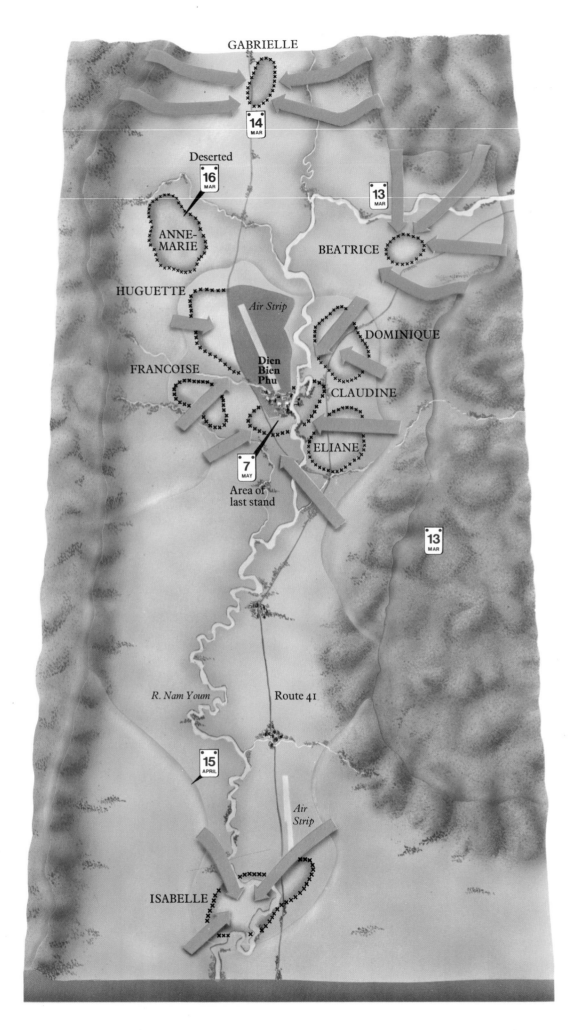

GABRIELLE

14 MAR

Deserted

16 MAR

13 MAR

ANNE-MARIE

BEATRICE

HUGUETTE

Air Strip

DOMINIQUE

FRANCOISE

Dien Bien Phu

CLAUDINE

ELIANE

7 MAY

Area of last stand

13 MAR

15 APRIL

R. Nam Youn

Route 41

Air Strip

ISABELLE

Right: The French positions around Dien Bien Phu, each of which could be – and was – tackled in isolation by the Viet Minh (*orange*). On the ground, the French stood no chance without unchallenged control of the air – and the solid chain of Viet Minh AA guns ringing the valley was a key element in the battle. The French garrison was far too weak to break out of its inner perimeter and loosen the stranglehold which the Viet Minh maintained from their positions on the heights.

of the Foreign Legion, a battalion of Moroccan *Tirailleurs,* of non-Communist Vietnamese and Thai infantry. There was a sapper battalion, three catering units and a transport company consisting of 127 vehicles – trucks, jeeps, and ambulances. A small tactical air force of five fighter-bombers operated from the airfield, and there were four C-47 transport planes and a helicopter for evacuating casualties. To crown this impressive achievement, the French flew in ten M24 Chaffee light tanks ; and by March 1954 the garrison of Dien Bien Phu had risen to 10,133 men.

The village and airstrip were ringed by five defensive positions forming a circle one-and-a-half miles across : in clockwise order 'Dominique', 'Eliane', 'Claudine', 'Françoise' and 'Huguette'. North of this inner circle lay a northward-pointing triangle of outer positions, 'Anne-Marie', 'Béatrice' and 'Gabrielle'; and the southernmost strong point, 'Isabelle', lay three miles south of the village. All in all, the defence complex built up at Dien Bien Phu resembled a long slim oval, stretching nine miles from 'Gabrielle' to 'Isabelle' and two miles across at its widest point, between the outer perimeters of 'Anne-Marie' and 'Béatrice'.

This was the spiky bait which Giap was expected to swallow. He was in fact planning to do so – with five Viet Minh infantry divisions and one artillery division, 70,000 men in all. The Viet Minh troops were backed up by a great force of 60,000 male and female auxiliaries, devoted patriot natives detailed to build roads and hump ammunition and supplies along those roads once built. Giap's fire-power was overwhelming: 144 field guns of 105-mm and 75-mm, 48 120-mm mortars and 30 75-mm recoilless guns. On their way were 12 six-barrelled rocket launchers, Soviet 'Katyushas', that on arrival were dug into deep firing positions with narrow slits, and which the French gunners were to find virtually impossible to hit.

Up on the heights ringing Dien Bien Phu the Viet Minh built up a ring of anti-aircraft guns, over 180 strong, with calibres ranging from 12.7-cm to 37-mm – a flak barrage greater than the anti-aircraft defences of the Ruhr in the Second World War. Such was the opposition preparing to assault the garrison of Dien Bien Phu by the end of the second week of March 1954. The French airborne strategists had hoped to lure a muscle-bound yokel to his doom; what they found was something of a Frankenstein monster.

Giap waited until his forces had swelled to a superiority of eight to one over the French, then fixed D-Day for 12 March.

The Viet Minh attack

Giap opened his offensive with the one

Dien Bien Phu complex had suffered a humiliating defeat – and the Viet Minh had inflicted losses of seventy-five per cent.

Braving the flak that streamed up from the surrounding heights, another air-borne paratroop battalion, the 5th Vietnamese, was dropped into the perimeter on 14 March – but these reinforcements had barely familiarized themselves with their new surroundings before the Viet Minh attacked again at 6 p.m. This time their objective was the northernmost strong point, 'Gabrielle', held by a battalion of Algerian *Tirailleurs* and Legion mortar troops. After a desperate night's battle against impossible odds – the Viet Minh threw eight battalions into the attack – 'Gabrielle' went the way of 'Béatrice', with only one strong-point holding out at dawn. Eager to avenge the shame of the previous night's defeat, two Foreign Legion companies counter-attacked with a battalion of Vietnamese paratroops and six of the Chaffee tanks, extricating the last 150 men of 'Gabrielle's' garrison.

Frantic reinforcements

After these spectacular opening successes the Viet Minh held their hand for an uneasy fortnight, digging cover trenches to get as close as possible to the remaining French strong points before the next attack, while the defenders of Dien Bien Phu frantically set about strengthening their own defences. Almost at once, however, the garrison suffered another setback. On the night of 16-17 March the 3rd Thai Battalion, posted in 'Anne-Marie', deserted the position. This mass defection triggered off a number of desertions by North African and Vietnamese soldiers who slipped away from their posts and hid along the banks of the Nam Youm river.

More reinforcements were dropped into the perimeter between 16 and 27 March: Lt.-Col. Bigeard's 6th Battalion of Colonial Paratroops, together with a field hospital and staff. These reinforcements included 400 volunteers who were making their first jump – ample proof, if any were needed, of the severity of Dien Bien Phu's plight. Unable to open out the perimeter and deploy their fire-power as planned, hemmed in by a largely invisible enemy, menaced at every turn by the Viet Minh guns – there was no longer any serious chance of tipping the battle the way the French wanted it to go, let alone any conviction that it was the Viet Minh who were being lured to their doom.

Above: Emergency air cover, though short-lived, for the trapped garrison. These are Curtiss Helldivers from the carrier *Arromanches*, resting on an emergency airstrip before making the long and perilous flight inland to Dien Bien Phu. They were not enough: only a permanent 'cab-rank' of ground-attack aircraft would have stood a chance of pinning down the Viet Minh

Below: French 105-mm howitzer crew in one of the Dien Bien Phu strong points. As with the Germans over Stalingrad, French propaganda waxed confident about the course of the battle. 'Three thousand Viets were left on the barbed wire,' boasts the caption to this picture. 'Reinforcements have been parachuted and the following days spent in violent artillery duels.' But the French artillery proved quite unable to destroy the Viet Minh artillery in its positions

thing the French had never expected to encounter: a pulverizing long-range artillery bombardment, raging throughout the twelfth and thirteenth and – a grim lesson of what the Viet Minh had already accomplished with their preparations and deployment – destroying two of the C-47s and a fighter-bomber on the airstrip. Then, at 5.15 p.m., the Viet Minh swarmed forward for their first direct confrontation, selecting the 'Béatrice' strong point as their target for attack. This was held by a battalion of the Foreign Legion, 800 strong, and was totally cut off by the assault. By 9 p.m. the French headquarters in Dien Bien Phu could contact only one position in 'Béatrice' and by midnight this, too, had gone. Only 200 shaken survivors managed to struggle through the Viet Minh lines and rejoin the main garrison. Within forty-eight hours of the first gun opening fire, the impregnable

The April fighting

The second phase of Giap's offensive was heralded on the night of 30 March, when his engineers triggered off a mine which tunnellers had placed beneath 'Eliane's' perimeter. This was followed by the resumption of the artillery bombardment and an attack by two Viet Minh divisions against both 'Eliane' and 'Dominique'. A four-day battle ensued, punctuated with repeated attacks and counter-attacks. Then, on 2 April, another Viet Minh division attacked 'Huguette'. Dien Bien Phu's defences were now being squeezed by a converging attack on three fronts, but Bigeard staved off total disaster by leading desperate counter-attacks. For the first and only time since the battle started, a glimmer of the original French strategy was realized: the Viet Minh fell back, having suffered enormous casualties.

The last reinforcements

Having survived the crisis of 30 March–2 April by the skin of their teeth, the garrison received what would prove to be their last reinforcements: another two companies of the Foreign Legion and two more battalions of Colonial Paratroops, bringing the number of paratroop battalions in the perimeter up to seven.

Throughout April, Giap was building up for what he planned to be the final attack. He had urgent political reasons for wanting to bring the battle to a close with a triumphant finale, because on 26 April the Geneva Conference on the Far East opened. The attention of the world was now focused on Dien Bien Phu; if the siege dragged on through the debate on Indo-China, scheduled for 8 May, the non-Communist powers were bound to insist on a cease-fire and thus let the French extricate the garrison. But if Ho Chi Minh's representatives went to the conference table with a resounding victory fresh in their pockets the prospects would be very different indeed.

The last stand

Giap's final attack opened on 1 May to the familiar pattern: a numbing bombardment followed by a dense infantry attack by night. Once again it was a blow at the heart, aimed at the strong points of 'Claudine', 'Dominique' and 'Eliane'. By now, however, the French were down to three days'

rations and their ammunition was also fast running out, but they managed to beat off their tormentors until the sixth. Then Giap played his trump card and turned the 'Katyusha' rocket launchers loose on the battered and rapidly shrinking perimeter of the French garrison, which by dawn on the seventh was down to a rough oblong half-a-mile square.

As the Viet Minh came in for the kill, Bigeard counter-attacked for the last time, with the last surviving tank – commanded by a wounded officer who had had the plaster casts cut from his arms to allow him to join the crew. The final pockets of resistance fell piecemeal, like the squares of the Old Guard at Waterloo – there never was a formal surrender. When the Geneva Conference turned its attention to Vietnam on the following day, the Viet Minh delegates could display their victory to a shocked world.

Aftermath and losses

At its peak, the Dien Bien Phu garrison numbered 16,554 men, of whom more than 3,000 were killed in the fighting and another 10,000 vanished during the march into captivity and Communist 're-education'. A bare 3,000 survivors remained. The price the Viet Minh had had to pay was light: 8,000 dead and 15,000 wounded for the victory that won that stage of the war. On 2 June the French and Viet Minh in Geneva began talks on a cease-fire that would lead to the recognition of North Vietnam – born, like the State of Israel, in battle.

Below : Approaching the end: a grim-faced Algerian carries away the body of a dead comrade

CHAPTER NINETEEN
THE SIX-DAY WAR
5th–10th JUNE 1967

Never have so many been beaten by so few, in so little time

Background

THE Six-Day War of June 1967 is natural ammunition for the wishful argument that 'violence never settles anything'. It was the third joint Arab attempt in twenty years to wipe the state of Israel off the map. Like its predecessors, it was an utter failure. It saw Israel claw great chunks of territory from her three assailants, and it did absolutely nothing to diminish the crackling tensions of the Middle East. The war was, in short, a latter-day parable of the futility of battle. In itself it was military perfection under a glass case, the model *blitzkrieg* as it should be fought – yet failing to yield, as decisive victories are supposed to, a lasting peace for the victor.

Tell an Israeli, however, that 'violence never settles anything' and he might well retort that violence settled the fate of six million of his people in the Second World War, and that the survivors and heirs of the Holocaust are never going to forget it, let alone meekly acquiesce in their own destruction. In 1948–9 and 1956 they shattered their enemies and kept their young nation in being; in 1967 they had to do it again. No matter that the war brought no lasting peace; the State of Israel had survived again, and for Israelis that was more than enough.

When the Second World War ended, attempts to share out Palestine between the Jews and the Arabs were doomed to failure as far as pleasing both parties were concerned – the thing could not be done. Up until the Six-Day War, Israel's frontiers were the ones her army had hammered out during the War of Independence in 1948, and they could hardly have been weaker. Every natural feature favoured the Arabs in their ceaseless but unco-ordinated attempts to pressurize Israel out of existence.

From 1949 to 1967, four-fifths of Israel's territory lay within range of Arab medium artillery – a sobering fact for outsiders to remember. Comparatively low-lying, Israel's straggling boundaries were ringed by commanding heights, all held by hostile Arabs. From the north-east, Syria menaced the upper Jordan valley from the forty-mile-long Golan Plateau. Jordan's hold on the West Bank of the river formed a bulging salient that pinched Israel into a ten-mile-wide wasp waist; north of Tel Aviv, Jordanian guns could land their shells right into the Mediterranean. From the south-west, Egypt could inflict a triple bite on Israel. The Gaza Strip on the Mediterranean coast jutted nearly thirty miles into Israeli territory; the long desert frontier between the Gaza Strip and the Gulf of Akaba offered ready access on a 220-mile front; and Eilat, Israel's lone port at the head of the Gulf of Akaba, could be totally blockaded by Egypt from Sharm-el-Sheikh and the Tiran Straits at the southern end of the Gulf.

These appalling strategic weaknesses were coupled with persistent Arab harass-

Previous pages : A column of Israeli jeeps packing anti-tank recoilless guns reaches the Mount of Olives in Jerusalem

Below left : A hummock of camouflage net in the Negev desert conceals an AA gun on the Sinai Front

Below right : Wiped out on a desert airfield – what was left of an Egyptian MIG after the crushing Israeli attacks from the air. The charred barrels of the fighter's guns can be seen amid the wreckage at centre left

Above: Vigilance: an Israeli patrol aboard a personnel carrier, with the ever-present menace of Arab-controlled mountains dominating the skyline

ment in the form of artillery and rocket bombardments, and terrorist infiltration which has plagued Israel throughout her existence. All this, however, had the profoundest effects on the creation from scratch of Israel's armed forces. Her enemies had armies and air forces that bore the stamp of their former colonial masters; Israel had to build an army, an air force and an overall defence strategy tailored to meet perpetual crisis and the spectre of total defeat. As Dr Johnson reminds us, when a man knows that he is to be hanged tomorrow, it concentrates his mind wonderfully.

Israel's policy of launching reprisals for every major instance of Arab harassment produced uniquely close teamwork between the Israeli Air Force and commando, paratroop and small hit-and-run armoured columns, expertise that bore triumphant fruit in the Sinai campaign of 1956 and the Six-Day War of 1967. When faced with a war of aggression by one or all three of her Arab neighbours, Israel's only chance lay in a pre-emptive attack to demolish the developing menace outside her frontiers. But there could be no question of a prolonged war. From a tiny populaton of under 2.5 million Israel could mobilize about 264,000 combatants within seventy-two hours, but only at the cost of suspending the country's normal industrial and commercial life. For Israel, full mobilization was like major surgery without an anaesthetic, and only a lightning operation could save the patient from dying under the surgeon's knife.

Sinai, 1956: the 'Hundred Hours'

When the first trial came in 1956, Israel had the luck to face only one opponent: Egypt. Emboldened by his arms deal with the USSR in September 1955, Nasser planned the conquest of Israel; first by economic strangulation – closing the Suez Canal and Tiran Straits to Israeli shipping, blockading Eilat – and eventually by invasion. For all his posturing as the champion of the Arab League, he was left to do the fighting alone, owing to the self-interest and caution of Jordan and Syria. On 29 October the Israelis struck first, their targets being the Egyptian forces massing on the Sinai frontier. Three columns stabbed west into the Gaza Strip and Sinai peninsula, driving west to join up with the paratroops dropped far in the rear of Nasser's front-line units. Within 100 hours of the commencement of operations, the Israelis had reached the Suez Canal and Sharm-el-Sheikh, lifting the blockade of Eilat and opening the way

The Six-Day War, 1967

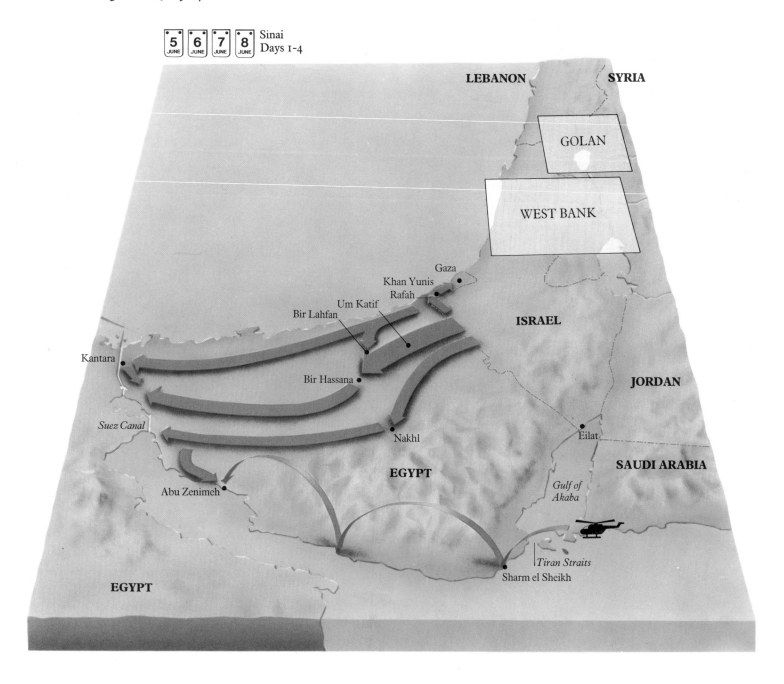

5 JUNE **6** JUNE **7** JUNE **8** JUNE Sinai
Days 1-4

LEBANON SYRIA

GOLAN

WEST BANK

Gaza
Khan Yunis
Rafah
Um Katif
Bir Lahfan
ISRAEL
Kantara
Bir Hassana
JORDAN
Suez Canal
Nakhl
Eilat
SAUDI ARABIA
EGYPT
Gulf of Akaba
Abu Zenimeh
Tiran Straits
EGYPT
Sharm el Sheikh

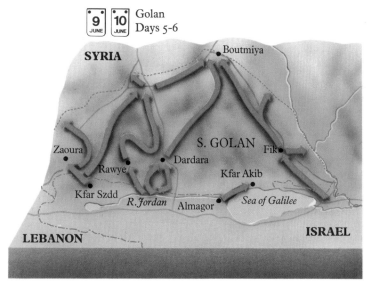

9 JUNE **10** JUNE Golan
Days 5-6

SYRIA
Boutmiya
Zaoura
S. GOLAN
Fik
Rawye
Dardara
Kfar Akib
Kfar Szdd
R. Jordan
Almagor
Sea of Galilee
LEBANON
ISRAEL

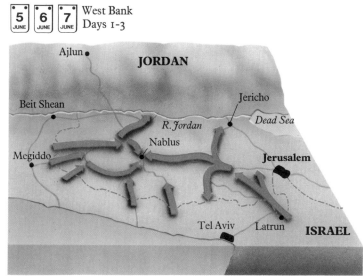

5 JUNE **6** JUNE **7** JUNE West Bank
Days 1-3

Ajlun
JORDAN
Beit Shean
Jericho
Dead Sea
R. Jordan
Nablus
Megiddo
Jerusalem
Tel Aviv
Latrun
ISRAEL

to Cairo – only to be left on their own by the Anglo-French *débâcle* prompted by the Israeli initiative. By the end of January 1957 Israel had reluctantly evacuated Sinai apart from the Gaza Strip, and that followed in March.

The Arab build-up

Over the following ten years, as the USSR continued to rearm Egypt and encourage Nasser in his professed crusade against Israel, the Middle East became a happy hunting-ground for arms salesmen. As a counter-balance to the powerful new Soviet influence in Egypt, and very soon in Syria as well, the USA agreed to the re-inforcement of Israel with Mirage III jets, Mystère and Ouragàn fighter-bombers, Patton, 'Super-Sherman', Centurion and French AMX tanks. In the face of growing solidarity between Egypt and Syria it became increasingly likely that Israel's next raid would be on two fronts, not one, but her strategy remained unchanged. If Egypt was the corner-stone of a daunting new Arab alignment, then Egypt must be the first objective of a pre-emptive

strike. Israel could contemplate a multi-front war of limited duration – provided that her new, all-jet air force could destroy the main Arab air forces at once and guarantee her army air cover and support.

The run-up to the 1967 war was an-nounced by the intensifying of raids by Yasser Arafat's 'Fatah' terrorists, based in Syria and Jordan. These were met with the usual Israeli reprisals, which were shrilly de-nounced by the Arab world and the USSR as Israeli aggression. Throughout May 1967 Nasser built up Egyptian forces in the Sinai peninsular and pressurised the United Nations Emergency Force buffer troops, which had patrolled the frontier since 1957, out of the Gaza Strip and Sharm-el-Sheikh. Finally he not only announced another closure of the Tiran Straits (23 May) but demanded that Israel give up Eilat as well. After another tense week in which it became quite clear that the USA was going to do nothing to help Israel by exerting diplomatic or any other kind of pressure, on the night of 3 June 1967 the Israeli Cabinet voted for war. D-Day would be in forty-eight hours, on the morning of the fifth.

Above: Israeli spearhead – a 'Super-Sherman' tank with supporting motorized infantry

Opposite: The three-stage course of the Six-Day War – Sinai/Jordan/Golan Heights, with airlifted Israeli combat teams completing the occupation of the Sinai coastline. If Nasser's dream of a united Arab world, combining to wipe Israel off the map, had proved anything but illusory, Israel would probably have gone under in 1967. As it turned out, Israel never had to worry about a tightly co-ordinated Arab war strategy and was able to tackle her three enemies piecemeal from the moment her forces seized the initiative

Above : After the exhausting but decisive battles of the first 48 hours, Israeli Centurion tank crews enjoy their first rest. One of the most demanding actions was at Um Katif on the Sinai sector, where formidable Egyptian defences were not cleared until noon on the second day. In every tank-versus-tank encounter, however, superior Israeli tactics and marksmanship proved decisive

Overture, Day One: Israel's air blitz

The objective of Brigadier Hod, Israel's air force commander, was to destroy the Egyptian air force on the ground. He accomplished this by waiting until the Egyptian MiG-21s had flown their normal dawn patrols and returned to base. He then sent in massed Israeli air strikes to hit simultaneously at 7.45 a.m.

As a bonus, Field-Marshal Amer, the Egyptian air force commander, was airborne when the Israelis struck; his plane was unable to land for an hour-and-a-half, depriving the Egyptian air force of orders from the top during its fiery but brief annihilation. By the time Amer was able to command he no longer had an air force; after savaging seventeen airfields the Israeli pilots had wiped out nearly 300 of the Egyptian aircraft.

Mendacious claims of victory in the air on the part of the Egyptians prompted the intervention of Jordan and Syria, and after a brief rest to refuel and rearm, the Israeli pilots repeated their triumph against Jordanian and Syrian airfields shortly after noon. One strike sufficed for each air force, raising the tally of Arab aircraft destroyed on Day One to 374 'certs' and 34 'possibles'. Israeli losses were limited to 18. It was the quickest, most complete victory in the history of air warfare; by nightfall on 5 June, unchallenged in the air, the Israelis could concentrate on giving full air support to their ground forces.

The first forty-eight hours – Sinai and West Bank

The first two days of the war saw the Israelis run into spirited Egyptian and Jordanian resistance, with the Arab troops confident and fighting determinedly from their defensive positions. They believed the lies they were told about their own aircraft, actually non-existent long before noon on Day One, being engaged to the hilt over Israel, and looked forward confidently to enjoying full air support on the morrow. When, on Day Two, all the Arabs got were savage Israeli air strikes and increasingly effective ground attacks, their morale began to wilt rapidly from the top down. Brave, devoted, well-equipped yet atrociously led, the Arab troops of the Six-Day War deserved far better officers than they had.

For their part the Israeli strike forces – normally consisting of an armoured brigade and a brigade of mechanized infantry – had the resilience not to be fought to a halt by the resistance they ran into. They worked to broad overall directives, not minutely-detailed operational plans like the Arab forces. (For this the Arabs had their Soviet advisers to thank.) The Israeli forté was improvisation, bypassing, refusing to squander their strength against unexpected cores of resistance, generally keeping the battle moving until their aircraft could enter the fray and the vital breakthroughs were achieved.

On Day One the Tal strike force attacked

the Gaza Strip and overran the Egyptian defences round Rafah, but failed either to reduce the Strip itself or break out to the west through Jiradi. The Yoffe strike force, driving west into Sinai close to the south, advanced painfully twenty-five miles through loose desert sand only to be halted at Bir Lafhan as evening came on. The Sharon strike group came up against formidable Egyptian defences at Um Katif, barely ten miles over the frontier, and it took the Israelis until noon on Day Two to clean out its strong points and trenches.

For the Israelis, the Jordan front remained of secondary importance until victory was secure in Sinai, and the opening moves on the Jerusalem-West Bank sector came from the Jordanians in the form of artillery and mortar bombardments late in the morning of Day One. Initial Israeli moves against Jordan were limited, concentrating on taking out the forward Jordanian artillery. On Day Two they stepped up their attacks, taking the Latrun Salient and surrounding Jerusalem, driving deeper into Samaria from the north. Like the Egyptians, the Jordanians fought well; their worst enemy was the pessimism of their C.-in-C., General Riad.

By nightfall on Day Two, the Egyptians and Jordanians had completely failed to deprive the Israelis of the initiative on the Gaza, Sinai or West Bank-Jerusalem fronts. The Israeli strike groups had broken open all the forward Arab positions and had forced the Arab generals to accept that withdrawal was inevitable. The Syrians, who had undertaken to come to

Below : A summit of emotion reached by the victors of few other wars in history – Israeli troops by the Wailing Wall in Jerusalem

Jordan's aid, had done precisely nothing, reinforcing Jordan's rapidly-growing sense of insecurity and improving Israel's chances for further advances towards the Jordan river.

Day Three: the flood breaks loose

On Day Three the Israelis exploited the successful break-in on the Sinai front achieved during the first two days. They surged forward on all three of their main axes, pushing along the coastal, central and southern lines of advance into central Sinai, relentlessly keeping up the pressure and denying the Egyptians any respite in which to turn and make a stand on their third defence line. By nightfall, the leading Israeli units were all within twenty-five miles of the Suez Canal.

Above all else, however, Day Three – 7 June 1967 – marked the total collapse of resistance on the Jordanian front and gave both the State of Israel and international Jewry one of the most glorious dates in their history. For it was on Day Three that Israeli troops stormed into the City of Jerusalem and reached the Wailing Wall, and this was the emotional climax of the war. Aggressive advances by the Israeli columns probed inwards and joined up; by the afternoon the fleeing Jordanians were thinking only of making a stand on the east bank of the Jordan. More than content with the capture of the whole of the Jordanian left bank, the triumphant Israelis halted along the line of the river. By the afternoon of Day Four a cease-fire had been accepted.

Day Four: the end in Sinai

Penned into a ribbon of territory twenty-five miles wide on the east bank of the Suez Canal, the Egyptians tried to make a stand on Day Four in order to pass maximum troops and *matériel* back into the Egyptian mainland. Some of the most intense tank-versus-tank fighting took place on this day, with over 1,000 tanks taking part on both sides – but again the expertise of the Israeli tank crews and unremitting air attacks carried the day. The Northern strike force was the first to reach the Canal (about 8 p.m.), at Kantara, followed by the Tal and Yoffe strike forces between 2 a.m. and 3 a.m. on the Fifth Day. Racing to reach the Suez Canal before a cease-fire could be concluded, few of the Israeli armoured units got there with more than thirty per cent of their full strength, owing to breakdowns and lack of fuel. The pace had been terrific; men and machines had been pushed to the limit of endurance – but nonetheless the Fourth Day of the war brought the Sinai campaign of 1967 to a triumphant conclusion for the Israelis.

Days Five and Six: storming the Golan Heights

With morale sky-high at having eliminated any further danger from two out of their three Arab foes, the Israelis assaulted the formidable Syrian positions on the Golan Heights. Their objective was to keep the assault moving on as wide a front as possible, any limited breakthrough being extremely vulnerable to Syrian counter-attack. Huge air strikes and superb teamwork on the ground between sappers, infantry and tank crews won the Israelis a five-mile-wide bridgehead by the evening of Day Five, and by 11 a.m. on Day Six the Syrian Command on the Golan, paralysed by the breadth of the Israeli offensive, had lost control of the battle. By 6.30 p.m., when a cease-fire came into force, Israeli troops had occupied every commanding feature on the Golan.

Aftermath and losses

In the six days Israel had overrun about 26,000 square miles of Arab territory in an offensive war on three fronts, their losses being an absurdly low 778 killed, 2,586 wounded and 21 captured (five of these were killed by Arab mobs). Official Arab figures have never been released but are estimated to have been about 15,000 killed and 53,000 wounded. The three Arab countries lost over 400 aircraft and about 1,000 tanks.

Buffers of occupied territory now surrounded the state of Israel, but the humiliation of her enemies was soon dispelled by lavish Soviet aid. The guerilla war continued, with Lebanon as the main base. Israel now had to administer 1,385,000 Arabs; before the war only 300,000 Arabs had been living in Israel. The Six-Day War, unforgettable victory though it was, created as many problems as it temporarily solved for Israel. Six years and three months later, Israel was fighting once more for her life in the War of Yom Kippur.

THE BATTLE OF THE FUTURE

'*Maybe someday they'll get everything nice and tidy and we'll have that thing we sing about, when "we ain't a-gonna study war no more." Maybe. Maybe the same day the leopard will take off his spots and get a job as a Jersey cow, too.*'

So speaks the soldier hero of Robert Heinlein's *Starship Troopers*, a deeply disturbing novel of interstellar war. As a prophecy it seems sound enough, for wars continue and will continue to be fought round the globe. All attempts to bring about a genuine world peace through international co-operation have proved useless. Despite the awful lessons of two world wars, of Hiroshima and of Nagasaki there is still every chance of the ruin of the northern hemisphere in a conventional and thermonuclear Third World War.

One fact, however, is crystal-clear : there will never be another self-contained battle between the armies or groups of armies of two nations preceded by march and counter-march, the two sides groping for a convenient battle-ground on which to fight, the mutual drawing-up of lines of battle, and an engagement ending with one side beaten and chased from the battlefield by the victors. For the face of battle was changed for ever by the First World War, which replaced the conflict of rival international groups of armies, expanding battle zones tenfold.

The deserts of the Middle East formed the last theatre in which battles could be fought in virtual isolation from the rest of the world. But even Second Alamein, last of the set-piece desert battles between two rival armies, formed part of a much greater strategy. Montgomery's 8th Army, attacking at Alamein, was really no more than the right wing of a huge enveloping Allied

attack, with the left wing invading Algeria and Tunisia over 1,100 miles away. And in all four of her wars with the Arab powers Israel has been forced, like Germany in the two world wars, to fight on at least two and frequently three fronts. Nor was the Vietnam War solely what some left-wing idealists claimed it to be : a struggle between southern decadence and the progressive liberation forces of the north. Vietnam was a proxy war between the American and Russian superpowers, with a controlling influence in south-east Asia as the over-riding strategic objective.

Apart from ushering in the age of huge Moloch-battles raging on for weeks and months, the First World War introduced a new phase in the evolution of armies and weapons. This was the gradual replacement of 'labour-intensive' armies – relying on the infantryman with his rifle and bayonet – with 'capital-intensive' armies. These were much smaller and armed with weapon-systems operated by technicians, rather than cannon-fodder soldiers armed with simple weapons. (This had already happened with naval warfare ; by the time

Left : Test firing of a 'Patriot' surface-to-air (SAM) missile. As the Middle East wars have amply demonstrated, SAM defences have become one of the biggest headaches for tactical air forces trying to do their job of disrupting enemy ground movements. Equipped with radar and heat-seeking sensors, modern SAMs have a formidable tenacity and reach, and form one of the most important elements in the air umbrella over the battlefield

Britain introduced the 'Dreadnought' battleship in 1906 warships had become highly technological weapon-systems, demanding skilled crews for efficient operation.) The First World War introduced the process on land, with the tank and military aircraft used for ground attack. Cambrai was the first battle in which modern weapon-systems appeared *en masse* on a battlefield, helping troops to fight and win in the utterly hostile environment of a war of fire-power versus flesh and blood.

The Second World War virtually completed the process. By 1945 no land offensive had a chance of succeeding if the enemy had control of the air, no matter how strong the attacker was in armour and mobile fire-power on the ground. It was still possible for outnumbered forces to hold off superior numbers of attackers, but never for long if the attackers had control of the air. The Allies landed in Normandy on

Towards the end of the war the Germans were experimenting with rocket-missiles – not just surface-to-air missiles to knock down enemy aircraft, but surface-to-surface missiles for long-range bombardment and anti-tank missiles with hollow-charge warheads for fighting enemy armour at close range. As early as 1943 the Germans had a guided air-to-surface missile capable of sinking the Italian battleship *Roma*; by 1945 the Americans had the 'Bat', one of which, on its first trial in combat, sank a Japanese destroyer at the missile's maximum range of twenty miles. Rapid improvements in electronic and miniaturization since 1945 have extended this accuracy to ground forces – as witness the success of Egyptian troops with Russian-built 'Sagger' missiles against Israeli tanks in October 1973.

Nuclear weapons – the continuing debate

The advent of nuclear weapons in 1945 changed strategy first, introducing the spectre of total destruction at home without the means to reply. Then the American-Russian arms race, with lesser powers clamouring for 'a bomb' of their own, seemed to indicate that the human race had finally gone mad. But in fact it had two most unexpected results. The first, and most obvious, is that Hiroshima and Nagasaki are still the only victims of nuclear attacks, nearly thirty-five years after atomic weapons first became a reality. Had not the first, crude atomic bombs been tested 'for real' at the end of the Second World War, in a period hardened to the grossest atrocity, it is inconceivable that far more powerful nuclear weapons would not have been used in later years, with no foreknowledge of what they could do.

It is precisely this foreknowledge that has made the two nuclear-armed superpowers extremely careful in managing crises and confrontations. In any other period before 1945, crises like the Berlin Airlift, Quemoy and Matsu, the Cuban Missiles of 1962 and the imminent defeat of Egypt in 1973 – all would have led inevitably to total war. Since nuclear deadlock was reached, both the USSR and the USA have repeatedly pulled back from the brink without instinctively reaching for the sledge-hammers. But this in turn has dangers. America and her NATO partners no longer enjoy parity in conventional weapons with the USSR and the Warsaw Pact countries;

Above: 'Poseidon' multi-head submarine-launched strategic missile, a weapon which has helped convert the prospect of 'total' war from a glorious adventure to mutual suicide

Opposite, above: Sikorsky TR716 attack helicopter: a fast, hard-hitting gunship able to operate against tanks

Opposite, below: Harrier 'jump-jets' can operate from improvized sites in woodland clearings as well as orthodox airfields

6 June 1944; the Germans kept them penned in until 25 July – but it was the Allies' total control of the air which made the containment of the Normandy beachhead an impossible task. 'If it's black it's British, if it's silver it's American, if you don't see it at all it's the *Luftwaffe*', was the bitter watchword of the German infantry in Normandy.

Ironically, the Germans had been the first to recognize this new fact of military life and see to it that advancing divisions took along their own anti-aircraft defences.

there is still every danger of the hesitation to use nuclear weapons being exploited by the still tremendous power of conventional land armies.

The USSR has effectively broken the nuclear deadlock by building up an enormous deployment of conventional armed forces. It is armed with excellent tanks, troop carriers, mobile artillery and anti-aircraft armament (both guns and missiles), and backed by a swarming and well-equipped air force. Geography allows the Warsaw Pact countries to reinforce themselves continually by land while forcing NATO to rely on airlifts and seaborne convoys. In short, the Warsaw Pact host deployed against NATO is geared up for the biggest *blitzkrieg* of all time, a knockout assault which NATO, thanks to twenty years of defence economies, lacks the resources to control or defeat.

Forecast for a Third World War

The pretext for such an assault will be some event in West Germany which the NATO governments see as solvable and Moscow sees as intolerable. NATO would hope for a

period of gradual diplomatic breakdown, allowing the West to get its airlifts, convoys and mobilizations ready; the Warsaw Pact countries could motor straight into battle. Its spearhead units could come through the frontier wire with no initial bombardment, without even firing a shot, leaving the British, German or American forces in the line of fire to take the enormous plunge and start the shooting.

As in 1939, the first instinct of all governments would be to limit the conflict, and diplomatic notes would fuss to and fro while the Soviet armour continued to advance, bypassing cores of resistance in true *blitzkrieg* style, searching for the weak spots in the thin NATO cordon while the flood built up behind. Over the battlefield NATO aircraft would brave Warsaw Pact anti-aircraft missiles and artillery flak, advancing with the Pact armour, in attacks on the interminable columns below. To help the ground-attack aircraft get through, fighters would dog-fight with their opposite numbers, using high-performance cannon and air-to-air missiles. As the clash of armour moved to its crisis, NATO would rely heavily on helicopter gunships flying below treetop level and briefly soaring up to fire, as well as on anti-tank guided weapons in the hands of the infantry.

Darkness would bring no respite; aided by infra-red sights and scanners, the battle would continue through the night. The NATO armies would very probably manage to hold out for the first two days but by day three, and certainly day four, they would be

running into real trouble. This would stem not merely from losses – though these would be grievous, and the Warsaw Pact countries can stand them better than NATO – but from the lack of instant and abundant replenishment of ammunition and above all missiles. The expenditure of missiles, as the Middle East wars have shown, would be enormous – but over fifteen years of sustained economy at the expense of NATO's supply services would probably not have been put to rights. Thus by the fourth day – unless they had been granted the sort of supply miracle denied the German 6th Army at Stalingrad – the NATO forces would be approaching the total exhaustion of all types of missile.

Attrition – a dirty word in military circles ever since the trench massacres of the First World War – would make a nonsense of the excellence of NATO's weapons and training. Without replenishment ammunition and missiles, those weapons would be highly expensive and impotent junk. Once unchallenged in the air, able to roam at will along the battle area and far beyond it, the Warsaw Pact air forces would give their armoured columns on the ground absolute mastery in hours rather than days. Long before the end of the first week, the NATO front would be broken beyond repair, as likely as not in more than one sector.

Nuclear release

As the moment of total collapse approached the NATO commander-in-chief would have only one card left to play: the use of tactical nuclear missiles to wither the battle into temporary immobility. Denied the accuracy and limited destructive power of the neutron warhead thanks to popular ignorance and political expediency, he would have to use weapons far less accurate, less efficient and more widely destructive. To do so would court immediate retaliation in kind, which would only slow the land battle further; but it would also bring the world to within a hair's breadth of the ultimate disaster: a nuclear exchange around the entire northern hemisphere.

Is it fanciful or 'scare-mongering' to point out that if a burning fuse stuck in a powder-keg is not extinguished or broken, that powder-keg will explode? The troops and the weapons for the last of all land battles are ready; and one of the lessons of history is that if troops and weapons are kept ready for long enough, sooner or later they are used. The battle of the future is more than likely to realize a dream that has obsessed military theorists down the ages, only this time with hideous finality: the *schlact ohne morgen*, the 'battle without a morrow'.

Above : A far cry from the days when a general stood on a hill and surveyed the battle. This is the Boeing AWACS ('Airborne Warning and Control System') – a flying headquarters designed to control the battle from the air by electronics

Opposite, above : Kiev, first of Russia's carrier fleet. Carriers remain the only sure way of providing instant air support anywhere in the world. The West has concluded that there is no future for the big carrier and is busily scrapping them. The Russians think otherwise

Opposite, below : Deliberately produced to fool hostile weapon systems geared to high speeds, the Fairchild A-10A features low speed and a mighty weapons load delivered 'on the deck'

SELECT BIBLIOGRAPHY

Alden, John R., *History of the American Civil War* (MacDonald, 1969)

Barnett, Corelli, *Marlborough* (Eyre Methuen, 1974)

Catton, Bruce, *Never Call Retreat* (Gollancz, 1966)

Clark, Alan, *Barbarossa* (Hutchinson, 1965)

de Ste Croix, P., *Airborne Operations* (Salamander Books, 1978)

Duffy, Christopher, *Austerlitz* (Seeley Service, 1977)

Hibbert, Christopher, *Agincourt* (Batsford, 1964)

Horne, Alistair, *The Fall of Paris : The Siege and the Commune*, 1870–1 (Macmillan, 1965)

Horne, Alistair, *To Lose a Battle : France 1940* (Macmillan 1969)

Howarth, David, *A Near Run Thing* (Collins, 1968)

Hunt, Sir David, *A Don at War* (William Kimber, 1966)

Lefebvre, Georges, *The French Revolution*, Vol. 1: *From its Origins to 1793* (Routledge and Kegan Paul, 1966)

Macksey, Kenneth, *To the Green Fields Beyond* (Royal Tank Regiment, 1966)

O'Ballance, Edgar, *The Third Arab–Israeli War* (Faber and Faber, 1972)

Selby, John, *The Thin Red Line of Balaclava* (Hamish Hamilton, 1970)

Terraine, John, *Mons* (Batsford, 1960)

Woolrych, Austin, *Battles of the English Civil War* (Batsford, 1962)

Yoder, Don, *Iwo Jima* (Purnell's *History of World War 2*, part 6, 1974)

ACKNOWLEDGMENTS

Photographs and illustrations were supplied or are reproduced by kind permission of the following:

The Marquess of Anglesey and the National Trust 33, 37 (Ian Graham)
Bildarchiv Preussischer Kulturbesitz, Berlin 96–7, 99, 103, 107, 111, 121–2, 123, 124 *top*
Bodleian Library, Oxford 17 *top and bottom*, 19 *bottom*
British Library, London 14–15, 16, 19 *top*, 26 *top left*, 158
Camera Press 158
Peter Clayton 9 *top*
By kind permission of the Lieutenant General commanding Coldstream Guards 80 (A.C. Cooper)
Cooper-Bridgeman Library 66–7 (Courtesy of Christie's), 78–9 (Royal Academy of Arts, London)
Daily Telegraph Colour Library 166 *bottom* (John Marmaras), 169 (Anthony Howard)
Mary Evans Picture Library 26 *bottom*, 42, 48–9, 52 *bottom*, 69, 82, 85 *bottom*, 86, 102 *bottom*
John R. Freeman 21, 25, 27, 51
Gettysburg National Military Park 88–9, 93 *bottom*
Photographie Giraudon, Paris 52 *top*, 56–1, 58, 59, 60, 13
Michael Holford Library 13
Imperial War Museum, London endpapers (A.C. Cooper), 83, 104, 110 *bottom*, 115, 118, 119, 127 *bottom*, 128–9 (A.C. Cooper), 130 *top*, 133 (A.C. Cooper)
Keystone Press Agency 122, 124 *bottom*, 127 *top*, 156–7
Leeds City Art Galleries 2–3
Louvre, Paris 8 (Françoise Foliot)
MacClancy Press Ltd. 142 *top*, 148–9, 150 *and* 151 *top* (US Defense Dept. Marine Corps.)
Magnum Photographs 166 *top*, 167, 170, 171 (Charles Harbutt)
His Grace the Duke of Marlborough 30–1
J. G. Moore Collection, London 9 *bottom*, 10, 11, 12 *top and bottom* (British Library), 41 (Courtesy of Washington and Lee University, Virginia, USA), 70, 113, 116,
126 *bottom*, 131, 132, 140 *bottom*, 141 *bottom*, 142 *bottom*, 143 *bottom*, 151 *bottom* (US defense Dept. Marine Corps), 174 *top* (Thompson OSF/Roger Viollet, France), 174 *bottom* (Chrysler Corp. USA), 175 (Martin Marietta Aerospace, USA), 176 (Lockheed Corp. USA), 177 *top* (Sikorsky Aircraft, USA), 177 *bottom* and 178 *top* (Central Office of Information, Crown Copyright), 178 *bottom* (Fairchild Industries, Maryland, USA), 179 (US Air Force)
Musée de l'Armée, Paris 50, 54, 55, 61, 64, 64–5, 106
National Army Museum, London 34 *top and bottom*, 36, 38–9, 76–7, 77, 85 *top*
National Portrait Gallery, London 22–3, 32, 40
Peter Newark's Historical Pictures 98, 108, 110 *top*
Peter Newark's Western Americana 91 *top and bottom*, 92, 95
Novosti Press Agency 1, 117, 140, 141 *top*, 146 *top and bottom*
Popperfoto 159, 161, 162 *top and bottom*, 163
Ridge Press, New York 90
By kind permission of the Lieutenant Colonel commanding the Scots Guards 81 (A.C. Cooper)
Ronald Sheridan 4–5, 6–7, 164–5
Society for Cultural Relations with the USSR 138
Staatsbibliothek Berlin 100, 102 *top*, 126 *top*
Stadtische Galerie, Landesmuseum, Hanover 26 *top right*
Victoria and Albert Museum, London 73, 87
Walker Art Gallery, Liverpool 71
Collection of Washington and Lee University, Virginia, USA 93 *top*
Weidenfeld and Nicolson Archives 29 (J. Tillotson), 103
Yale University Art Gallery 46–7

All possible care has been taken in tracing the ownership of copyright material in this book. If any owner has not been acknowledged the publishers apologize and will be glad of an opportunity to rectify the error.

Maps by David Worth and Jennifer Mexter

INDEX